Transforming Education through the Arts

This timely book takes up the challenge of maintaining programs in the arts in the face of unrelenting pressure from two directions: the increasing focus on literacy and numeracy in schools, teamed with the cut-backs in public funding that often affect the arts most severely.

Drawing on the wealth of evidence already available on the impact of the arts, including the findings of a landmark experimental study in Australia, this text considers:

*   the social and educational impact of neglecting the arts
*   research evidence on engagement in the arts
*   why there is a need for educational reform
*   how to transform schools through engagement in the arts.

This challenge to arts education exists at a time where an increasing number of students are becoming disengaged from the traditional schooling model that appears ill-suited to the needs of the twenty-first century and to the ways young people learn in a globalised, high-tech knowledge world. *Transforming Education through the Arts* provides illustrations from around the world that clearly show how the arts have transformed learning for disengaged students and established their worth beyond doubt in settings where the disengagement of students has hitherto been presented as an intractable problem.

Transforming Education through the Arts is an indispensible tool for policymakers and practitioners in school education and for academic and postgraduate students with an interest in the arts. It is also highly relevant to the work of individuals and organisations in the philanthropic sector and those in the wider community who place a priority on closing the gap between high- and low-performing students.

Brian Caldwell is Managing Director and Principal Consultant at Educational Transformations, Australia, and Professorial Fellow and former Dean of Education at the University of Melbourne.

Tanya Vaughan is a scientist and Senior Consulting Researcher at Educational Transformations, Australia, where she is Chief Investigator for the landmark Australian studies on student engagement in the arts.

Transforming Education through the Arts

Brian Caldwell and Tanya Vaughan

Routledge
Taylor & Francis Group

LONDON AND NEW YORK

First published 2012
by Routledge
2 Park Square, Milton Park, Abingdon, Oxon OX14 4RN

Simultaneously published in the USA and Canada
by Routledge
711 Third Avenue, New York, NY 10017

Routledge is an imprint of the Taylor & Francis Group, an informa business

British Library Cataloguing in Publication Data
A catalogue record for this book is available from the British Library

Library of Congress Cataloging in Publication Data
Caldwell, Brian.
    Transforming education through the arts /
    by Brian Caldwell and Tanya Vaughan.—1st ed.
    p. cm.
    Includes bibliographical references and index.
    1. Arts in education I. Vaughan, Tanya. II. Title.
    NX280.C35 2012
    700.71—dc23
    2011023773

ISBN: 978–0–415–68701–0 (hbk)
ISBN: 978–0–415–68702–7 (pbk)
ISBN: 978–0–203–15249–2 (ebk)

Typeset in Garamond
by Swales & Willis Ltd, Exeter, Devon

MIX
Paper from
responsible sources
FSC® C004839

Printed and bound in Great Britain by
TJ International Ltd, Padstow, Cornwall

Contents

Figures

Tables

Foreword

I am not an artist by any definition. I am not even a good art critic. In fact, I know nothing about the arts — either as a creator or learned admirer. But I am a staunch defender of arts education. So I am grateful to Brian Caldwell and Tanya Vaughan, who send a loud, evidence-based, and much-needed message to parents, teachers, school leaders, and most important, education policy makers around the world: the arts are essential 'to national creativity and to the wellbeing of the individual citizen.'

I might have become a Picasso or Mozart or perhaps even a male version of Lady Gaga, but I never had the opportunity to try painting or singing to know my talents or lack thereof. Born in a poor village in China in the 1960s, I did not see a violin until college, did not play with crayons until I came to the United States in my late twenties, and did not know of the existence of art galleries before graduating from college. All through my primary and secondary education, I had a highly focused curriculum— mathematics, Chinese language, and later English. But that was not by choice, rather than by necessity: we did not have the resources, no art teachers, no supplies, no galleries, and no access to the arts.

The arts, as Caldwell and Vaughan masterfully document in *Transforming Education through the Arts*, are fundamental to us as human beings. Besides their utilitarian value in cultivating economically valuable creative talents and innovative spirits, the arts add undeniable value to the human society. Moreover, they are simply enjoyable. Any one of these is reason enough to make the arts an essential element of any educational experience, whenever possible.

Thus I don't understand why anyone in their right mind wants to take the arts out of their children's educational experiences. Unfortunately that is precisely what the leading education reformers are doing, especially in some Western developed nations. From the United States of America to Australia, some Western countries have recently embarked on a journey to improve education by almost exclusively focusing on numeracy and literacy. The arts have, naturally, been disappearing from many children's school experiences.

What is worse and more disheartening is that while the arts have been increasingly squeezed out of all children's curriculum, those who are fortunate to be born into families and communities with the means, can find them outside school; those who cannot afford it are deprived of the opportunities entirely, just like me. This is becoming increasingly dangerous in the twenty-first century, when artistic capabilities and creativity are becoming even more cherished assets and when arts are the only experiences that engage some children. The disadvantaged children, without access to the arts at home or in their neighborhood, are now deprived of the experience in school. It is not only morally cruel but also practically discriminating: the wealthy have a rich, well-balanced education while the poor have an impoverished experience focusing on literacy and numeracy.

It is my hope that, after reading this book, you will be compelled by the evidence and logic presented to actively defend the arts as an essential element of education for all children.

Yong Zhao
Presidential Chair and Associate Dean for Global Education
University of Oregon
November 2011

Preface

We began the research reported in these pages, as we should, as dispassionate scholars who had been commissioned to study the impact of an innovative program in the performing arts in the upper primary years in schools in relatively disadvantaged settings.

On the basis of the evidence we gathered, which was consistent with findings in similar or related projects elsewhere around the world, we have grave concerns that there are fundamental 'design flaws' in efforts to improve or transform schools that are sidelining the arts.

Current governments may have drifted off-course in their policies but the fault lies just as much with previous governments in (mostly) Western nations, accentuating the widening bifurcation of the sciences and the arts over more than a century to the particular detriment of the arts. We write this with heavy hearts because we are both scientists by training.

While this bifurcation must change and the efforts of governments must increase, the contributions from the public purse should be supported, if not exceeded, by the wider community including the philanthropic and non-profit sectors. The good news we learnt as our work progressed is that private effort is increasing steadily.

As far as our Australian research is concerned, we wish to thank The Song Room (TSR), a non-profit organisation committed to providing programs in the arts where none exist, for the commission to Educational Transformations to enable us to undertake the study reported in Chapters 5 to 8. We acknowledge, in particular, the leadership and guidance of Chief Executive Officer Caroline Aebersold, and the contribution of the Macquarie Group Foundation that funded the research. The Song Room also provided an additional grant to support the preparation of the manuscript.

We are exceedingly grateful to our colleague Dr Jessica Harris, Senior Consulting Researcher at Educational Transformations based in Brisbane, for her skilful leadership in undertaking the case studies reported in Chapter 8 and to Project Manager Anna Kitney who assisted with organisational arrangements and the collection of data. The Australian Council for Educational Research (ACER) made available its Social-Emotional and Wellbeing (SEWB) survey and provided an independent analysis of the findings. The Department of Education and Training in New South Wales gave its approval to conduct the research.

We are delighted that Yong Zhao, Presidential Chair and Associate Dean for Global Education at the University of Oregon, kindly agreed to write the Foreword. He is a pre-eminent educator on the world stage at this time, being much in demand for his extraordinary capacity to understand the need for a broad and rich curriculum. He is a passionate advocate for the arts, as is evident in his blog which is read by thousands (http://zhaolearning.com) from which we draw in Chapter 3.

Above all, we acknowledge the assistance of principals, parents, teachers and students in 10 schools in the western suburbs of Sydney who gathered information and shared their views so freely. We are not able to name them in the book but we have extended our thanks in more personal ways.

The outcome is a major contribution to worldwide understanding of the critically important role of the arts in education and of the pitfalls, indeed the dangers of neglecting them in well-intentioned but ultimately misguided efforts in school reform.

Abbreviations

AARE	Australian Association for Research in Education
AITSL	Australian Institute for Teaching and School Leadership
ACMF	Australian Children's Music Foundation
ACER	Australian Council for Educational Research
ACARA	Australian Curriculum, Assessment and Reporting Authority
ACT	Australian Capital Territory
ANOVA	Analysis of Variance
CCE	Creativity, Culture and Education
CoCA	Centre of Contemporary Arts
DHS	Dandenong High School
FHL	Festival for Healthy Living
GU	Griffith University
ICA	Inner City Arts
ICEA	Index of Community Socio-Educational Advantage
LBOTE	Language Background Other Than English
LTTA	Learning Through the Arts
NAPLAN	National Assessment Program – Literacy and Numeracy
NBYO	New Brunswick Youth Orchestra
NCEE	National Centre on Education and Economy
NCLB	No Child Left Behind
NFER	National Foundation for Educational Research
NSW	New South Wales
MCEECDYA	Ministerial Council for Education, Early Childhood Development and Youth Affairs
PASW	Predictive Analytics Software
PISA	Program for International Student Assessment
QACI	Queensland Academy for Creative Industries
QAHS	Queensland Academy for Health Sciences
QASMT	Queensland Academy for Science, Mathematics and Technology
QUT	Queensland University of Technology
SES	Socio-Economic Status
SEWB	Social-Emotional Wellbeing
TA	Teaching Artist

TFA	Teach for America
TIMSS	Trends in International Mathematics and Science Study
TSR	The Song Room
OECD	Organisation for Economic Co-Operation and Development
SOTA	School of the Arts, Singapore
VCASS	Victorian College of the Arts Secondary School

1   The social and educational costs of neglecting the arts

In a powerful critique of Australia's preoccupation with national testing in literacy and numeracy, Richard Gill, then director of the Victorian Opera, declared that 'this abhorrent method of assessing children, teachers and their students needs to stop now'. He argued that the tests and associated transparency in results for all schools in the country on the My School website have 'nothing to do with the education of a child' (Gill 2011: 15). He went on:

> Evidence is now available that schools all over the country are cutting back on arts education to devote more time to subjects that make children literate. It can demonstrably be proven that activities used in teaching for the national tests destroy individuality, stifle creativity, stultify thought and make all children respond in the same way – a sort of educational circus in which the children are the trained animals and the teachers the poorly paid ringmasters.
>
> (Gill 2011: 15)

Critics in comparable countries, notably England and the United States, argue along the same lines. What will it mean to a nation if Richard Gill is correct and, moreover, the curtailment of arts education not only robs students of the intrinsic benefit of an artistic experience but further reduces the performance of students in literacy and numeracy? Moreover, what will it mean to a nation if such a cut-back increases the gap between high- and low-performing students on these same tests and decreases the life chances of students, even to the extent of increasing the probability they may subsequently be involved in crime or other anti-social behaviour?

Our purpose in *Transforming Education through the Arts* is to critically examine these issues and provide evidence that Australia and similar nations will benefit from greater rather than lesser engagement in the arts in school education.

Indeed, we go further and contend that a major design flaw has opened up in these nations and that school education, especially in the public sector, is at risk unless corrective action is taken as a matter of urgency.

Major themes

Schools and school systems around the world face the challenge of maintaining programs in the arts in the face of unrelenting pressure from two directions. One is the justifiable focus on literacy and numeracy, often accompanied by high-stakes testing that is exerting pressure on other areas of learning and teaching. The other is cut-backs in public funding, with international evidence suggesting that programs in the arts are often the first to suffer. The paradox is that study after study reveals the benefits of student participation in the arts.

The challenge described here is occurring at the same time that an increasing number of students are becoming disengaged from schooling. Part of the blame in the view of many observers is that school systems are trapped in a traditional model of schooling that is ill-suited to the needs of the twenty-first century and to the ways young people learn in a globalised, high-tech knowledge world. Disengagement occurs across all strata of society but is acute in highly disadvantaged settings where there is often a risk of involvement in juvenile crime. It seems that improvement in current approaches to schooling is not enough and change on the scale of transformation is required.

Among the many concerns of educators as far as recent attempts at reform are concerned is the narrowing of the curriculum, especially when the focus has been on literacy and numeracy, and schools have had to operate in a regime of high-stakes testing. This focus is often at the expense of the arts and pedagogies that endeavour to nurture innovation, creativity and problem-solving. These trade-offs have been especially noteworthy in schools in disadvantaged settings.

Governments in many nations in the Western world seem to be at their wits' end in devising policies that will close the gap in achievement between high- and low-performing students. Among strategies that have been adopted are new curricula, often at the national level; high-stakes testing programs with unprecedented levels of transparency; performance pay for teachers; structural change through different approaches to governance and choice; and reform in initial teacher education. Yet countries like Australia, England and the United States still lag behind countries in Scandinavia and East Asia. While there are exceptions, it is proving very difficult to achieve improvement on the scale of transformation, especially in schools in highly disadvantaged settings.

Foundation in research

Transforming Education through the Arts builds the case for the arts to be at the centre of efforts to achieve such a transformation. It draws on the wealth of evidence already available on the impact of the arts but includes the findings of a landmark experimental study in Australia that puts the case beyond doubt in settings where disengagement of students has hitherto presented as an intractable problem. There are powerful implications for all stakeholders, including policymakers and the wider community. The case for expanding the involvement of the non-profit philanthropic sector in new kinds of partnerships is presented. Illustrations are provided from around the world of how the arts have transformed learning for disengaged students. Strategies for policy and practice are provided that leave no doubt about the 'why' and the 'how'.

The findings from research around the world provide the touchstone for an evidence-based approach in this book. Particular attention is given to ground-breaking research in several of the most disadvantaged communities in Australia

(Western Sydney in New South Wales) in state schools which did not previously offer programs in the arts. An intervention by the national non-profit arts organisation The Song Room (TSR), with the support of a high-profile foundation (Macquarie Group Foundation) to provide such programs in primary schools has led to gains on almost every measure of student achievement and wellbeing. Particularly noteworthy is the fact that these gains have been on indicators that are predictive of engagement in juvenile crime. Teaching was conducted by successful artists.

The Australian research is a rare example of experimental design in education wherein the performance of students in schools that offered programs in the arts was compared with the performance of students in matching schools that did not offer such programs. The effects were much larger than expected and the findings suggest strategies that should be adopted if levels of achievement and wellbeing are to be raised.

The book sets the findings in national and international research in the context of efforts around the world to achieve improvement on the scale of transformation, defined as significant, systematic and sustained change that secures success for all students in all settings. International research on the impact of the arts is summarised along with studies of conditions that predict the incidence of juvenile crime. Case studies of successful practice in different countries are provided and these include descriptions of approaches to learning and teaching which proved to be instrumental in achieving the desired outcomes. Implications for policymakers and professionals are offered. These implications will challenge several current strategies to improve schools.

In Chapter 1 we document the social and educational costs of neglecting the arts in schools and school systems. In England, the Cambridge Primary Review drew attention to this and proposed a new curriculum with a central place for the arts. In the United States, the arts are often the first programs to be cut as states and school districts introduce savage cuts in funding. It took a major effort to get the arts on the agenda in the national curriculum in Australia. These developments are puzzling given that high-performing nations on international tests of literacy and numeracy such as the Program for International Student Assessment (PISA) protect the arts; for example, China, Finland, Japan, Korea and Singapore. It is even more puzzling given the wide gap between high- and low-performing students in countries such as Australia, England and the United States when evidence to date and to be developed further in the book shows how the arts can help close the gap.

What do we mean by 'the arts'?

The draft of the Australian Curriculum for the arts provides a useful starting point for explaining what we mean by 'the arts':

> We experience and engage in the Arts through sensory, cognitive and affective dimensions of perception. We make sense of the Arts within our three realms of experience:

- the realm of personal experience
- the realm of our relation to others and the society we experience
- the realm of people, places and objects which lie beyond our direct experience.

Through the five art forms we create representations of these three realms.

(ACARA 2010a: 4)

Dance, drama, media arts, music and visual arts are the five art forms in the Australian Curriculum, and these were considered to be 'reasonably distinct' although 'organically connected, and not easily separable in some contexts' (ACARA 2010a: 4).

Finland, which consistently performs well in PISA, specifies nine forms of the arts in its national curriculum which include literacy arts, performing arts (circus, theatre) and visual arts (architecture, visual arts and craft) (Finnish National Board of Education 2011).

The arts have been part of human history and have encouraged human expression in daily life and cultural ceremonies. The origins were explored by Nathan (2008):

> Our ancestors knew the arts were synonymous with survival. We created art to communicate emotions: our passions, jealousies, and enduring conflicts. We designed pageants to dramatise the passing of seasons and other more temporal events. Daily life, communication, and rituals were circumscribed and delineated in a range of artistic expressions.
>
> We went into battle with the sounds of trumpets, piccolos, and drums all over the globe. We buried our dead with song and even dance. We created theatre that proposed solutions to our woes. We drew pictures of our kings and queens, and also cave drawings to tell the history of our day. Was this our primitive form of expression, or were we informing future generations in a way that language will never do alone? In short, the performing and visual arts have been the foundation of our recorded existence. I believe the arts are key to how we educate ourselves.
>
> (Nathan 2008: 177)

A distinction is made between arts and culture, with culture considered in part to refer to 'any combination of race, gender, social practices belonging to a distinct human group and not necessarily to artistic content' (ACARA 2010a: 4). In her evaluation of arts education in Iceland, Bamford described the importance of the arts to 'reflect unique cultural circumstances' (Bamford 2009: 51). The Singapore Art Syllabus (primary and lower secondary) notes that 'through making art, our students learnt to reflect and express their uniqueness by communicating their thoughts and emotions using images and objects' (Ministry of Education Singapore 2008: 1). The relationship between culture and the arts is described in the following terms:

> [All] art making and artworks are culturally mediated, and the meanings they express are directly related to the culture in which the artists and audiences live.

The Arts are shaped by their culture, its history and traditions and in turn help to shape and re-shape it.

(ACARA 2010a: 4)

The case for the arts

In this section we summarise the case for the arts by (a) examining their contribution to overall economic wellbeing, (b) exploring the relationship between the arts and science, (c) noting their place in a balanced curriculum, (d) establishing the arts as a human right, and (e) describing how they might support those who are most vulnerable. This is a general introduction to the theme. In Chapters 4, 6 and 7 we summarise more highly focused research on the impact of engagement in the arts.

Arts education and creative nations

The importance of 'the creative class' in successful economies has been well documented by Richard Florida, who reported that there is 'broad agreement among economists and business forecasters that the growth of the overall economy will come in the creativity or knowledge-based occupations and in the service sector' (Florida 2005: 29). He documented growth in the creative sector, especially, and also the service sector, compared to sharp declines in the manufacturing and agricultural sectors, and reported that 'nearly all of the growth in jobs [in the United States] has come in two fields: expert thinking and complex communications' (Florida 2005: 31). Florida compared the performance of nations as far as creativity is concerned:

- The creative class accounts for more than 40 percent of the work force in nine countries: Netherlands (47 percent); Australia (43 percent); Sweden, Switzerland, Denmark, Norway (all 42 percent); Belgium, Finland (both 41 percent); and Germany (40 percent) (Florida 2005: 137).
- The Global Talent Index has two dimensions: Human Capital and Scientific Talent. On the Human Capital Index, measured by the percentage of the population with a bachelor's or professional degree, the top-ranked nations are the United States, Norway, Denmark, the Netherlands and Canada. On the Scientific Talent Index, measured by the number of research scientists and engineers per million people, the top-ranked nations are Finland, Japan, Sweden, Norway, the United States, Switzerland and Denmark. When the two indices are combined, the top-ranked nations are Finland, Japan, Norway, Australia, Iceland, the Netherlands, Sweden and Canada. The United States ranked 9th, the United Kingdom 13th, Germany 18th and France 22nd (Florida 2005: 144–45).
- Along with technology and talent, tolerance is one of three factors in economic growth in the twenty-first century. The Global Tolerance Index has two dimensions: Values and Self-Expression. Sweden, Denmark, the Netherlands, Norway, Japan, Germany, Switzerland, Iceland, Finland and New Zealand are the leaders (Florida 2005: 151).

- The Global Creativity Index provides a measure of national competitiveness based on the three factors accounting for economic growth: technology, talent and tolerance. The 12 top-ranked nations are Sweden, Japan, Finland, the United States, Switzerland, Denmark, Iceland, the Netherlands, Norway, Germany, Canada and Australia, ahead of the United Kingdom (15th), France (17th) and New Zealand (18th) (Florida 2005: 156).
- Nations can be 'talent magnets' in respect to the proportion of university students who come from other countries. Top-ranked countries are Australia, Switzerland, Austria, Belgium, the United Kingdom, Germany, France, Sweden, Denmark, New Zealand, Ireland and the United States (Florida 2005: 148). The United States has the highest number of foreign students in absolute terms, accounting for 36 percent of the world total (Florida 2005: 147).

Florida contends that:

> America will continue to be squeezed between the global talent magnets of Canada, Australia and the Scandinavian countries, who are developing their technological capabilities, becoming more open and tolerant, and competing effectively for creative people; and the large emerging economies of India and China, who rake in a greater share of low-cost production and are now competing more effectively for their own talent.
>
> (Florida 2005: 238)

He argues that reform at the school level is critical to long-term economic success. Writing of the United States, he contends that 'we can no longer succeed – or even tread water – with an education system handed down to us from the industrial age, since what we no longer need is assembly-line workers. We need one that instead reflects and reinforces the values, priorities and requirements of the creative age'. Florida argued that 'at its core, education reform must make schools into places where human creativity is cultivated and can flourish' (Florida 2005: 254).

Several observations are in order. While Florida was considering creativity in general terms, he developed several carefully specified and highly regarded indices which measured capacities that are developed through the arts, notably, tolerance, that included values and self-expression. Nations that have placed arts education at risk, including the United Kingdom and the United States, tend to rank below those that have not followed this course, including Sweden, Denmark, the Netherlands, Norway, Japan, Germany, Switzerland, Iceland, Finland and New Zealand. Australia appears to be following the UK and the United States, so a re-calculation is likely to reveal a lower ranking.

Relationship between the arts and science

In their keynote address to the Second World Conference on Arts Education sponsored by UNESCO and held in Seoul in May 2010, Robert Root-Bernstein and Michelle Root-Bernstein declared that 'the arts have always been and will always be at the centre of creative practice in every discipline in every culture' (Root-Bernstein and Root-Bernstein 2010: 2). They developed an argument on the role of the arts in the 'high-level pursuit of science, invention and business beyond the value of arts in and of themselves'. Robert Root-Bernstein is a professor in the Physiology Department at Michigan State University. Michelle Root-Bernstein is a Kennedy Centre teaching artist and member of the Adjunct Faculty at Michigan State University.

They summarised the thesis proposed over a century ago by J.H. van't Hoff, a Nobel Prize winner in Chemistry, that the arts foster scientific creativity. They referred to a study of more than 200 biographies that affirmed the thesis, noting that Galileo was an artist and craftsman, Kepler a musician and composer and Sir Humphrey Davy a poet. Their own research found that 'artistic or craft talent turns out to be typical of Nobel Prize winners and other eminent scientists' (Root-Bernstein and Root-Bernstein 2010: 3). For example:

> Dorothy Hodgkin, British Nobel laureate, said that she learned to think in three dimensions as a crystallographer because of the art lessons given to her by her mother, who was a professional artist and archaeologist. While still a teen, Hodgkin illustrated her parents' archaeological finds, and she used her skill to illustrate her own crystallographic discoveries as well.
>
> (Root-Bernstein and Root-Bernstein 2010: 4)

Moreover:

> We found that compared with typical scientists, Nobel laureates are at least 2 times more likely to be photographers; 4 times more likely to be musicians; 17 times more likely to be artists; 15 times more likely to be craftsmen; 25 times more likely to be writers of non-professional writing, such as poetry or fiction; and 22 times more likely to be performers, such as actors, dancers or magicians.
>
> (Root-Bernstein and Root-Bernstein 2010: 7–8)

Writing in *Sparks of Genius, the 13 Thinking Tools of the World's Most Creative People* (Root-Bernstein and Root-Bernstein 1999) they found a common set of 13 thinking tools: observing, imaging, abstracting, pattern recognising, pattern forming, analogising, empathising, body thinking, dimensional thinking, modelling, playing, transforming and synthesising. They offered three strategies to educate for creativity, as the twenty-first century challenges us to do:

1　Teach tools for thinking, so that students learn to develop imaginative skills and conceive their own personal, original ideas.
2　Teach the creative process, so that students learn how conceived ideas are realised and implemented; how poems, experiments, dances, theories, paintings and policies are created and made.
3　Implement a multi-disciplinary education that places the arts on an equal footing with the sciences, so that students learn the imaginative thinking and expression that lead to discovery and invention. Like reading, writing and

math, the practice of the arts – and the development of correlative talents – should be required for all students in all grades through college.

(Root-Bernstein and Root-Bernstein 2010: 28–29)

Arts education in the curriculum

One of the most influential people in shaping the curriculum of schools is Harvard University's Howard Gardner. He developed the idea of 'multiple intelligences' more than a quarter of a century ago in which music and movement, in particular, find their place (these intelligences are the awkwardly named linguistic, logical-mathematical, spatial, bodily-kinaesthetic, musical, interpersonal and intrapersonal). There would be few initiatives in curriculum development that have not drawn on his work. It is noteworthy that in *Five Minds for the Future* (Gardner 2006), Gardner included the arts among requirements for learning in schools: 'I believe it is essential for individuals in the future to be able to think in the ways that characterise the major disciplines. At the pre-collegiate [school level] level, my own short list includes science, mathematics, history and at least one art form' (Gardner 2006: 31).

One of the most powerful statements on the value of the arts is contained in the draft outline of what should be addressed when the arts are included in Australia's national curriculum, implementation of which is scheduled for 2013. It identifies the arts as a major driver in the development of a 'creative nation' in the sense described by Richard Florida. Five art forms are specified: dance, drama, media arts, music and visual arts. The rationale is set out in the draft statement (ACARA 2010a) in the following terms:

> The Arts are fundamental to the learning of all young Australians. The Arts make distinct and unique contributions to each young person's ability to perceive, imagine, create, think, feel, symbolise, communicate, understand and become confident and creative individuals. The Arts in the Australian curriculum will provide all young Australians with the opportunity to imagine and creatively engage, personally and collectively within their real and imagined worlds. Engagement in all the Arts, shapes our thought and activity, and makes a significant contribution to the broader community. Each of the Arts assists in developing identity, confidence, social participation and inclusion. Cultural diversity and indigenous cultural heritage are integral to all art forms.
>
> The Arts have a special relationship with learning, in that the Arts can be learned and can be used as a tool by which to learn something else. Fully understanding the Arts involves critical and practical study. Through critical and practical study students have the opportunity to explore, experiment, create, analyse and critique, and ultimately discover multiple meanings in artwork.
>
> (ACARA 2010a: 3)

The place of the arts in the economy is noted ('The Arts is one of Australia's major industries') and the 'creative industries' are considered to 'embrace a wide range of arts-based or related industries. They are knowledge-based and innovative, often focusing on commercial application, employment and economic outputs'. Australia already has a secondary school that addresses this area in the Queensland Academy for the Creative Industries (QACI) described in Chapter 9.

It is proposed that students engage in arts education across all year levels and that it be compulsory for all young Australians from kindergarten to Year 8. The K-8 curriculum will be presented in bands (K-2, 3–4, 5–6 and 7–8) with 160 hours of learning across all five art forms in each band. As described in Chapter 10 when policy implications are addressed, this will present a major challenge in Australia where, as in comparable countries, the arts have been sidelined.

Arts education as a universal human right

UNESCO considers education in the arts to be a universal human right, implying that its absence or sidelining is a breach of the Convention on the Rights of the Child. A 'road map for arts education' was prepared at the First World Conference on Arts Education held in Lisbon in March 2006. It included the following statement:

> Culture and the arts are essential components of a comprehensive education leading to the full development of the individual. Therefore, Arts Education is a universal human right, for all learners, including those who are often excluded from education, such as immigrants, cultural minority groups, and people with disabilities.
>
> (UNESCO 2006: 3)

The road map cited Article 27 in the Universal Declaration of Human Rights: 'Everyone has the right freely to participate in the cultural life of the community, to enjoy the arts and share in scientific advancement and its benefits'. It cited the Convention on the Rights of the Child: 'The education of the child shall be directed to . . . The development of the child's personality, talents and mental and physical abilities to their fullest potential' (Article 29) and 'State parties shall respect and promote the right of the child to participate fully in cultural and artistic life and shall encourage the provision of appropriate and equal opportunities for cultural, artistic, recreational and leisure activity' (Article 31).

Arts education and student wellbeing

The arts and arts education feature in several accounts of programs in special education and the support of students with special needs. Oliver Sacks is Professor of Clinical Neurology at Columbia University. The title of his book *Musicophilia: Tales of Music and the Brain* (Sacks 2007) has sunk into public and professional consciousness. It is a powerful affirmation of the arts and arts therapy in education. He referred to autistic people

> who may be unable to perform fairly simple sequences involving perhaps four or five movements or procedures – but who can often do these tasks perfectly well

if they set them to music. Music has the power to embed sequences and to do this when other forms of organisation (including verbal forms) fail.

(Sacks 2007: 237)

Sacks paid particular attention to people with Williams syndrome (less than one in ten thousand children) who have a 'strange mixture of intellectual strengths and deficits', with most having an IQ of less than 60. He wrote that 'even as toddlers, children with Williams syndrome are extraordinarily responsive to music', observing that 'the three dispositions which are so heightened in people with Williams syndrome – the musical, the narrative, and the social – seem to go together' (Sacks 2007: 329).

Sacks explained how the condition involves the 'micro-deletion' of 15 to 25 genes on one chromosome (out of 25,000 or so genes in the normal genome) and concludes that the syndrome affords 'an extraordinarily rich and precise view of how a particular genetic endowment can shape the anatomy of a brain and how this, in turn, will shape cognitive strengths and weaknesses, personality traits, and perhaps even creativity' (Sacks 2007: 311).

An initiative in Victoria (Australia) is the Festival for Healthy Living (FHL) based at the Royal Children's Hospital in Melbourne. The impetus comes from recognition that one in five children and adolescents experience mental health problems, with half of these experiencing difficulties at school and in their social development. It takes account of research which has shown that the performing arts may make a contribution to good mental health (details at www.rch.org.au/fhl). It is best understood in the context of national initiatives under the rubric of Mind Matters, an Australian government initiative in mental health that acknowledges that 'schools that have a system that recognises a range of success, including academic, community service, sport, art and cultural leadership will enhance individual and collective mental health and wellbeing' (Commonwealth of Australia 2010: 15).

Bell Shakespeare is a national touring theatre company specialising in works by William Shakespeare which has consistently provided education programs of varied compositions to urban, rural and remote communities throughout Australia since its inception in 1990. Twenty percent of its annual turnover ($10 million) is dedicated to this work. Income is drawn from box office revenue, the private sector, and government at both federal and state level. Four key learning initiatives are student master classes, residencies, juvenile justice programs and 'Actors at Work' which form part of a broader program that enables Bell Shakespeare to reach approximately 80,000 students and 600 teachers annually. The Bell Shakespeare learning initiatives provide 'innovative methods of approaching Shakespeare texts in English and drama classrooms' (The University of Sydney 2011). A key focus of the initiatives is the involvement of disadvantaged and marginalised participants. John Bell the artistic director and founder of Bell Shakespeare described the impact of the program: '[it] broadens our horizons, transports us to worlds beyond our knowledge and reminds us of the extraordinary power of human creativity' (Bell Shakespeare 2011).

The arts are becoming an area of specialisation in some special schools. An outstanding example is the Port Phillip Specialist School in Melbourne that caters for a range of children with special needs from 2.8 to 18 years of age. It has developed a

Visual and Performing Arts Curriculum that reflects 'a child-centred approach where our teachers and therapists use the power of concrete experiences delivered through dance, drama, music and visual arts as a way to immerse our students in a deeply engaging learning environment' (see www.portphillip.vic.edu.au). Comprehensive accounts of the school and the role of the arts are contained in James (2011).

The sidelining of the arts

The sidelining of the arts reflects the bifurcation in the disciplines of learning that has existed since at least the nineteenth century. Paul Johnson drew attention to the problem in *Creators* (Johnson 2006) where he described the work of men and women of outstanding originality, including Chaucer, Shakespeare, J.S. Bach, Jane Austen, Victor Hugo, Mark Twain, Picasso and Walt Disney. In an affirmation of what can be accomplished in arts education, he declared that 'creativity is inherent in us all' and 'the only problem is how to bring it out' (Johnson 2006: 3). Johnson believes that 'the art of creation comes closer than any other activity to serving as a sovereign remedy for the ills of existence' (Johnson 2006: 2).

Looking back over the centuries, Johnson reminded us that 'throughout history, no real distinction was made between the exercise of skill or even genius in the arts and science'. He recalled that 'Renaissance studios, especially in Florence . . . buzzed with artist scientists', concluding that 'the truth is that until the nineteenth century, there was a single culture of learning' (Johnson 2006: 277). We can observe the resulting bifurcation in trends in education, with events in England chosen here to illustrate the consequences of curtailment in arts education.

The report of the Cambridge Primary Review of policy and practice in England was published under the title *Children, Their World, Their Education* (Alexander 2010a). Project Director Robin Alexander delivered the Miegunyah Distinguished Lecture in the Dean's Lecture Series at the Melbourne Graduate School of Education in March 2010 on the topic 'The Perils of Policy: Success, Amnesia and Collateral Damage in Systematic Educational Reform' (Alexander 2010b). Many of the fears in Australia about the dysfunctional effects of national testing, an excessive focus on and unrealistic expectations for standards, the narrowing of curriculum, and high levels of stress for students and teachers have been borne out in experience in England.

Alexander was careful not to make comparisons or offer recommendations about the implications for Australia, but the message was not lost on his audience. We sensed that many were shell-shocked, especially when he drew comparisons of England with Finland, which has no national tests, has decentralised decision-making, and provides high levels of school and teacher autonomy. Finland has a high-performing school system where students do not start school until they are seven. Finland is in the top ranks of nations as far as creativity is concerned, as illustrated in the work of Richard Florida cited above. All but about two percent of students attend public (state) schools.

Also sobering was the way Alexander contrasted the 'spin' of government, overstating outcomes, with the 'substance' of the reforms, which mostly reflect flat-lining in achievement:

> This is not, or not only, about reducing prescription overall. In the first instance, it requires a much more confident – perhaps even aggressive – assertion of the educational importance of the arts and humanities in human development, culture and education, and a refusal to capitulate to narrowly-conceived criteria of 'relevance'. Ministerial support for the arts in education tends to sound token and insincere, whether or not it is. Authoritative official enquiries on the arts, creativity and culture are warmly applauded, and then disappear without trace.
>
> (Alexander 2010a: 252)

A new primary curriculum was recommended in the Cambridge Review, with the first recommendation as follows:

> [The proposed curriculum] addresses and seeks to resolve the problems of present and past arrangements, especially: overload, micro-management from the centre, the distorting impact of testing and the national strategies, the dislocation of English/literacy, the qualitative imbalance between 'the basics' and the rest, the marginalisation of the arts and humanities, tokenism in respect of aims, and the muddled discourse of subjects, knowledge and skills.
>
> (Alexander 2010a: 275)

The proposed curriculum domains are: arts and creativity; citizenship and ethics; faith and belief; language, oracy and literacy; mathematics; physical and emotional health; place and time; science and technology (Alexander 2010a: 494).

Budget cuts by the coalition government in the UK have led to the abolition of a program to improve the teaching of the arts in English schools. Creative Partnerships, a £38.1 million per year initiative, enabled professional musicians, artists and actors to work with schools for nearly a decade. Routledge has published five books in its Creative Teaching/Creative Schools series for teachers at Key Stages 2 and 3, drawing from experiences in Creative Partnerships.

Administered by Creativity, Culture and Education (CCE), a national charity, the funding came from the Arts Council, which had to abandon the program when the government reduced its grant. Acclaimed actor Sir Ian McKellen deplored the decision: 'In my visits to schools the stimulus of meeting people from outside is clear. It lets children know that there are people who care about them in the world beyond their school' (cited by Thorpe 2011). Affirmation of the economic benefits of programs in the arts is contained in a report of Pricewaterhouse Coopers that showed that 'every £1 of investment in Creative Partnerships generated £15.30 in economic benefits' (Pricewaterhouse Coopers 2010: 3).

The findings of the Pricewaterhouse Coopers study are probably the best illustration of the costs and benefits of programs that are the focus of attention in this book. While larger in scope and reach, Creative Partnerships is the best counterpart we could locate in international practice that matched the program of TSR in Australia.

CCE is 'a national organisation which aims to transform the lives of children and families by harnessing the potential of creative learning and cultural opportunity to enhance their aspirations, achievements and skills' (Pricewaterhouse Coopers 2010: 3). It manages two programs:

Creative Partnerships which is the flagship creative learning program designed to foster long-term partnerships between schools and creative professionals to inspire, open minds and harness the potential of creative learning; and Prevent, which brings together creative agents, cultural practitioners and schools in key geographical areas to channel the expression of young people through filmmaking, poetry and writing in order to challenge extreme ideologies.

(Pricewaterhouse Coopers 2010: 3)

Based on information provided by CCE, the study reported that from 2002–3 to 2008–9, services were provided to 2,148 schools including nursery (44), primary (1,428), secondary (542) and other (134). The number of projects over the same period of time was 10,828 including nursery (281), primary (6,139), secondary (3,345) and other (1,063). A total of 791,436 students were involved including early years (12,959), reception to Year 6 (336,966), Years 7–9 (323,552) and Years 10–11 (117,959) (Pricewaterhouse Coopers 2010).

Using a methodology that was consistent with requirements in the Treasury Green Book the study concluded that 'overall, Creative Partnerships is estimated to have generated or is expected to generate a net positive economic benefit of just under £4 billion. Expressed as a ratio of benefits to the costs, we estimate that every £1 invested in the program delivers £15.30 worth of benefits' (Pricewaterhouse Coopers 2010: 3).

The report cited an earlier study of the National Foundation for Educational Research (NFER) that found that students who had participated in Creative Partnership activities made the equivalent of 2.5 grades better progress at GCSE than students in other schools not engaged in such activities (Kendall *et al.* 2008). Pricewaterhouse Coopers estimated the increase in the number of students who gained five good grades at GCSE which would lead to engagement in further and higher education and, thus, higher levels of lifetime earnings. It was concluded that 'we estimate that total net benefits of Creative Partnerships are just under £8 billion' (Pricewaterhouse Coopers 2010: 4).

While the NFER study found no statistically significant impact on learning outcomes in upper primary, Pricewaterhouse Coopers (2010: 5) suggested that tests at this level are not sensitive to the types of skills that students would normally acquire as a result of their participation in the program. Deeper analysis suggested that there would be a net economic benefit of £1.9 billion if upper primary students continued their engagement in the secondary years when most of the economic benefits would be achieved (in the GCSE Years 10 and 11).

In our view these are important findings, suggesting that there will be a noteworthy loss of economic benefits if the program is abandoned. There would, of course, be a social loss through lower levels of achievement and engagement in further and higher education.

An important note

It is important that we acknowledge that the sidelining of the arts and the other dysfunctions we described above are not universal and that, even in the same countries or school systems or schools, there are outstanding programs in the arts. We offer many examples throughout the book. Also, where sidelining has occurred, we do not attach blame to school or school system leaders whose hands have been tied, often by narrowly focused high-stakes testing that leaves little room to manoeuvre, or by cutbacks in funding that remove or provide insufficient resources to schools to do what they know is right if the needs of their students are to be met. We also acknowledge that the merits that we ascribe to the arts apply to other aspects of the curriculum such as sport, but it is the arts that are our priority and chief cause of concern in this book. However, on the broader scene, and taking account of trends described here and in subsequent chapters, there is something fundamentally wrong when all that we know about quality and balance in education, if not the yearning of the human spirit, have been jeopardised.

Chapter outline

Chapter 1 has set the context, explained what is meant by 'the arts', presented in general terms the case for the arts, and documented the social and educational costs of neglecting the arts in schools. The starting point for Chapter 2 is an explanation of what is meant by 'transformation'; then follows an account of strategies that have been adopted to achieve it, with reference to the inclusion of the arts in several instances.

Chapter 3 develops the themes introduced in Chapters 1 and 2. Among the many concerns of educators is the narrowing of the curriculum, especially when the focus has been on literacy and numeracy and schools have had to operate in a regime of high-stakes testing. This focus is often at the expense of the arts and pedagogies that have endeavoured to nurture innovation, creativity and problem-solving. These trade-offs have been especially noteworthy in schools in disadvantaged settings.

Chapter 4 summarises research on the impact of arts education. There is, for example, a substantial body of research that indicates that engaging students in the arts can lift performance on a range of indicators of achievement and wellbeing, including those indicators related to a propensity to be involved in juvenile crime. There is also an impressive body of evidence that points to low achievement being a factor in a young person turning to crime. There have been few studies in any setting that investigate the relationships among these variables and even fewer that have involved students in matched schools. This chapter also describes what is occurring in Australia and other nations on the involvement of the philanthropic sector in school education, with a particular focus on the arts.

Chapter 5 describes methodologies for research that will illuminate the issues raised in Chapters 1 to 3 and that will also address the need for more matched schools 'quasi-experimental' research. We describe how such research was conducted in Australia in highly disadvantaged settings. An intervention by a national non-profit arts organisation (TSR), with the support of a high-profile foundation (Macquarie Group Foundation) has led to the offering of such programs in primary schools in these settings. The research is a rare example of quasi-experimental design in education wherein the performance of students in schools that offered programs in the arts was compared with the performance of students in matching schools that did not offer such programs. We provide a detailed account of the methodology for this research, the findings of which are reported in Chapters 6 to 8.

The starting point for Chapter 6 is a summary of findings around the world on the impact of the arts on student achievement. The major findings of the Australian study in the areas of student achievement (school tests, national tests) and student attendance are then reported. Comparisons are made between student performance in schools participating in the arts and those in matching schools that did not participate. Comparisons between the initial and longer-term arts programs provide evidence of the impact on student achievement and attendance for prolonged participation in the arts. Illustrative findings are:

- Attendance was significantly higher for the longer-term arts program and initial arts program cohorts in comparison to the students who had not participated in the arts.
- Literacy results were significantly higher for the longer-term arts program cohort in comparison to students who did not participate in arts program.
- Students' grades in science and technology were significantly higher for students who had participated in an arts program compared to those who had not participated in such a program.

Findings are displayed in a series of illustrations and discussed in the light of related research from around the world that was summarised at the start of the chapter.

The starting point for Chapter 7 is a summary of findings from around the world on psychological outcomes. The major findings of the Australian study are then presented in the broad area of student wellbeing, as measured in the Social-Emotional Wellbeing survey (SEWB) developed and validated by the Australian Council for Educational Research (ACER). Student responses are compared for schools participating in the arts and a matching set of schools that do not participate. The longer students are in the program the stronger their sense of wellbeing. Illustrative findings are:

- The percentage of students at the highest levels of overall SEWB was highest for the longer-term arts program, at an intermediate level for the initial arts program, and lowest for those who had not participated in the arts program.
- The percentage of students at the highest levels of resilience shows a gradual decrease from the highest level for the longer-term arts program students, to an intermediate level for the initial arts program students and the lowest level for the non-participating students.
- Male students who participated in arts programs showed significantly lower agreement with the statement 'I very feel stressed' compared to male students who had not participated in arts programs.

- The students' responses to the statement 'During the past six months, I have felt so hopeless and down almost every day for one week that I have stopped doing my usual activities' showed a statistically significant difference for female students in the longer-term program in comparison to those who had not participated in an arts program.

Findings are discussed in the context of related research from around the world that was summarised at the start of the chapter.

There have been several rich accounts of what actually occurs in schools when impact on educational and psychological outcomes has been demonstrated. The key features are summarised at the start of Chapter 8. Then follows an account of how things are done in four schools in the Australian study where outcomes of the kind reported in Chapters 6 and 7 have been achieved. The four schools were comprised of two schools with long-term engagement in the arts (Willow Brook and Margaret Park) and two schools that had just started (Bonvilla and Curraburra). While outcomes are documented, particular attention is given to processes and pedagogies that account for impact. Illustrative findings are:

- The confidence of students was reported to increase through participation in classes and the performance aspects of the arts program.
- The behaviour of students showed improvement through their participation in the arts program.
- The confidence gained from arts programs was described as 'spilling over' to other areas such as academic studies.
- The arts program had a positive influence on student attendance in all schools in the case studies.
- The program was found to increase the confidence of teachers to teach music.

The findings are discussed in the context of similar studies in other nations.

In Chapter 9 we return to the wider context of efforts to raise the levels of achievement of students, especially in Western nations and, in particular, disadvantaged settings. The focus in this chapter is on schools and how schools can design and deliver programs in the arts that will help achieve a turnaround. The role of the philanthropic sector is described. We canvass the possibility that introducing or re-instating programs in the arts may constitute a 'disruptive innovation' on a scale that is similar to the challenge of dealing with 'disruptive innovation' in response to developments in technology.

In addition to a summary and synthesis, Chapter 10 offers implications for policymakers in the public and private sectors with an interest in school transformation and the nurturing and harnessing of the creative spirit. We conclude that a major design flaw has opened up in countries like Australia, England and the United States and that school education, especially in the public sector, is at risk unless corrective action is taken as a matter of urgency.

Significance

For many centuries the arts have been at the centre of education and society in a holistic view of human development. In more recent times there has been a bifurcation of endeavour that has led to the arts being sidelined when the curriculum has narrowed or there has been a need to cut public expenditure. This is despite evidence of the contribution the arts make to national creativity and to the wellbeing of the individual citizen. The social and economic costs will be high in nations that have succumbed under these circumstances.

Among the harms that result from this bifurcation is the possibility that the gap between the experiences of students in different kinds of schools could widen rather than narrow. We cited the views of Richard Gill, then director of the Victorian Opera. In another contribution to the public debate he explained how this scenario is unfolding:

> It is an embarrassment that large numbers of school-age children are not receiving any music education at all. It is also disgraceful that large numbers are receiving substandard, watered-down versions of music . . . It is ridiculous there are private schools with facilities like conservatoriums, practice rooms, recital halls and every instrument known to mankind because the parents can afford it and the divide between the rich and the poor, between state and private, is getting bigger all the time.
>
> (cited by Tarica 2011: 17)

It is extraordinary that this is the current state of affairs in Australia and other nations where the capacities that may be nurtured through the arts have been identified as essential in the twenty-first century. We explain what is required in Chapter 2.

2 The challenge of transforming schools

Why have our schools drifted off-course? Why did it all go so wrong when momentum was building for an expanded role for the arts in education? We address these matters in Chapters 2 and 3. The starting point is to describe intentions that should have secured a place for the arts as an apparently unprecedented effort was made to lift the performance of schools. We do this in three parts: first, to describe the momentum that seemed to be building toward the end of the twentieth century; second, to summarise what research tells us about the factors that account for success in high-performing school systems; and third, to indicate likely and preferred directions for the future of schools. In each part we refer to the place of the arts. We draw on some of the landmark reports and publications over more than two decades to make the case.

Trajectory at the turn of the century

While there has always been concern for improvement in the performance of schools, a key marker was the report in the United States entitled *A Nation at Risk* (National Commission on Excellence in Education 1983). However, there were counterparts in other nations that did not have the same international profile. The Thatcher Conservative government in the United Kingdom had already made the reform of the nation's schools a top priority, culminating in the famous 1988 Education Reform Act. In Australia, the Quality of Education Review Committee completed its work in 1985, led by Professor Peter Karmel, one of the most influential figures in school reform in the country (Quality of Education Review Committee 1985). Each state government was soon pursuing a vigorous reform agenda.

Rather than summarise the various reports, it is sufficient to provide a narrative of the overall thrust of the reform effort. Brian Caldwell and Jim Spinks did this in *Leading the Self-Managing School* (Caldwell and Spinks 1992). They suggested that trends in education were of a magnitude and consistency that they could be described as 'megatrends' in the sense popularised by John Naisbitt in the 1980s (for example, Naisbitt 1982). Ten megatrends in education were described:

1 There will be a powerful but sharply focused role for central authorities, especially in respect to formulating goals, setting priorities, and building frameworks for accountability.

2   National and global considerations will become increasingly important, especially in respect to curriculum and an education system that is responsive to national needs within a global economy.

3   Within centrally determined frameworks, government [public] schools will become largely self-managing, and distinctions between government and non-government [private] schools will narrow.

4   There will be unparalleled concern for the provision of a quality education for each individual.

5   There will be a dispersion of the educative function, with telecommunications and computer technology ensuring that much learning that currently occurs in schools or in institutions of higher education will occur at home and in the workplace.

6   The basics of education will be expanded to include problem-solving, creativity and a capacity for life-long learning and re-learning.

7   There will be an expanded role for the arts and spirituality, defined broadly in each instance; there will be a high level of connectedness in the curriculum.

8   Women will claim their place among the ranks of leaders in education, including those at the most senior levels.

9   The parent and community role in education will be claimed or reclaimed.

10 There will be unparalleled concern for service by those who are required or have the opportunity to support the work of schools.

(Caldwell and Spinks 1992: 7–8)

While the terminology may have changed since these were formulated it is fair to say that it was a good reading of what had transpired or was under way, with one notable exception: 'There will be an expanded role for the arts . . . defined broadly . . . there will be a high level of connectedness in the curriculum' (Caldwell and Spinks 1992: 7–8). As illustrated in Chapter 1, any trend in respect to the arts, even a megatrend, is in the opposite direction.

Caldwell and Spinks developed the narrative in *Beyond the Self-Managing School* after reviewing trends from 1992 to 1997 (Caldwell and Spinks 1998). These were consolidated in descriptions of three 'tracks for change':

A review of developments around the world suggests that there are three different movements under way. The image of a 'track' rather than 'stage' seems appropriate, because the three movements are occurring at the same time in most places: schools, school systems and nations vary in the distance they have moved down each track:

Track 1: Building systems of self-managing schools
Track 2: Unrelenting focus on learning outcomes
Track 3: Creating schools for the knowledge society

(Caldwell and Spinks 1998: 11)

As far as Track 3 was concerned, the authors concluded that it was difficult to specify the many innovations that were involved in 'creating schools for the knowledge

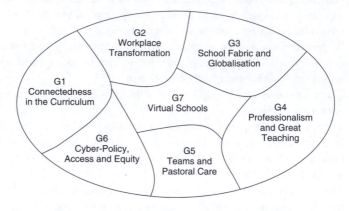

Figure 2.1 Schooling for the knowledge society illustrated in a *gestalt* (based on Caldwell and
        Spinks 1998: 13)

society'. It seemed better to describe what was involved as a *gestalt*: 'a perceived
organised whole that is more than the sum of its parts'. The *gestalt* is illustrated in
Figure 2.1 above.

While the terminology may have changed in some respects, the short descriptions
of each element below (based on Caldwell and Spinks 1998: 11–12) suggest that the
gestalt continues to take shape in most respects, but not in the arts.

- *G1 Connectedness in the Curriculum*: Dramatic change in approaches to learning and
  teaching is in store as electronic networking allows 'cutting across and so challenging the very idea of subject boundaries' and 'changing the emphasis from
  impersonal curriculum to 'excited live exploration' (citing Seymour Papert in
  Papert 1993).
- *G2 Workplace Transformation*: Schools as workplaces are transformed in every
  dimension including the scheduling of time for learning and approaches to
  human resource management.
- *G3 School Fabric and Globalisation*: Everything from building design to the size, shape,
  alignment, and furnishing of space for the 'knowledge worker' in the school is
  transformed. In one sense, of course, the school has no walls, for there are global
  learning networks. Much of the learning that previously called for the student to
  be located at school occurs in many places, at home, at school, and at the upper
  level years of secondary schooling and for lifelong learning, at the workplace.
- *G4 Professionalism and Great Teaching*: A wide range of professionals and para-pro-
  fessionals support learning in an educational parallel to the diversity of support
  that can be found in modern health care. The role of the teacher is elevated, for
  it demands wisdom, judgement and a facility to manage learning in modes more
  complex and varied than ever.
- *G5 Teams and Pastoral Care*: A capacity to work in teams is more evident in
  approaches to learning, given the primacy of the work team in every formulation
  of the knowledge society.

- *G6 Cyber-policy, Access and Equity*: The issues of access and equity will drive public debate until such time as prices fall to make electronic networks as common as the telephone or radio, and that may soon be a reality, given trends in networked computers.
- *G7 Virtual Schools*: The concept of the virtual organisation or the learning network organisation is a reality in the knowledge society. Schools take on many of the characteristics of such organisations, given that learning occurs in so many modes and from so many sources, all networked electronically.

The concept of connectedness in the *gestalt* was described in terms of the role of the computer but there is little evidence that momentum was building for an expanded role for the arts. However, an interesting exception was emerging in England where a major feature of the reform agenda was the creation of specialist secondary schools, with the arts and music being two of 11 specialisms.

The movement got under way during the Conservative years in the establishment of so-called 'city technology colleges' but a range of specialisations emerged during the Labour years from 1997. This meant that, while schools were expected, if not required, to address the national curriculum, they could choose one specialism (in later years they could offer more than one). By 2004 the specialisms were technology, language, arts, music, sports, science, engineering, mathematics and computing, business and enterprise, and humanities. Schools in rural areas could offer a rural specialisation. Schools had to satisfy several conditions, including a school improvement plan and capacity to secure support from the business sector, broadly defined, related to the field of specialisation. In return the school received additional funding from government. Schools were supported throughout by the Specialist Schools Trust, now the Specialist Schools and Academies Trust, originally the Technology Colleges Trust. The arts colleges specialise in the performing arts including music, dance and drama, and visual or media arts.

By 2010, almost all of England's 3,100 secondary schools offered at least one specialism. The focus is now on creating as many academies within the secondary sector as possible, these having a much higher degree of autonomy than the 'self-managing' secondary schools that were created in the 1988 Education Reform Act. By mid-2011, there were 629 academies, up from 203 in May 2010 when the coalition government was formed.

The characteristics and expected impact of the arts in specialist arts colleges were set out in A Vision Paper for Arts Education prepared by the Specialist Arts Colleges National Headteacher Group (Specialist Schools and Academies Trust n.d.). These extend the 'case for the arts' set out in Chapter 1.

- Through creating, performing and enjoying a wide range of cultural experiences, students have the chance to develop new interests, raise their aspirations and develop untapped potential. The needs of individual students can be met through creative approaches.
- Participation in the arts develops confidence, motivation and raises self-esteem. It engages students in taking responsibility for their learning and that of others;

it develops project management skills, creative thinking and problem-solving skills.

- Learning about the arts and having opportunities to take part in cultural activities, provide powerful ways to further students' personal and social skills. Taking part in arts activities can complement formal learning and can reach out in new ways to students who may have drifted away from formal education; there is also evidence to suggest that improved behaviour and engagement amongst challenging students can come as a result of participation in the arts.

- Cultural activities can have a profound impact on attitudes and develop the very skills that employers in the creative industries say that they are looking for in the future workplace: an entrepreneurial attitude, creativity, ability to work in a team, imagination and discipline.

- Participation and performance in drama, music, dance and singing can improve students' levels of fitness and enhance their sense of wellbeing, driving them on to bigger and better things.

- Involvement in the arts can lead to positive social outcomes including greater community cohesion and an improved sense of social responsibility.

- High standards of discipline amongst [students] come from a deep engagement in the arts education.

Until the middle of the last decade it was possible to make comparisons between the performance of specialist and non-specialist schools. The Specialist Schools and Academies Trust released a report each year comparing performance using student grades at the GCSE level. The trust also used a robust value-added measure. In 2005, according to the trust, 938 specialist schools out-performed 1,993 non-specialist schools in every area of specialisation (Taylor and Ryan 2005: 79). Comparisons for arts colleges are summarised in Table 2.1. The indicator is the percentage of students receiving high grades in the range from A* (top grade) to C. Specialist schools out-performed non-specialist schools for each of five sub-specialisations.

Comparisons like those reported in Table 2.1 have proved contentious. Apart from an ideological critique on the part of those wedded to the concept of the 'standard comprehensive school', some have suggested that the differences are due to a degree of selectivity on the part of specialist schools. It is an argument with merit even though no more than 10 percent of students may be selected on the basis of their prior achievement in the area of specialisation. However, once value-added comparisons were included in the analysis, the relative advantage of specialist

Table 2.1 Comparing performances of arts colleges with other schools (percentage of students receiving grades in the range A* to C)

Classification	Art/design A*–C (%)	Drama A*–C (%)	Performing arts A*–C (%)	Media A*–C (%)	Music A*–C (%)
Arts colleges	64.3	65.4	53.7	56.2	65.0
Other schools	60.0	62.3	44.9	50.9	58.5

Source: adapted from Taylor and Ryan 2005: 81

over non-specialist schools was maintained. Other explanations of the comparative advantages include more effective management, since the schools must have a well-developed improvement plan to be accepted, and the additional cash that was provided by government.

As far as arts colleges are concerned, a study by Smithers and Robinson from the Centre for Education and Employment at the University of Buckingham found that a student attending a music school was more likely to get a high grade in physics than a student at a science school. Indeed, students at science schools were also ranked below those from language schools and mathematics and computer schools. However, the authors challenged the conclusion that specialist schools drove-up standards and that arts colleges made a special contribution. For example, it was found that about one-fifth of science schools chose the specialisation because they were traditionally weak in this area and it was thought it was easier to attract good science teachers if a specialisation was offered. Apart from the additional cash, it was pointed out that music and language schools tended to enrol a higher proportion of middle-class students who had higher levels of attainment on entry. The researchers concluded that 'Our interpretation is that specialist schools policy has proved useful as a general programme for freshening up a tired comprehensive system' and that 'it may not be too much of an over-simplification to say that the sum total of research on specialist schools shows that good schools plus extra funding do better' (cited by Garner 2009).

In summary, an initial reading of the trajectory of school reform toward the end of the twentieth century suggested that there would be an expanded place for the arts. However, while narratives placed a sharp focus on the importance of innovation and creativity, there was little change for the arts. An interesting exception emerged in England when a major plank in the reform effort encouraged secondary schools to adopt a specialisation, with the arts being one specialisation out of 10, with schools still offering the broad national curriculum. At first sight, arts colleges at the secondary level out-performed matching non-specialist schools but recent research suggests that other factors accounted for the claimed benefits of specialisation. The sidelining of the arts in primary schools in England was described in Chapter 1.

Factors that account for success in high-performing school systems

Two widely-read and highly-respected reports by McKinsey & Company have systematically documented the factors that account for success in high-performing or dramatically improving schools and school systems. The findings are summarised here together with an assessment of the place of the arts.

The McKinsey Report on *How the World's Best-Performing School Systems Come Out on Top* (Barber and Mourshed 2007), referred to here as the first McKinsey report, is one of the most widely read studies in recent times. Among its striking findings is that 'the available evidence suggests that the main driver of the variation in student learning at school is the quality of the teachers' (Barber and Mourshed 2007: 12).

Investing in intellectual capital of teachers can be a costly business but the first McKinsey report makes clear that an exclusive focus on securing higher levels of financial capital may have little impact on learning. It cited one study that found that performance had declined or plateaued in several countries between the 1970s and 1990s despite increases in expenditure. For example, real per student expenditure in Australia had increased by 270 percent but student achievement had declined by 2 percent. The corresponding figures for New Zealand were an increase of 223 percent and a decline of 10 percent, respectively (Barber and Mourshed 2007: 10). Top-performing country Finland is not top-spending, adjusting for purchasing power parity. The first McKinsey report provides a summary of its findings in the form of key questions and parameters or policy settings based on best practice. These are reproduced in Table 2.2.

The report is silent on the matter of curriculum and approaches to teaching and learning except in its finding that the best systems in the world attract to teaching the top 10 percent of the academic cohort and ensure that staff remain at the forefront of knowledge and skill in their professional fields. Outstanding support is provided to students who fall behind.

The second McKinsey report entitled *How the World's Most Improved School Systems Keep Getting Better* (Mourshed *et al.* 2010) also warrants attention. While the authors' claim in the title that they are reporting on 'the world's most improved school systems' is open to debate, they document what has occurred in 'systems that have achieved significant, sustained, and widespread gains in student outcomes on international and national assessment from 1980s onward' (Mourshed *et al.* 2010: 17). There were 18 countries in their sample (a total of 20 systems including three from the United States). These were classified on a robust evidence base in four 'journeys': poor to fair ('achieving the basics of literacy and numeracy'), fair to good ('getting the foundations in place'), good to great ('shaping the profession') and great to excellent ('improving through peers and innovation'). There were six common interventions: (1) revising curriculum and standards; (2) reviewing reward and remunerations structure; (3) building technical skills of teachers and principals, often through group or cascaded training; (4) assessing student learning; (5) utilising student data to guide delivery; and (6) establishing policy documents and education laws. It is noteworthy that innovation was a theme in only one journey, namely, from great to excellent.

Five of the 20 systems in the second McKinsey report are on the journey from great to excellent during which innovation is a theme: Hong Kong, Ontario, Saxony, Singapore and South Korea. The authors described the environment for these journeys in the following terms: 'In the final frontier of school improvement, the journey from great to excellence, systems focus on creating an environment that will unleash the creativity and innovation of its educators and other stakeholder groups' (Mourshed *et al.* 2010: 50).

Overall, it seems that the second McKinsey report is primarily concerned with an improvement agenda and, beyond that, moving to excellence, with a place for innovation in the final stages of the journey. It concludes that 'leaders follow a common "playbook", irrespective of system performance level, culture or geography' (Mourshed *et al.* 2010: 110). There are five steps in this playbook: (1) decide on what is 'non-negotiable', (2) install capable and like-minded people in the most critical positions, (3) engage with stakeholders, (4) secure resources for the non-negotiable, and (5) get 'early wins' on the board quickly (Mourshed *et al.* 2010: 110–14).

Table 2.2 Key questions and policy settings based on best practice as identified in the first McKinsey report

Question	Best in the world
Getting the right people to become teachers	
• What is the average academic calibre of people who become teachers?	Among the top 10 percent of each cohort
• How is the teaching profession viewed by university students and recent graduates?	One of the top 3 career choices
• How rigorous are selection processes in teacher training?	Rigorous checks designed to assess teaching potential; e.g. teaching practice, literacy and numeracy tests
• What is the ratio of places in initial teacher education courses to applications?	1:10
• How does starting compensation for teachers compare to other graduate salaries?	In line with other graduate salaries
Developing effective instructors	
• What is the total amount of coaching new teachers receive in schools?	More than 20 weeks
• What proportion of each teacher's time is spent on professional development?	10 percent of working time is used for professional development
• Does each teacher have an exact knowledge of specific weaknesses in their practice?	Yes, as a result of everyday activities occurring in schools
• Can teachers observe and understand better teaching practice in a school setting?	Yes, teachers regularly invite each other into other's classrooms to observe and coach
• Do teachers reflect on and discuss practice?	Yes, through both formal and informal processes in schools
• What role do school leaders play in developing effective instructors?	The best coaches and instructors are selected as leaders
• How much focused, systematic research is conducted into effective instruction and then fed back into policy and classroom practice?	Research budget equivalent to US$50 per student each year focused on improving instruction
Ensuring every student performs well	
• What standards exist for what students should know, understand and be able to do?	Clear standards appropriate to system performance
• What system-wide checks exist on the quality of school performance?	All schools are aware of their strengths and weaknesses
• What action is taken to tackle underperformance?	Effective mechanisms to support all failing students; minimal performance variation between schools
• How is funding and support organised?	Funding and support are focused where it can have the most impact

Source: Barber and Mourshed 2007: 41

There were three main findings (Mourshed *et al.* 2010: 33–34) as far as strategy for each stage of the journey is concerned:

1   It's a system thing, not a single thing: There is a common pattern in the interventions improving systems use to move from one performance stage to the next, irrespective of geography, time, or culture. These interventions, which we term the 'improvement cluster', are mutually reinforcing and act together to produce an upward shift in the trajectory of the system. Though there is a different cluster of interventions for each stage of the system's journey (poor to fair, fair to good, good to great, great to excellent), there is a dominant pattern throughout that journey.

2   Prescribe adequacy, unleash greatness: There is a strong correlation between a school system's improvement journey stage and the tightness of central control over the individual school's activities and performance. Systems on the poor to fair journey, in general characterised by lower skill educators, exercise tight, central control over teaching and learning processes in order to minimise the degree of variation between individual classes and across schools. In contrast, systems moving from good to great, characterised by higher skill educators, provide only loose, central guidelines for teaching and learning processes, in order to encourage peer led creativity and innovation inside schools, the core driver for raising performance at this stage.

3   Common but different: Our findings indicate that six interventions occur with equal frequency across all the improvement journeys, though manifesting differently in each one. These six interventions are: revising curriculum and standards, ensuring an appropriate reward and remuneration structure for teachers and principals, building the technical skills of teachers and principals, assessing students, establishing data systems, and facilitating the improvement journey through the publication of policy documents and implementation of education laws.

(Mourshed *et al.* 2010: 33–34)

The report provides examples of interventions for each of the three findings. For the first finding, in the journey from great to excellent ('it's a system thing, not a single thing'), these interventions included collaborative practice among educators, decentralising pedagogical rights to schools and teachers, creating rotation and secondment programs across schools and between centre and schools, providing additional administrative staff, sharing innovation from the front-line, and funding for innovation (Mourshed *et al.* 2010: 51). For the second finding ('prescribe adequacy, unleash greatness'), the report concludes that 'lower-performing systems focus on raising the floor, while higher performing ones focus on opening up the ceiling' (Mourshed *et al.* 2010: 52). For the third finding ('common but different'), particular attention is given in the journey from great to excellent to 'attracting top talent', with teachers' base salary significantly above per capita GDP (Mourshed *et al.* 2010: 62).

While the second McKinsey report refers to 'revising curriculum and standards' there are no accounts of the particular ways this is done as systems move from 'great' to 'excellent' for which there is a general finding of 'unleashing greatness' and nurturing creativity and innovation. Examples of changes in curriculum tend to refer to schools and school systems at the start of the journey, and these tend to sharpen the focus on literacy and numeracy. The arts are not mentioned once in either the first or second McKinsey reports which are concerned more than anything else with policy and process rather than innovation and content of the curriculum (except for literacy and numeracy).

Likely and preferred directions for the future of schools

So far in this chapter we have described how momentum seemed to be building for an expanded role for the arts as the school reform movement took shape from the 1980s, yet accounts of how the world's best-performing and most improved systems achieved their success rarely if ever referred to the place of the arts. References to curriculum were usually limited to a focus on literacy and numeracy and acknowledgement that the truly outstanding performers provided a high level of professional empowerment and encouragement of innovation. Nevertheless, proposals for further reform in education invariably call for dramatically different approaches that re-capture the momentum of earlier times.

As far as Australia is concerned, the Melbourne Declaration on Educational Goals for Young Australians (Ministerial Council for Education, Early Childhood Development and Youth Affairs) MCEECDYA 2008 made clear that successful learners should be able to do the following:

- develop their capacity to learn and play an active role in their own learning
- have the essential skills in literacy and numeracy and are creative and pro-ductive users of technology, especially ICT, as a foundation for success in all learning areas
- are able to think deeply and logically, and obtain and evaluate evidence in a disciplined way as the result of studying fundamental disciplines
- are creative, innovative and resourceful, and are able to solve problems in ways that draw upon a range of learning areas and disciplines
- are able to plan activities independently, collaborate, work in teams and communicate ideas
- are able to make sense of their world and think about how things have become the way they are
- are on a pathway towards continued success in further education, training or employment, and acquire the skills to make informed learning and employ-ment decisions throughout their lives
- are motivated to reach their full potential.

(MCEECDYA 2008: 9)

While many people reject the nomenclature, the so-called twenty-first-century skills are generally considered to include those in the Cisco (2008) report entitled *Equipping Every Learner for the 21st Century* which proposed that all learners:

- Are to acquire a range of skills including problem solving and decision-making, creative and critical thinking, collaboration, communication and negotiation, and intellectual curiosity.
- Receive tailored instruction.
- Connect to their communities.
- Continue learning through their lives.

(Cisco 2008: 9)

While not explicitly mentioned, engagement in the arts is clearly consistent with intentions set out in the Melbourne Declaration and the Cisco Report. The latter made clear that far-reaching change is required (Cisco 2008):

Our education systems continue to reinforce traditional approaches to teaching. Changing this will require leaders to develop a compelling vision of 21st century learning, communicate it with passion, and ensure that it is translated into action at all levels of the system. The transformation will need to be holistic; from government ministries to principals and classroom teachers. It will also require a holistic reform of education delivery, to align incentives and provide resources for teacher training, curriculum development, accountability, and assessment [in the following areas]:

- Teachers: Great teaching is at the heart of successful learning. Great 21st century teachers will weave 21st century skills into core subjects through new pedagogy, enlivened by collaborative technologies. New and proven instructional approaches and digital resources will become a core toolkit for 21st century teachers. This transformation will require new forms of teacher training and professional development.
- Curriculum and assessment: In the future, curricular reform will most likely be required to balance core subjects and new 21st century skills. This will also require fresh thinking about performance measures to overcome legitimate concerns that there has been limited progress toward recognising and rewarding skill development that cannot be detected in an end-of-term assessment.
- Accountability for outcomes: Accountability will be more essential than ever in 21st century education systems. School leaders will be accountable to students; questioning if school is staying relevant to their lives. Policy leaders will be accountable to employers and citizens; questioning if the system is effectively preparing young people to help meet national aspirations. It will also be important to measure accurately the impact of new skills and pedagogy in the classroom to bring about new and improved outcomes.

(Cisco 2008: 15)

Milton Chen is former executive director of The George Lucas Education Foundation and one-time director of research at Sesame Street. He is well-placed to document innovations that are consistent with what is proposed by Cisco, as he does in *Education Nation: Six Leading Edges of Innovation in our Schools* (Chen 2010). These six innovations are summarised below. They are, in fact, sets of strategies and collections of related practices that together form a *gestalt* in the sense illustrated earlier in the chapter.

The Thinking Edge: 'the most basic prerequisite to creating an Education Nation is changing our thinking about the enterprise itself – the learning process, the role of students, teachers and parents, and what is possible given the opportunities afforded by technology' (Chen 2010: 11). An illustration of 'the thinking edge' is to turn 'either/ or' debates into 'both-and' syntheses. Chen lists 10; for example, rather than teacher-centred instruction or student-centred learning he offers a synthesis: 'teachers are vital in a student-centred classroom, but they play a different role when technology is the platform for content and collaboration' (Chen 2010: 23).

The Curriculum Edge: 'the curriculum edge represents the growing trend of transforming and reorganising the most fundamental educational activities; what students are taught and how their learning is assessed. This edge recognises that today's curriculum has not kept up with the rapid pace of change in every discipline. The very definition of what a course is, how it is organised, and what it covers needs to be reconceived for advances in twenty-first century knowledge' (Chen 2010: 35). Chen provides an impressive array of examples of 'the curriculum edge' in hundreds of schools across the United States. He explicitly refers to initiatives in the development of twenty-first-century skills.

The Technology Edge: 'until every student has his or her own computer, the benefits of using them on a regular, ongoing basis are undercut' (Chen 2010: 87). Chen provides a host of illustrations to establish the case for the role of technology, making explicit the links to twenty-first-century skills. While he documents the extraordinary growth in the number of school students taking online courses, he is careful to acknowledge that attending a 'bricks-and-mortar' school will continue to be important. He has reservations about the position taken by writers such as Christensen, Johnson and Horn (2008) in *Disrupting Class* that online learning is a competitive force 'that finally will challenge the dominance of bricks-and-mortar schools relying on teachers in physical classrooms' (Christensen *et al.* 2008: 111).

The Time/Place Edge: which 'represents the destruction of the old view of education happening within the four worlds of the classroom' (Christensen *et al.* 2008: 139).

The Co-Teaching Edge: Chen acknowledges that teachers are the most important resource in securing the success of students but describes partnerships with others who can support the effort, including parents, professionals in other fields and students (Chen 2010).

The Youth Edge: Today's students:

are marching through our schools, carrying a transformational change in their pockets in the form of powerful handheld devices. Yet this generation, 95 percent of the stakeholders in education and the ones who stand the most to lose from a poor education, are often left out of the conversation about how to change it.

(Chen 2010: 213).

Chen captures an important feature in the following description of the twenty-first-century learner:

In the traditional classroom, a student's main job is to sit, listen, take good notes, do the homework, memorise facts, figures, and formulae, and repeat this information back in quizzes and tests. The twenty-first century student uses technology to actively seek out reliable and high-quality information, analyse these sources, and utilise them in producing a product of his or her knowledge. In the traditional classroom, the teacher works hard and the students rest. In classrooms emulating the modern workplace, the students should be the ones working the hardest.

(Chen 2010: 237)

Chen draws on policies and practices that are already in place in many schools. Except for their consistency with what the second McKinsey report describes for the journey from 'great' to 'excellent', there is little in either the first or second McKinsey report to suggest that these should be 'mainstreamed' as a matter of urgency. Not surprisingly, since he worked for The George Lucas Education Foundation, Chen gives special attention to one particular art form in his advocacy of further change in the Curriculum Edge, namely, the 'language of images':

Among all the ways in which the human species communicates using words, pictures, and sound, the school system overwhelmingly prizes books, text, and writing at the expense of photography, cinema, or music. The curriculum is a verbal curriculum. Yet cinema can unify all media – the written and spoken word, images, and sound – into one transcendent experience.

(Chen 2010: 65)

Chen cites George Lucas in arguing that schools fail to build on the affinity young people have for music:

They know music. They may not know the grammar of music . . . We go through school and learn the grammar of English . . . Somehow in the education system, these need to be balanced out so that kids can communicate using all forms of communication.

(Chen 2010: 67)

Significance

School reform has extended over three decades in nations such as Australia, England and the United States. Unprecedented amounts of money have been devoted to the effort, yet levels of achievement have only marginally improved if results on tests of international student achievement such as PISA are a guide. Strategies associated with high performance or dramatic improvement have been documented and these have tended to focus on a relatively narrow range of outcomes and have been concerned largely with process, albeit on important matters such as the quality of teaching. There has been consistent advocacy over this period of a holistic view of education, the desirability of connectedness in the curriculum and an expanded role for the arts. The so-called twenty-first-century skills have emphasised creativity and innovation for which the importance of the arts should be assumed. However, there is a disjunction between what has been advocated and what lies at centre-stage in the reform agenda. The outcome is the apparent sidelining of the arts, as documented in Chapter 1.

It is disconcerting that progress is slow and that connectedness in a holistic view of learning has been impaired despite a consensus among those whose business it is to make connections between education, economy and society. It is profoundly disappointing that neither the first nor the second McKinsey report could find much evidence that these connections were being made.

3   Pitfalls in educational reform

In Chapter 3 we undertake a deeper analysis to explain why the arts have been sidelined. The focus is on what should be central to the education reform effort, namely, the curriculum and associated pedagogies rather than structures and processes, which are important but should be secondary, complementary or facilitative. We start with an analysis of mis-alignment of the reform effort in Australia, generalising to comparable countries, and offer support from experts who interpret the evidence in the same way. We conclude by suggesting mis-alignment on a grand scale in two respects: (1) education, economy and society; and (2) passion, strategy and trust.

A framework that helps explain why the arts have been sidelined

The development of a national curriculum is one of the most exciting and worthwhile projects in Australian education in many years. Priority has been given to the development of a curriculum in the arts. Australia is one of only three of 21 nations around the Asia-Pacific that do not already have a national curriculum, the others being Canada and the United States. No country could be more fortunate to have outstanding leaders of the effort in the persons of Professor Barry McGaw, Chair of the Australian Curriculum, Assessment and Reporting Authority (ACARA) and Dr Peter Hill, CEO of ACARA. McGaw is former head of the education division of the Organisation for Economic Co-Operation and Development (OECD) and served before that as chief executive officer of ACER. Hill was head of the school system in Victoria until the early 1990s before assuming positions at the University of Melbourne, the National Centre on Education and Economy (NCEE) in the United States, and the Hong Kong Examinations and Assessment Authority. They have unparalleled knowledge in curriculum, assessment and reporting.

However, no matter how well designed a national, or any other, curriculum might be, expectations will be frustrated if other strategies to achieve the transformation of schools, no matter how well-intentioned, do not align with it. Such a mis-alignment explains why the arts have been sidelined, in countries such as Australia, England and the United States.

In *Why not the Best Schools?* Brian Caldwell and Jessica Harris proposed a 10-point 10-year strategy for achieving the transformation of a nation's schools, with transformation defined as significant, systematic and sustained change that secures success for all students in all settings (Caldwell and Harris 2008: chapter 9). The strategy was developed about two-thirds of the way through an eight-year sequence of projects focusing on the transformation of schools. The groundwork was laid from 2004 to 2007 in 73 seminars and workshops involving about 4,000 school and school system leaders from 11 countries. These events involved input from Brian Caldwell, Jessica Harris and Jim Spinks but the centre-piece in most instances were scores of short case studies from school leaders about how their schools had achieved, or were making progress in achieving, transformation as defined above. The purpose of the workshops was to further share and test ideas. It was an iterative program with findings from one event being fed in to those that followed. Hypotheses were created to explain how transformation was achieved. A progress report of findings was provided by Caldwell and Spinks (2008).

A series of focused national studies was conducted to test these hypotheses, funded by the Australian government and Welsh Assembly government. They were conducted in Australia, China, England, Finland, Wales and the United States. The findings were reported by Caldwell and Harris (2008) and in a series of country reports. These findings are of two kinds, one being descriptions of four kinds of capital (intellectual, social, spiritual, financial) that should be strengthened and aligned if transformation is to be achieved. The other findings were in the form of a concise set of strategies to guide policymaking and policy implementation in efforts to achieve the transformation of schools. They were intended to be immediately adaptable to Australia because the Australian government led by Kevin Rudd and later by Julia Gillard was determined to create an 'education revolution'. The framework is relevant to any country that has the same intention, especially nations from which data were gathered in the seminars and workshops described above. The 10-point 10-year strategy was as follows:

1 A national curriculum is designed that is broad enough and sufficiently adaptable to ensure the professional judgement of a highly-skilled profession will prevail at the school level ('national curriculum').

2 Initial teacher education is transformed to ensure all teachers have a Master's degree and remain at the forefront of knowledge and skill through continuous professional development ('teacher education').

3 New structural arrangements are designed to ensure diversity of programs in the post-compulsory years in an effective constantly-changing alignment of education, economy and society ('program diversity').

4 National testing of all students is minimised as the highest levels of knowledge and skill are developed by teachers and those who support them ('national testing').

5 The wider community, including business, is seriously engaged in design and delivery with public and private funds deployed through networks of foundations and trusts ('community engagement').

6 Transparent needs-based mechanisms are designed to ensure the efficient deployment of public and private funds ('transparent funding').

7   Innovative approaches to governance are introduced along the lines of pub-
    licly-funded no-fee charter schools to ensure that public schools maintain
    their appeal to parents ('innovative governance').
8   School ownership ceases to be a factor in determining the amount of public
    funds that are disbursed to schools ('school ownership').
9   Higher levels of school autonomy in the public sector are achieved within a
    framework of accountability and choice ('school autonomy').
10 Most schools in the public sector are rebuilt or redesigned to make them
    suitable for learning and teaching in the 21st century ('school design').

(Caldwell and Harris 2008: 171)

The various alignments that are necessary to achieve transformation are illustrated
in the matrix in Table 3.1, which represents a 'force field' of strategies to achieve
the transformation of schools. Ideally, there should be perfect alignment among the
strategies. Illustrations of mis-alignment are contained in the fourth line which shows
the 'force field' for national testing.

Not all elements in the matrix are relevant, but most are. For example, there
must be alignment between national testing and national curriculum, teacher
education, program diversity, innovative governance, school autonomy, and school
design.

Two examples of mis-alignment are described below, one related to assessment,
the other to teachers' bonuses.

Mis-alignment Case 1: Assessment

The contrast between assessment in Australia, England and the United States and, for
example, Finland and New Zealand, is illuminating. Finland and New Zealand draw
on a wide range of qualitative and quantitative approaches and stress the importance
of judgement in balancing the two. Assessment in the arts is accommodated.

Much has been written about the performance of Finland on international tests
of student achievement such as the Program for International Student Assessment
(PISA). Its reputation is well-deserved; although it should be pointed out that it
did not do so well in the Trends in International Mathematics and Science Study
(TIMSS) when it participated, prior to its switch to PISA. Many reasons are offered
in explanation of Finland's performance in PISA, including the quality of its teachers,
the relatively high degree of school autonomy, an outstanding approach to providing
support to its students, and the capacity of schools to adapt the broad national
curriculum to the mix of student needs at the local level. A report that compared
performance in the United States with other countries, citing results in PISA 2009,
drew attention to other features of schooling in Finland:

The emphasis on learner-centred, collaborative instruction and a future oriented,
relevant curriculum that focuses on creativity and problem solving has made
PISA *the* international test for reformers promoting constructivist learning and
21st-century skills. Finland implemented reforms in the 1990s and early 2000s

Table 3.1 Force field of strategies to achieve the transformation of schools illustrated in mis-alignments that may arise from narrowly-focused high-stakes testing (X)

Strategy	National curriculum	Teacher education	Program diversity	National testing	Community engagement	Transparent funding	Innovative governance	School ownership	School autonomy	School design
National curriculum	—									
Teacher education		—								
Program diversity			—							
National testing	X	X	X	—			X		X	X
Community engagement					—					
Transparent funding						—				
Innovative governance							—			
School ownership								—		
School autonomy									—	
School design										—

that embraced the tenets of these movements. Several education researchers from Finland have attributed their nation's strong showing to the compatibility of recent reforms with the content of PISA.

(Loveless 2011: 11)

In addition to the foregoing, it is important to note that Finland does not have a national testing program, so that schools are freed up from the pressures associated with such an approach. However, it is equally important to note that teachers have high levels of skill in assessing students and personalising learning, especially in respect to the way specially trained staff provide immediate support for students who fall behind. All of these factors are likely to contribute to the ranking of Finland on various indices of creativity, performing well above Australia, England and the United States (Florida 2005) reported in Chapter 1.

New Zealand is also a top performer in PISA. It has a better balanced approach to assessment than Australia, England and the United States. A discussion paper of the Ministry of Education makes this clear (Ministry of Education 2010). Here are two excerpts that highlight the importance of both quantitative and qualitative data:

> Assessment information consists of *quantitative* and *qualitative* data. The nature and content of the information will differ depending on the immediate purpose for its collection and the level of the sector at which it is collected. A range of rich assessment data will be captured and shared at the school-level. Subsets of information will be made available with appropriate qualitative and quantitative context to other agencies in the education system to enable them to fulfil their roles.
>
> (Ministry of Education 2010: 50)

> The Ministry maintains that the publishing of raw, highly aggregated assessment data without qualitative context information will both undermine this collegial environment and subvert the reliability of the assessment data collected. The Ministry of Education considers that it is not appropriate to compare schools on a simplistic and misleading basis. This is a consistent position held by successive Governments in New Zealand and dating back at least to the 1998 Green Paper entitled *Assessment for Success in Primary Schools*.
>
> (Ministry of Education 2010: 50)

Finally, in this reference to the way things are done in New Zealand, the discussion paper highlights the importance of 'overall teacher judgements' that are based on both 'tacit information' and 'explicit information' that are drawn from multiple sources:

> Teachers are expected to make professional judgments about student progress and achievement in relation to what is expected by the appropriate standard of reference. These qualitative judgments are termed *overall teacher judgments* because they are 'on balance' judgments made across a range of information and across the range of skills, knowledge and understanding expected at any given reference

point. They make use of tacit information held by the teacher as well as a range of explicit information collected by the teacher from multiple sources.

(Ministry of Education 2010: 16)

It is incumbent on us to suggest a better way to achieve alignment and ensure a proper focus is placed on the arts. We will do this with a scenario. Writing a scenario is a useful technique for thinking about the future. A scenario is not a prediction. It describes an alternative future, either probable or preferred, with a narrative that credibly explains the pathways from the present to that future (Caldwell and Loader 2010).

Here is a narrative for an alternative future that describes how we might reverse current and likely trends as far as impact of high-stakes testing is concerned while we nurture innovation and creativity. An adaptation of this scenario formed part of Brian Caldwell's evidence to the Senate Inquiry into the Administration and Reporting of NAPLAN (National Assessment Program – Literacy and Numeracy) Testing and in a presentation at the 2010 International Education Research Conference of the Australian Association of Research in Education (AARE) (Caldwell 2010). Footnotes illustrate the evidence of support for particular elements (see page 46).

It is 2020. There is now a higher level of transparency and more assessment in Australia's schools than in the past. However, approaches associated with NAPLAN and the My School website at the start of the decade, when every student in Years 3, 5, 7 and 9 was required to do several 40 to 50 minute, mostly multiple choice 'high-stakes' national tests each year, have been abandoned. A united profession and the public at large soon realised that expectations had not been realised and the scheme was become increasingly and seriously dysfunctional. It inhibited rather than supported the transformation[1] of schools. There was marginal improvement in student achievement in the early part of the decade but results soon flat-lined.[2] There was anecdotal evidence of 'gaming the system'. Changes in levels of achievement against national standards are now, in 2020, monitored through periodic testing of samples of students in jurisdictions around the country.

Long-overdue reforms in teacher education starting in 2011 meant that teachers became expert in skilful assessment, diagnosis of need and immediate support of their students in an unprecedented and comprehensive approach to personalising learning.[3] Every school has teachers and other professionals on call who give immediate support to their colleagues to ensure that no student falls behind.[4] A re-modelled national agency prepares tests that schools can choose if they wish, but the high level of professional skill ensures that most schools design their own and use an array of approaches to assessment. This agency works through each jurisdiction to monitor schools to ensure they are doing this well.[5]

Parents obtain real-time online reports of how their sons and daughters are progressing,[6] and online comparisons of schools in My School were phased out from 2012. They were of dubious validity, difficult to understand and the subject of seemingly endless debates among academics, policymakers and practitioners.

Teaching to the test and the narrowing of the curriculum are dysfunctions of the past. The curriculum has been broadened to address the range of knowledge and skills demanded in the 21st century.[7] Schools have far more autonomy than in the past,[8] with many opting for an international rather than national curriculum, but they operate within robust frameworks of accountability. Innovation and creativity flourish and there has been a resurgence in the arts and science. New world-class facilities have been an important factor in attracting able people to the profession.[9] There is a passion that has not been evident for several decades.

In this scenario, by 2020: 'innovation and creativity flourish and there has been resurgence in the arts and science'. We have much to do to if these outcomes are to be achieved.

Mis-alignment Case 2: Teacher bonus

The second case of mis-alignment moved to centre-stage in Australia in 2011 in the prime minister's announcement about a teacher bonus scheme. According to Brian Caldwell (Caldwell 2011a, 2011b) the scheme is poorly designed, has no successful counterpart in comparable countries, and is almost certain to be abandoned or postponed. It is astonishing under these conditions that $425 million was set aside in the Commonwealth budget for 2011–12 as an initial payment on the final cost of $1.3 billion.

The intentions may be commendable. After all, there can be no disagreement that high-quality teaching is the most important school-based factor in accounting for student achievement, and that high-quality teaching should be recognised and rewarded.

It cannot be implemented in the time frame announced by the prime minister. A total of 25,000 teachers or 10 percent of the workforce will receive their bonus in 2014 based on appraisals in 2013. This means that 250,000 teachers must be appraised according to an agreed and valid framework. No such framework exists. The Australian Institute for Teaching and School Leadership (AITSL) has been charged with developing one and has, to its credit, secured agreement on a set of teaching standards. There are 37 standards, with a different set for each of four categories of teachers, creating 148 different standards. There are currently no agreed evidence-based approaches to determining how each standard will be measured. Implementation in 2013 will likely be no more than a hastily contrived tick-the-box approach that will de-professionalise rather than enhance the profession.

International experts on school improvement give such schemes the thumbs-down. Canada's Michael Fullan (University of Toronto) concluded that 'performance-based merit pay is a nonstarter' and that 'when common sense tells you it won't work, when no research exists that backs up the claim for merit pay . . . it is time to give up the ghost [of merit pay]' (Fullan 2010: 84 and 91). He noted that performance pay is used in virtually no other profession.

Fullan has been the chief education advisor to the government of Ontario in Canada, one of the best performing systems in PISA. Along with Alberta, another province in Canada, it is not far behind Finland in PISA. Neither system has adopted or plans to adopt a bonus system or merit pay (nor has Finland).

As described in Chapter 2, McKinsey & Company has released two well-researched and highly regarded reports on reform in education which list the factors that account for high performance or dramatic improvement. In *How the World's Best-Performing Systems Come Out on Top* (Barber and Mourshed 2007), there is no mention of bonuses or performance pay. In *How the World's Most Improved School Systems Keep Getting Better* (Mourshed *et al.* 2010), among 20 national or sub-national systems, there are no examples of bonuses or performance pay except for three systems that moved from 'poor' to 'fair': Western Cape (South Africa), Madhya Pradesh (India) and Minas Gerais (Brazil), none of which are relevant to Australia, England or the United States. Those systems that have moved from 'fair' to 'good', 'good' to 'great' or 'great' to 'excellent' ensured that teachers were paid appropriately, preferably significantly above GDP per capita.

The prime minister also raised the possibility that scores in NAPLAN and information on the My School website might be used. Apart from concerns about the validity of scores and comparisons (Caldwell and Vaughan 2011a), with evidence that many schools are 'gaming' the system (for example, encouraging some students not to sit the tests or providing excessive coaching) there is no provision for assessing the performance of teachers in areas other than literacy and numeracy, for example, in the arts. There are many reasons why NAPLAN should not be used to make judgements about the performance of individual teachers but, should the approach prevail, grave harm will be done to efforts to offer the full range of curriculum in schools.

Independent authoritative support for mis-alignment

The mis-alignments described above were identified through an analysis of a 'force field' of multiple strategies for the transformation of schools, as identified by Caldwell and Harris (2008). There is independent authoritative support for the primary source of mis-alignment and evidence is cited here from two eminent scholars (Yong Zhao and Diane Ravitch) and from the highly regarded think tank at the RAND Corporation.

Yong Zhao is Presidential Chair and Associate Dean for Global Education, College of Education at the University of Oregon. In *Catching Up or Leading the Way: American Education in the Age of Globalization* (Zhao 2009) he highlighted the achievements of America on various indicators of innovation and creativity, including the number of patents, the number of Nobel Prizes and leadership in science and medicine. He argued that these achievements could not be gained if American education at all levels was as poor as it is often painted to be. National reports over several decades continue to highlight its weaknesses. Zhao acknowledged these weaknesses, and was highly critical on a range of matters, including aspects of curriculum. However, he connected student experiences in schools with the aforementioned strengths, including diversity in curriculum and extra-curriculum programs, the encouragement of individuality, and the extensity and intensity of team-oriented programs. He acknowledged that these strengths are viewed by some as weaknesses when the criterion is performance on international tests. However, he noted that several high-performing nations seek to emulate the United States in its areas of strength:

> While the United States is moving toward more standardisation and centralisation, the Asian countries are working hard to allow more flexibility and autonomy at the local level. While the United States is investing resources to ensure all students take the same courses and pass the same tests, the Asian countries are advocating for more individualisation and attending to emotions, creativity and other skills. While the United States is raising the stakes on testing, the Asian countries are exerting great efforts to reduce the power and pressure of testing.
>
> (Zhao 2009: 63)

> As we enter a new world rapidly changed by globalisation and technology, we need to change course. Instead of instilling fear in the public about the rise of other countries, bureaucratising education with bean-counting policies, demoralising educators through dubious accountability measures, homogenising school curriculum, and turning children into test takers, we should inform the public about the possibilities brought about by globalisation, encourage educational innovations, inspire educators with genuine support, diversify and decentralise curriculum, and educate children as confident, unique, and well-rounded human beings.
>
> (Zhao 2009: 198)

Zhao provides a regular blog posting at http://zhaolearning.com. His post on 26 February 2011 on the topic 'Entrepreneurship and creativity: Where do they come from and how not to destroy them' is recommended. It included the following:

> I found it amazing that a president [Obama] who spends time [coaching] his daughter's basketball team and who sends his children to a private school that believes 'all our students have within them the light of creativity and can learn much of value from their own and others' and thus provides rich art, music, and sports programs and teaches foreign languages starting from Pre-K, wants only more math and science for other people's children. It is equally amazing for the Secretary of Education [Duncan], whose love for basketball helped him get to Harvard, [find] his wife, and become close friends with a man who made him the Secretary of Education, to think other people's children should only focus on getting good test scores on the so called core academic subjects. Somehow, arts, music, sports, foreign languages, or any subjects other than English, mathematics, and science have been considered soft or 'useless' in American education reforms judging from the Federal education funding priorities or public statements made by the political leaders. These are also the programs that are typically first to be cut or reduced when schools face financial difficulties or need to improve student test scores to meet AYP [Annual Yearly Progress].
>
> (Zhao 2011)

Diane Ravitch is Research Professor of Education at New York University and a senior fellow at the Brookings Institution. From 1991 to 1993 she was Assistant Secretary for Education and Counsellor to Secretary of Education Lamar Alexander in the administration of President George H. W. Bush. President Clinton appointed her to the National Assessment Governing Board, which oversees federal testing. After previously supporting testing and extensive choice, including charter schools and the engagement of the philanthropic sector, she has reversed her positions. Her strongest criticism is levelled at the testing movement and, among other things, the way it has narrowed the curriculum, including the arts.

The title of Chapter 2 in her book *The Death and Life of the American School System* (Ravitch 2010) is 'Hijacked! How the Standards Movement Turned into the Testing Movement'. She elaborated:

> How did testing and accountability become the main levers of school reform? How did our elected officials become convinced that measurement and data would fix the schools? Somehow our nation got off the track in its efforts to improve education. What once was the standards movement was replaced by the accountability movement.
>
> (Ravitch 2010: 16)

At the heart of the problem, according to Ravitch, is the relationship between testing and the purposes of education:

> Not everything that matters can be quantified. What is tested may ultimately be less important than what is untested, such as a student's ability to seek alternative explanations, to raise questions, to pursue knowledge on his own, and to think differently. If we do not treasure our individualists, we will lose the spirit of innovation, inquiry, imagination, and dissent that has contributed powerfully to the success of our society in many different fields of endeavour.
>
> (Ravitch 2010: 226)

Significantly, Ravitch draws attention to the balanced curriculum in countries that should be providing the benchmark for Australia, England and the United States:

> Other nations that outrank us on international assessments of mathematics and science do not concentrate obsessively on those subjects in their classrooms. Nations such as Japan and Finland have developed excellent curricula that spell out what students are supposed to learn in a wide variety of subjects. Their schools teach the major fields of study, including the arts and foreign languages, because they believe that this is the right education for their students, not because they will be tested. They do the right thing without rewards and sanctions. Their students excel in the tested subjects because they are well-educated in many subjects that teach them to use language well and to wrestle with important ideas.
>
> (Ravitch 2010: 231)

In the arts, we should agree that all children deserve the opportunity to learn to play a musical instrument, to sing, to engage in dramatic events, dance, paint, sculpt, and study the great works of artistic endeavour from other times and places. Through the arts, children learn discipline, focus, passion, and the sheer joy of creativity. We should make sure that these opportunities and the resources to support them are available to every student in every school.

(Ravitch 2010: 235)

The RAND Corporation released a report in April 2011 proposing broader performance measures for education in the United States than those currently mandated for (No Child Left Behind (NCLB) Schwartz *et al.* 2011). It had this to say about the dysfunctions of narrow approaches to assessment as they concern the arts:

An additional, related benefit of an expanded system relates to the incentive effects that high-stakes measures impose . . . high-stakes accountability some-times leads to an increased focus on tested material at the expense of untested material. Such changes might result not only in important parts of the curriculum being neglected but also in the neglect of desirable competencies that are difficult to measure reliably on standardised assessments, such as communication and teamwork skills. An emphasis on achievement tests might also lead educators to neglect other aspects of students' educational experiences, such as the school's social and emotional climate. The research on effects of testing on these other aspects of schooling is limited, but there is some evidence that schools have reduced opportunities for students to participate in activities, such as arts and field trips, and that teachers worry about negative effects on students' engage-ment . . . A more balanced set of incentives might mitigate these risks, though it is clearly impractical to measure every input, process, and outcome of interest, and developers of these systems will need to weigh the costs and benefits of an expanded set of measures.

(Schwartz *et al.* 2011: 27–28)

The discussion paper on assessment of the Ministry of Education in New Zealand, cited earlier in the chapter, described the kind of re-focusing that is necessary in Australia and comparable countries. Part of this re-focusing is to reinforce if not re-capture time-honoured approaches to assessment, for example, in the arts. We know how to assess achievement in art, dance, drama, literature, music and singing. We have local, state, national and international competitions. They enrich our society and grow in strength as far as the economy is concerned. Prestigious awards are made. Teachers are trained in their assessment, which draws on both quantitative and qualitative data. Professional judgement is required. In many instances, there is a requirement for communication, creativity, innovation, problem-solving and teamwork – the so-called twenty-first-century skills.

While we are concerned in this book with the arts, it is worth highlighting how damage can be done in other subjects such as English. Writing in *Imagination Innovation*

Creativity: Re-visioning English in Education, Manuel, Brock, Sawyer and Carter (2009) set out to

> stress the importance of reconnecting and re-engaging with what teachers – and thereby, potentially, students – love about English: its unique capacity to engage the mind, the spirit and the heart; to stimulate imagination, curiosity and creative capacities through meaningful immersion in the stories of humanity, and to enrich and develop students' cognitive and affective command and understanding of language in all its expansive dimensions, contexts and purposes.
>
> (Manuel *et al.* 2009: 7)

They conclude that 'At a moment in Australian history when the National Curriculum is being developed, the warnings are here about the kind of testing that would defeat any well-intentioned move for richness and depth in that curriculum' (Manuel *et al.* 2009: 9). The same conclusion can be drawn for the arts.

In search of the perfect alignment

Is there a broader set of alignments that we should be striving for in education that also explains the mis-alignments that account for the sidelining of the arts? Two are described here: (1) education, economy, and society; and (2) passion, strategy and trust (Caldwell and Harris 2008).

Figure 3.1 illustrates an alignment between education, economy and society that schools are expected to address. The national curriculum has an important role to play in setting up the alignment. The 'compelling vision with high moral purpose' was described by Caldwell and Harris (2008) as 'success for all students in all settings'.

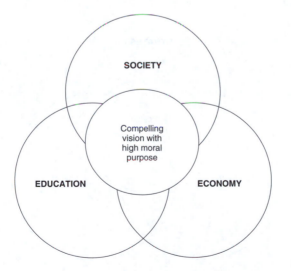

Figure 3.1 Education, economy and society (Caldwell and Harris 2008)

A typical disjunction between the three is illustrated in a statement that is often heard along the lines that 'I want to live in a society, not an economy'. However, a quality education and a strong economy contribute to a vibrant society.

The alignment has been strong in the past. An example is the alignment of schools and society in an agricultural economy, a situation that continues to prevail in communities in many countries. A similar alignment was evident in industrial times to the point that the curriculum was determined to a large extent by the requirements of factories and management in education reflected a 'factory model'. Such an alignment is still important in many countries. New alignments are necessary for education in a knowledge economy in which the technologies of learning have been transformed. Such alignments are not easy to establish and sustain, especially in the context of rapid change of a kind experienced over the last two decades. However, there is a major element missing and that is the arts, which play a much larger role in both economy and society than is reflected in current educational provision.

The second fundamental alignment is between passion, trust and strategy, as illustrated in Figure 3.2. This alignment may be viewed as a precondition for success in the first alignment in Figure 3.1. Passion, trust and strategy must be aligned with the vision. No amount of passion will suffice if well thought-out strategies are not designed and delivered. Passion in policymaking is ineffective if it does not engender trust. This concept was explored in a detailed account of the attempted decentralisation of schools in New South Wales (Caldwell and Vaughan 2011b). Those charged with policy implementation should be committed to the vision and the strategy. Determining the extent to which there is a relationship between passion and trust is an interesting way to analyse the impact of policy and practice in education.

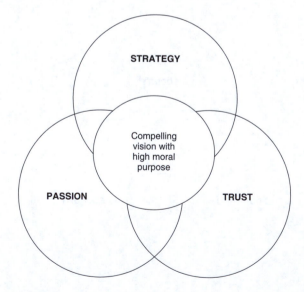

STRATEGY

Compelling
vision with
high moral
purpose

PASSION

TRUST

Figure 3.2 Passion, trust and strategy (Caldwell and Harris 2008)

Bill Clinton wished to be known as the 'education president'. I suspect Barack Obama wishes the same. In Australia, former Labour leader Kim Beazley wished to be known as the 'education prime minister'. It is likely that current Prime Minister Julia Gillard wishes the same. Few would doubt her passion. The key questions are 'Does she have the strategies to channel this passion to achieve the vision of success for all students in all settings? Do the public and the profession trust her to deliver?'

Former UK Prime Minister Gordon Brown set out his vision for education in a speech at the University of Greenwich in November 2007. He declared that 'education is my passion' and offered the following explanation:

> I make no apology for saying that education is the best economic policy. And I make no apology for wanting every child to be able to read, write and add up. But education has always been about more than exams, more than the basics, vital as they are. To educate is to form character, to shape values, and to liberate the imagination. It is to pass human wisdom, knowledge and ingenuity from one generation to the next. It is a duty and a calling. As Plutarch said, the mind is not a vessel to be filled but a fire to be kindled. And that is why we have such high ambitions. Not just because education is a matter of national prosperity, although it is certainly that. It is because education is the greatest liberator mankind has ever known, the greatest force for social progress. And that is why it is my passion.
>
> (Brown 2007)

This was a remarkable statement for within it is the alignment of education, economy and society, and it conveys passion. However, a strong case can be made that Brown's passion was not matched by strategies and, in the final analysis, he lost the trust of the electors.

Significance

There is a danger that the dysfunctional effects of current policy will inhibit passion in learning as well as innovation and creativity in schooling. In an eloquent statement in 2008, then minister for education in Australia, Julia Gillard (now prime minister), declared that 'All children have some gift and even some potential greatness within them. Finding that gift, nurturing it and bringing it to life is the responsibility of every single one of us'. Her words echo those of Sir Ken Robinson, who is a powerful advocate of an intensely personal approach to learning. Writing in *The Element* (Robinson 2009) he stated that:

> Education doesn't need to be reformed – it needs to be transformed. The key to this transformation is not to standardise education but to personalise it, to build achievement on discovering the individual talents of each child, to put students in an environment where they want to learn and where they can naturally discover their true passions.
>
> (Robinson 2009: 238)

But Robinson warned that the policy framework in England, now being replicated to a large extent in Australia, with parallels in the United States, will impair the nurturing of the 'gift' and 'potential greatness' of which Gillard spoke: 'Education is being strangled persistently by the culture of standardised testing. The irony is that these tests are not raising standards except in some very particular areas, and at the expense of most of what really matters in education' (Robinson 2009: 249).

It is astonishing that these mis-alignments have occurred in the face of robust evidence that engagement in the arts has a powerful impact of learning more generally. We review that evidence in Chapters 4, 6 and 7.

Notes (see pages 37 and 38)

1 Transformation is defined as significant, systematic and sustained change that secures success for all students in all settings.
2 This occurred in England in the first decade of the twenty-first century and evidence is emerging in most Australian states and territories.
3 A related standard is addressed in the teaching standards approved by MCEECDYA, as developed by AITSL, and recommended in the Review of Teacher Education and School Induction in Queensland.
4 These practices are major factors in accounting for success in Finland.
5 This approach is currently employed in New Zealand.
6 Several schools and school systems have made good progress in this approach.
7 A related international project in which Australia is a partner is now under way.
8 A national rollout of higher levels of autonomy for government schools will commence in 2015 and will be completed by 2018 ($480.5 million was included in the 2011–12 Commonwealth budget to get this under way).
9 A good start has been made, supported to some extent by initiatives in the contentious Building the Education Revolution project.

4 Research evidence on engagement in the arts

In this chapter we summarise research on engagement in the arts, drawing on the substantial body of evidence that indicates that engagement can lift performance on a range of indicators of achievement and wellbeing. This extends the general argument set out in Chapter 1. We also describe what is occurring in Australia and other nations on the involvement of the philanthropic sector in school education, with a particular focus on the arts. More evidence is provided in Chapters 6 and 7 to give an international context to Australian research.

The Australian research was commissioned by TSR, a non-profit organisation that provides programs in the arts for upper primary students. Students were in schools in highly disadvantaged settings and part of the brief was to examine the impact of indicators of students propensity to be involved in juvenile crime. There is an impressive body of research that points to low achievement being a factor in a young person turning to crime and this is also summarised in Chapter 4.

Research on related themes

Impact of the arts on student achievement

Music and arts initiatives have been shown to increase academic outcomes (Bamford 2006; Catterall *et al.* 1999), increase (IQ) (Schellenberg 2006), improve literacy (Bamford 2006; Hunter 2005; Spillane 2009) and numeracy (Catterall *et al.* 1999; Hunter 2005; Spillane 2009; Upitis and Smithrim 2003). Participation in the arts has been shown to encourage changes within the cognitive functions of the brain (Koelsch *et al.* 2005; Levitin and Triovolas 2009; Parsons 2001; Sacks 2007; Schlaug *et al.* 1995a; Schlaug *et al.* 1995b; Schlaug *et al.* 2005; Sluming *et al.* 2007; Wetter *et al.* 2009). Catterall (2005) proposed a theory on the transfer of learning through the arts which can be considered as 'change in knowledge, skills, dispositions, and orientations stemming from neural processes stimulated by learning in or participation in the arts' which encompassed two main points:

1   Arts learning and experiences, to varying degrees, reorganize neural pathways, or the way the brain functions. Extended and or deep learning in the arts reinforces these developments.

2   The development and re-organization of brain function due to learning in
the arts may impact how and how well the brain processes other tasks.

(Catterall 2005: 7)

The above studies show how learning in the arts can affect students' academic
outcomes. Further research is summarised in Chapter 6.

The impact of the arts on students was described by Catterall *et al.* (1999: 17) in
these terms: 'The arts do matter – not only as worthwhile experiences in their own
right . . . but also as instruments of cognitive growth and development and as agents
of motivation for school success'. Furthermore:

> The arts not only build our brains, they insulate them from our stress-full urban
> environments. In short, all children, and especially urban children, need the arts
> if they are to thrive and blossom to their full potential. We should not wait until
> our children are emotionally disturbed or incarcerated before we offer them the
> positive cognitive, social, medical and emotional benefits of a well-rounded arts
> education. To deny urban children arts education is societal child abuse. For
> those who feel that we can't afford arts education, we must remind them about
> the cost of a child who drops out of school or becomes incarcerated. A full edu-
> cation that includes the arts is the insurance we pay for our nation's democracy.
>
> (Creedon 2011: 36)

Catterall and colleagues used the National Educational Longitudinal Survey data
(NELS: 88), which included 25,000 students from the United States with 10 years
of longitudinal data, to perform an elegant and extensive analysis of the impact of
the arts. The studies identified three main sets of observations set out below that
included a focus on students from low socio-economic status (SES) backgrounds,
which makes the findings of particular interest in the context of the Australian study
reported in Chapters 6 to 8:

1   Involvement in the arts and academic success. Positive academic developments for children engaged in the arts are seen at each step in the research
– between 8th and 10th grade as well as between 10th and 12th grade. The
comparative gains for arts-involved youngsters generally become more pro-
nounced over time. Moreover and more important, these patterns also hold
for children from low socio-economic status (SES) backgrounds.
2   Music and mathematics achievement. Students who report consistent
high levels of involvement in instrumental music over the middle and high
school years show significantly higher levels of mathematics proficiency by
grade 12. This observation holds both generally and for low SES students
as a subgroup. In addition, absolute differences in measured mathematics
proficiency between students consistently involved versus not involved in
instrumental music grow significantly over time.
3   Theatre arts and human development. Sustained student involvement in
theatre arts (acting in plays and musicals, participating in drama clubs, and

taking acting lessons) associates with a variety of developments for youth: gains in reading proficiency, gains in self concept and motivation, and higher levels of empathy and tolerance for others. Our analyses of theatre arts were undertaken for low SES youth only. Our presumption was that more advantaged youngsters would be more likely to be involved in theatre and drama because of attendance at more affluent schools and because of parental ability to afford theatre opportunities in the community or private sectors.

(Catterall *et al.* 1999: 2)

Wetter and colleagues investigated the influence of music instruction on academic outcome in a retrospective study of students from Bern, Switzerland (Wetter *et al.* 2009). The study involved 53 children who practised music and 67 who did not. Significantly higher academic grades were found in the students who practised music in Grades 4, 5 and 6 in comparison to those who did not practise music. No significant difference was identified in Grade 3. The effects were consistent across the academic subjects that included mathematics and languages (French and German), with no significant difference identified for sports. Although the apparent lack of effect in Grade 3 could have been due to several factors, the authors proposed that length of time in music instruction may have been a contributing factor (Wetter *et al.* 2009).

Another study identified a link between length of music instruction and gains in IQ and academic achievement of 147 6–11-year-old students from Toronto, Canada (Schellenberg 2006). The longer the duration of the music instruction the higher the gains in intellectual functioning. Both studies retained their significant findings when they controlled for the economic situation of students (Schellenberg 2006; Wetter *et al.* 2009). Schellenberg's study, like that conducted by Wetter, found significant gains in all academic subjects rather than specific associations with some subjects. Wetter described the importance of music education:

At present, funding for music education is often reduced in order to save money. Music and arts are sometimes regarded as a luxury and as being of lesser significance for a child's education than other subjects such as mathematics or languages. We believe that such thinking is not justified because music is an important part of our culture and its exertion both involves many different skills and activates several areas of the brain. We believe that there are strong reasons why music has been our true companion for thousands of years until now, only some of these reasons and their implications have been discovered.

(Wetter *et al.* 2009: 372)

Wetter described how music appeared 'to induce structural and functional variations of central regions of the brain resulting in manifold implications' (Wetter *et al.* 2009: 372). Advances in imaging technology for neurobiology have enabled studies that investigated what specific areas of the brain were activated during the analysis of music and music performance (Koelsch *et al.* 2005; Levitin and Triovolas 2009; Parsons 2001). The neural systems underlying music were found to be distributed throughout the left and right hemispheres of the brain (Levitin and Triovolas 2009;

Parsons 2001: 211). Differences in brain symmetry and the size of specific regions (increased corpus callosum) and significantly increased grey matter in several regions of the brain have been identified in professional musicians (Schlaug *et al.* 1995b; Schlaug *et al.* 1995a; Schlaug *et al.* 2005). One area of the brain found to be increased in size was the corpus callosum which acts to connect the left and the right hemispheres of the brain. Interestingly although 'music processing shares some circuitry with spoken language processing', found within the left hemisphere, there is also the involvement of 'distinct neural circuits' (Levitin and Triovolas 2009: 226). Professional orchestral musicians have shown enhanced performance in a non-musical visuo-spatial task (three-dimensional mental rotation), with increased use of a specific area of the brain (Broca's area) in comparison to well-matched controls (Sluming *et al.* 2007). This study provided 'additional objective evidence to support the suggestion that the development and maintenance of musical performance abilities confers benefit on non-musical cognitive domains' (Sluming *et al.* 2007: 3804). These findings suggested that physical changes in the brain occurred through interaction with music, some of which are localised to regions associated with language processing (although they also have distinct neural circuits), indicating a link between music and language.

These forementioned findings are of even greater importance considering the plasticity of the brain, as explored in *The Brain that Changes Itself*, which presented evidence that new neuronal pathways can be created throughout life (Doidge 2010). A study at Harvard Medical School investigated what brain regions were activated that enabled the discernment between regular or irregular musical chord patterns in children (10 year olds) and adults with and without musical training (Koelsch *et al.* 2005). No significant differences were found between the groups. The authors concluded that 'humans have a general ability to effortlessly acquire complex musical knowledge, and to process musical information fast and accurately according to this knowledge'; this 'underlines the inherent interest of the human brain in music and thus stresses the biological relevance of music' (Koelsch *et al.* 2005: 1074). This study provided insight into the biological basis of the unique appeal of the arts to children.

Impact of the arts on student wellbeing

Participation in arts programs was seen to increase various psychological indicators such as resilience (Oreck *et al.* 1999), self-regulation (Hunter 2005; Oreck *et al.* 1999), self-esteem (Brice Heath and Roach 1999; Hunter 2005; Upitis and Smithrim 2003), identity (Oreck *et al.* 1999), self-concept (Catterall *et al.* 1999), self-efficacy and motivation (Bamford 2006; Catterall *et al.* 1999; Hunter 2005). Students who actively participated in various arts programs showed improvements in the behavioural indicators of empathy (Catterall *et al.* 1999; Hunter 2005), tolerance (Catterall *et al.* 1999), cooperation (Hunter 2005), skills of collaboration (Hunter 2005), and communication skills (Hunter 2005). The impact of the arts on psychological and behavioural indicators is extended in Chapter 7.

Catterall and Peppler (2007) analysed the impact of two visual arts programs on the self-efficacy and creativity of 103 eight year olds (Grade 3) from two major cities of the United States, Los Angles and St Louis. The communities surrounding the schools were affected by 'poverty, crime, drug-traffic and economic hardship' (Catterall and Peppler 2007: 545). The programs were provided by the Centre of Contemporary Arts (CoCA) and Inner City Arts (ICA) for 20- and 30-week blocks (equivalent to one-half and three-quarters of a school year, respectively) for 90 minutes twice a week and one hour per week, respectively (Catterall and Peppler 2007). The amount of time in program is of interest as the TSR program reported in Chapters 6 to 8 provides weekly one-hour lessons for six to eighteen months, which was similar to the ICA program. Value-added measurements were made from a pre- and post-test survey that measured self-efficacy and creativity of students in the arts, which were compared to a control group of 73 (Catterall and Peppler 2007). Significant differences were found, with higher gains for measurements of self-efficacy and creativity (originality), for those in the visual arts programs in comparison to the control group (Catterall and Peppler 2007). In consideration of the importance of 'the creative class' in successful economies, described in Chapter 1 (Florida 2005: 29), these gains in creativity were noteworthy. There were two main findings:

The primary finding is that participation in a sustained program of high quality visual arts instruction associated significantly with growth in our indicators of general self-efficacy. The mechanism seems to involve feelings of accomplishment in visual art and diverse positive interactions with peers and expert instructors surrounding the work . . . Self-efficacious children believe they can be agents in creating their own futures and are more optimistic about what the world has in store for them. The second finding is that the program had effects not only on self-efficacy beliefs, but also on children's originality . . . We argue that original thinking and self-efficacy may go hand-in-hand, and perhaps just as important that tendencies toward original thinking spawned by artistic learning may spill over or transfer to original thinking more generally. Confidence about the ability to generate novel solutions to problems or conceiving original pathways when facing a roadblock is a workable definition of self-efficacy. Original thinkers might be thought to have expansive as opposed to restrictive views of the world ahead.

What more does this suggest? We conclude that high quality visual arts education encourages sense of self-efficacy as well as creative, original thinking. Such outcomes befit all children. But they are particularly important when considering the lives of underprivileged children for whom educational and social advantages are scarce. These were the children we studied and the children to which our findings most readily apply. Participating in what we called high quality visual arts education allowed these children to feel more confident about their abilities and to have a greater sense of agency – these outcomes entwined with any artistic skills that ICA and CoCA cultivated. This begins to sound like an impact on the child's worldview, the ambitious notion with which we began this project. We do not claim to have captured worldview in all of its genesis and nuance, but our work does suggest that high quality arts education may provide children positive views of themselves and the worlds they will face.

(Catterall and Peppler 2007: 559)

The emotion of music (and more generally of the arts) goes beyond the boundaries of social and cultural constraints of human existence, it pierces the 'heart directly' (Sacks 2007: 301). Recent neurobiological evidence indicates that emotion inherent in music can be recognised regardless of large differences in culture and SES. The recognition of three basic emotional expressions (happy, sad and scared/fearful) from Western music by above that expected random chance, for listeners from Mafa (native African population) and Western participants (Fritz *et al.* 2009). This study was important as it enabled the examination of responses for two groups of listeners that were 'completely culturally isolated from each other', with the Mafa listeners not previously exposed to Western music (Fritz *et al.* 2009: 1). These studies indicated that music is inherently within us all, almost as if it was embedded in our DNA.

The ability of music (and the arts) to cross cultural boundaries may be one of the reasons it was so effective in the engagement of multicultural communities in disadvantaged settings (for example, one of the schools studied contained 92 percent of students from Language Backgrounds Other Than English (LBOTE)). The classroom of the recently migrated refugee would be dominated by talk in a foreign language which presents a territory of the unfamiliar. The universal language of music can reach into this classroom and engage the child through its ability to express emotions without cultural constraints. Furthermore, without the use of a common language the unique culture of the child can still find its own expression through the arts.

Risk factors for juvenile crime

Risk factors linked to juvenile crime are low academic achievement (Baltodano *et al.* 2005; Farrington 2003; Maguin and Loeber 1996; Pasko 2006), low school attendance (Baker 1998; Pasko 2006), and impulsivity (acting without prior thought) (Carroll *et al.* 2006; Farrington 2003). A low rate of school attendance has been shown to be a strong predictor of crime (Baker 1998; Pasko 2006).

A study of nearly 400 juvenile crime offenders in New South Wales (NSW) found that only one-third were still at school at the time they committed their first offence and more than one-third had been suspended or expelled (Weatherburn *et al.* 2007). Attendance at school and suspension (or expulsion) were significantly related to risk of re-offence in NSW juvenile offenders (Weatherburn *et al.* 2007). A peak in crime has been observed for secondary students aged 14–16 years (Years 9 and 10) (Baker 1998). Baker suggested that the link between truancy and crime may be a manifestation of poor school performance. Low academic achievement at high school has been shown to be associated with risk of juvenile offence (Baltodano *et al.* 2005; Farrington 2003; Maguin and Loeber 1996; Pasko 2006; Zabel and Nigro 2001). Baltodano *et al.* (2005) found that, although male youths from juvenile correction facilities were found to be below the mean on all measures of achievement, the majority were not more than one standard deviation below the mean. There was found to be no gender difference between boys and girls, with both groups equally likely to have failed academically (Pasko 2006). In contrast to the above findings, a meta-analysis of 118 research studies found that academic performance and delinquency were more strongly associated in males than in females (Maguin and Loeber 1996). Early-onset offenders were shown to display high impulsivity (Carroll *et al.* 2006; Farrington 2003) poor concentration (Farrington 2003), risk-taking (Farrington 2003), rapid cognitive tempo, poor mental inhibitory control (Carroll *et al.* 2006) and were unpopular with their peers (Farrington 2003). Troublesome and aggressive behaviour were predictors of later offending for boys aged eight to 10 (Farrington 2003). The above findings indicate relationships between juvenile crime and low academic achievement, poor school attendance and negative social behaviour.

The beginning of high school represents a key transition point developmentally that has been identified as important in the prevention of juvenile crime (National Crime Prevention 1999). Students who had committed an offence in year 7 formed 62.4 percent and 43.3 percent of the NSW secondary student population of boys and girls, respectively (Baker 1998). Early onset age for the first offences (10–14) has been linked to a higher rate of repeat offences (Chen *et al.* 2005) which take place over longer time periods (Farrington 2003). The transition to high school is thought to be particularly difficult to traverse, as it involves a 'transition to a new, larger, more demanding and less supportive school structure; the transition to puberty, with the associated need to establish one's own identity as an adult, independent of parents; and a transition to a new neighbourhood or peer group' (Homel 2005: 95). Increased juvenile participation has been observed in regions of economic and social disadvantage, which is thought to increase the rate of child neglect (Weatherburn and Lind 1997). Students from areas of economic disadvantage in Grades 5 and 6 precede transition to high school and form a cohort relevant to the study of the impact of the early intervention by TSR on the prevention of juvenile crime. Weatherburn and Lind (1997) described the benefit of preventative programs outside the justice system, 'agencies responsible for the health, education and welfare of children may actually be much better placed to deliver programs designed to prevent juvenile involvement in crime than those who are gatekeepers to the criminal justice system' (Weatherburn and Lind 1997: 48).

Arts initiatives

The study that is the centre-piece of this book was conducted as an independent evaluation of a program offered by a non-profit organisation (TSR). A summary of similar programs in Australia and other nations is provided here before turning to the methodology and findings in Chapters 5 to 8.

In their study of 35 arts interventions in Los Angeles, Stone *et al.* (1998) identified specific program features that were essential for pro-social impact on students. These were consistent with those reported by Bamford (2009) in a study of arts education in Iceland: 'active partnerships between schools and arts organisations and between teachers, artists and the community' and 'opportunities for public performance, exhibition and/or presentation' (Bamford 2009: 52). Bamford described active partnerships for arts education in these terms:

> Countries that have effective arts and cultural education generally have active
> partnerships across sectors, disciplines and organisations. The notion of an

active partnership involves the direct inclusion of a range of cultural and artistic organizations in all aspects of the planning and delivery. The best of these provide sustainable, long-term and reciprocal associations.

(Bamford 2009: 54)

Arts initiatives with extended time-in-program, such as ongoing sessions for students, were identified as important to the pro-social impact of the program (Stone *et al.* 1998). The importance of performance was described in *The Arts and Youth at Risk: Global and Local Challenges* (Brice Heath 2008) which identified four factors including 'high-risk expectations for collaborative exhibition, performance, or production' (Brice Heath 2008: xii). As summarised in Table 4.1 these provide a framework for the description and comparison of work by arts organisations in the non-profit philanthropic sector. The organisations chosen for review were two from Australia, TSR and The Australian Children's Music Foundation (ACMF); two from the United States, one of which spanned involvement in 10 states, Little Kids Rock, and another based in Florida, Dance – The Next Generation; El Sistema based in Venezuela, which has expanded throughout South America; and The Voices Foundation which is based in England.

The Song Room (TSR)

TSR is a not-for-profit organisation in receipt of grants from public and private sources that conducts free programs in the performing arts in schools where these are not currently offered. These programs are conducted by mutual agreement between TSR and participating schools. TSR delivers its programs to over 200 school communities each year and works with over 20,000 children every week. Programs are targeted to the 700,000 children in schools without specialist teachers in the arts in the most marginalised communities from every state/territory of Australia (The Song Room 2011a). Across Australia, approximately 45,000 students are engaged for a minimum of six months each year (The Song Room 2011a). Students typically participate for approximately one hour per week in each class. Instruction is provided by a teaching artist (TA), contracted to TSR and working in partnership with the classroom teacher at the school of placement.

TSR is a national program that encourages learning and development for underprivileged children through creative arts and music. TSR provides long-term, tailored workshop programs to various groups of disadvantaged children, including children at risk of juvenile crime involvement. TSR's additional emphasis on complementary performance programs, community holiday programs, capacity building and sustainability, and partnerships and collaboration (The Song Room 2011b) can be interpreted as equivalent to an emphasis on performance, complementary program components, extended time in program and ties with other community organisations, respectively (Stone *et al.* 1998). Ties to the community through the building of 'local community capacity' were considered to be essential to 'make a real difference . . . in the lives of children' through TSR (Saubern 2010: 12).

Table 4.1 Summary table of arts initiatives that include elements important for arts education

Arts initiative	Country	Number of participants since time of foundation	Extended time in program	Complementary program elements	Ties with other community organisations	Emphasis on performance and presentation
The Song Room	Australia	200,000 (approx)	6-month/ 12-month/ 18-month programs	Performances, community school holiday intensives, professional development, resource provision, online delivery	Arts and community organisations	Yes, at multiple levels
Australian Children's Music Foundation	Australia	2,200	12 month minimum	Annual song-writing competition	Juvenile justice centres	For most programmes
Little Kids Rock	United States	110,000	1 year	No	No	Yes
El Sistema	Venezuela	250,000	10 years for majority of students	Home visits, retreats and intensive workshops	Juvenile detention centres	Learning through performing
The Voices Foundation	England	7,000 (in 2005)	1 year	Continuation programs/special programs/singing steps workshop program	No	Showcase event/ singing celebration
Dance – The Next Generation	Florida	2,000	7 years	Summer outreach program	Yes	Yes

The Australian Children's Music Foundation

ACMF was established in 2002 by the distinguished Australian performer Don Spencer (ACMF 2011a). The music programs have a duration of a minimum of 12 months, within primary and secondary schools and juvenile justice centres (ACMF 2011a). The ACMF has four project streams: Music for Disadvantaged Schools Program, Music for Isolated and Indigenous Schools Program, Music for Hope Program (bushfire and natural disaster affected schools) and Youth at Risk Music Program (Juvenile Justice Centres and NSW Youth Drug and Alcohol Court Program) (ACMF 2011b). These programs involve the provision of weekly music tuition and the purchase of instruments (ACMF 2011b). The programs were developed in consultation with the schools and could involve a range of elements including percussion, song writing, hip-hop and choirs (ACMF 2011b). Don Spencer described the importance of music for the emotional wellbeing of children: 'Through music, children can find a way to express their emotions and channel their energy and abilities into something positive and creative' (Minnis Journals 2009).

El Sistema

The El Sistema is an example of an international program that has a strong emphasis on performance and community. It is a music education program established in Venezuela in 1975 by José Antonio Abreu, conductor, composer and economist, which has a specific focus on the performance of orchestral classical music as an agent of social change (The National System of Youth and Children's Orchestras of Venezuela 2009). El Sistema provides music instruction to 250,000 children who are taught in 270 music education centres or 'núcleos', the majority of which are within walking distance of areas of low SES (El Sistema 2011; EuroArts 2011a). The majority of students begin attending their 'núcleo' as early as age two or three and continue into their teenage years. They participate in the program for up to six days a week, three to four hours a day (El Sistema 2011). Orchestras have also been set up in juvenile detention centres (EuroArts 2011b). The program is built on the idea of learning through performance and has strong ties with the community (The National System of Youth and Children's Orchestras of Venezuela 2009). The El Sistema methodology is based on a philosophy of 'passion first/refinement second', with the goal 'to create a daily haven of safety, joy and fun that builds every child's self-esteem and sense of value' (The National System of Youth and Children's Orchestras of Venezuela 2009). José Antonio Abreu described the power of music on social development and community:

> It is evident that music has to be recognised as an element of socialisation, as an agent of social development in the highest sense, because it transmits the highest values – solidarity, harmony, mutual compassion. And it has the ability to unite an entire community and to express sublime feelings.

> (Rosen 2008: 20)

The transformative nature of El Sistema has inspired a host of new musical performance programs in 25 different countries with recent innovations in Australia, Canada, England, Scotland and the United States which all draw upon the El Sistema methodology (The National System of Youth and Children's Orchestras of Venezuela 2009). The El Sistema method was integrated into the ACMF new orchestra and choral music programs which emphasises inclusive (free music lessons and instruments to low SES students) and fun-based musical programs (The Australian Children's Music Foundation 2009). Programs based on the El Sistema model were found in many cites of the United States such as Baltimore, Chicago and New York (El Sistema USA 2010). In Canada, Sistema New Brunswick was launched in association with the New Brunswick Youth Orchestra (NBYO). NBYO President Ken MacLeod described the program as having the goal to 'influence children through music, to foster positive values such as discipline, teamwork, confidence and self-esteem, and to inspire in children a sense of hope, joy and the aspiration to succeed' (Orchestras Canada 2009).

Little Kids Rock

The Little Kids Rock organisation was established in 1996 by David Wish, a teacher who was frustrated by the lack of funding for his own public school (Little Kids Rock 2011a). The Little Kids Rock organisation has provided music education and instruments to over 110,000 children in 10 states in the United States public school system (Little Kids Rock 2011b, 2011d). It has a focus on popular music styles including rock, blues, rap and hip-hop (Little Kids Rock 2011e). The structure of the program has a pedagogical basis in immersion techniques of second language education and the Suzuki method (Little Kids Rock 2011f). Performance, composition, improvisation and recording are considered to be integral factors of the program (Little Kids Rock 2011e). The weekly program is provided free of charge to K-12 students (Little Kids Rock 2011g) in public schools with 50 percent or more of their students on the Free or Reduced Lunch program, and offered to other schools at a cost to the school (Little Kids Rock 2011c).

Dance – The Next Generation

The Sarasota Ballet School in Florida provides full scholarships for tuition for seven years for at-risk children under the title of Dance – The Next Generation (Sarasota Ballet 2011a). Older students in the program were reported to have consistently achieved between a three and one-half to four grade point average, which is equivalent to the grades between B+ and A+, and the majority have become honour roll students (Sarasota Ballet 2011b). Dance – The Next Generation has an annual enrolment of 100 (Sarasota Ballet 2011a) and students have participated in the program since 1991 (Ewing 2010). The scholarship program covered all expenses which included 'daily assistance with homework, nutrition, social etiquette, public-speaking, and, when necessary, counseling' and was a recipient of the Coming Up Taller award for Youth Arts and Humanities Programs for Excellence in 2002 (National Endowment for the

Humanities 2002). The goal of the program was the prevention of school drop-out for children aged from 8 to 18 (Sarasota Ballet 2011a). The aim of the program was described as having a key focus on helping children in need:

> The program provides a safe haven for these children and a way to improve their self-esteem, to learn responsibility and discipline, to gain confidence and, above all, to learn that regardless of their socio-economic status, they can achieve anything they want in life.
>
> (Sarasota Ballet 2011a)

The Voices Foundation

The Voices Foundation is a charitable organisation in England which provides partially funded singing-based programs to state primary schools (The Voices Foundation 2011b). It was established in 1993 by Susan Digby and was founded on the educational philosophies of Hungarian Zoltan Kodaly (The Voices Foundation 2011a). Unlike the programs provided by TSR and ACMF, which are customised to the local needs of the school, The Voices Foundation programs are based on the use of the voice of the child as 'the most appropriate medium for young children to develop aural skills as the children make the sounds themselves' (Hallam *et al.* 2005: 8) and are related to meeting the requirements of the National Curriculum (The Voices Foundation 2011a).

The Voices Foundation Primer contains the following three elements: whole school in-service training; the support of trained advisory teachers; and additional training for curriculum leaders to ensure long-term sustainability (Hallam *et al.* 2005: 4). An evaluation of the program which involved 11 schools found that confidence and musical understanding of teachers increased through their participation in The Voices Foundation Primer (Hallam *et al.* 2005; Rogers *et al.* 2008).

Shortcoming of the program were described in these terms:

> While the primer related well to the National Curriculum and satisfied most of its requirements concerns were expressed about the relative neglect of composing, listening and appraising and the lack of coverage of different genres, world musics and the use of instruments. Where schools had a strong tradition of instrumental tuition this was perceived as particularly important.
>
> (Hallam *et al.* 2005: 7)

Reduction in funding for the arts

Reduction in funding for the arts in schools presents a particular challenge. The reduction in funding for the arts internationally (Russell-Bowie 2009) has been a factor that has encouraged involvement of organisations in the philanthropic and business sectors (Renz and Atienza 2005). The majority of the organisations were involved in the provision of arts education to students from disadvantaged communities (Little Kids Rock 2011b; Sarasota Ballet 2011a; The Song Room 2011b) as described in this section of Chapter 4. Russell-Bowie (2009) described the effect of decreased funding for arts education:

> funding for music and other arts programmes, specialist music/visual arts/ drama/dance teachers, instruments, resources and teacher training has decreased significantly. In many countries, generalist elementary-school teachers are now expected not only to teach English, science, mathematics, social studies, physical education and many cross-curricular perspectives, but also to have the expertise and confidence to teach music, visual arts, dance and drama. This is despite the fact that many of them have not been adequately trained in any or some of these arts subjects.
>
> (Russell-Bowie 2009: 24)

Summary

The research reported in Chapter 4, to be extended in Chapters 6 and 7, indicates that engagement in the arts is associated with increased academic achievement, literacy, IQ, mathematics and attendance. Moreover, students tend to show improvement on psychological and behavioural indicators such as self-esteem, self-efficacy, motivation and empathy. There are various risk factors associated with juvenile crime, such as reduced school attendance, low academic achievement and negative behavioural indicators, and research suggests that participation in the arts serves to reduce the chances of subsequent engagement in juvenile crime.

The components of high-quality arts education include extended time in program, complementary program elements, ties with related community organisations and an emphasis on performance. These formed the framework for descriptions of six organisations in the philanthropic arts sector in Australia, the United States, England and Venezuela. TSR is an Australian initiative whose programs reflect the aforementioned components of high-quality arts education. It was observed that the decline in funding for the arts may lead to greater involvement of arts organisations from the philanthropic and business sectors.

Significance

Along with the general case for engagement in the arts set out in Chapter 1, there is thus a rich background in research on the impact of programs in the arts.

It is rare that one finds such consistent evidence in support of particular approaches in curriculum and pedagogy, especially where that evidence applies to improving the life chances of students in highly disadvantaged settings. There are examples of structures, processes and techniques (a more accurate description in some instances would be fads) that have been implemented nation-wide or system-wide that may have had a marginal impact or an early impact that subsequently flat-lines, but on the evidence before us, initiatives in arts education do not fall in this category.

It is against this background that further research was undertaken in Australia, the methodology and findings of which are reported in Chapters 5 to 8.

5   Methodology for Australian study

In this chapter we describe methodologies for research that will illuminate the issues raised in Chapters 1 to 4 and that will also address the need for more matched schools 'quasi-experimental' studies. We describe how such research was conducted in Australia in highly disadvantaged settings. An intervention by a national non-profit arts organisation TSR, with the support of high-profile foundations such as Macquarie Group Foundation, has led to the offering of such programs in primary schools in these settings.

The research is a rare example of quasi-experimental design in education wherein the performance of students in schools that offered programs in the arts was compared with the performance of students in matching schools that did not offer such programs. We provide a detailed account of the methodology for this research, the findings of which are reported in Chapters 6 to 8. The starting point is an overview of the methodology for the Australian study.

Overview of methodology

The purpose of the project was to determine the impact of TSR on indicators of student performance that were previously identified as related to potential engagement in juvenile crime as reported in Chapter 4.

TSR provides programs in music, drama, dance and visual arts for children in schools in socially disadvantaged settings across Australia. The research was funded by the Macquarie Group Foundation and focused in a region of high juvenile crime and socio-economic disadvantage on TSR programs of a musical nature, which included drumming, choir, body percussion and beat boxing. The Macquarie Group Foundation has played a key supporting role for the TSR, which included the funding of two other research projects, one of which was a study on young people from refugee backgrounds (Grossman and Sonn 2010). Richard Price of Macquarie Capital Advisors has served as chair of the TSR board since 2005.

The students in the study attended TSR classes once a week for a duration of approximately one hour per class. The TSR program was taught by TAs who have qualifications in music or arts along with teaching, youth work or similar qualifications and/or experience. The school classroom teacher was also present during the classes to participate, contribute to the program and enhance skills in the provision of arts education.

The study reported here was conducted in communities that had been identified in earlier research by the Department of Justice and Attorney-General in NSW as having relatively high levels of juvenile crime. However, there was no implication in the study that students for whom outcomes are reported have been or are likely to be involved in juvenile crime. They were involved in the study because they were in programs offered by TSR in schools in the aforementioned communities that agreed to participate or were in a matching sample of schools that did not offer the TSR program. Anonymity was assured for all students and the names of participating schools have been changed.

The methodology of the study reflects the purpose of the investigation and the research background set out in Chapter 4. The following includes the indicators of student performance selected for study, the selection of schools, research questions and approaches to the gathering and analysis of data.

Indicators of student performance

The indicators of student performance selected for study were as follows, reflecting the background of research findings summarised in Chapter 4:

- attendance, dropout, detention and suspension
- results on school tests and national tests in National Assessment Plan – Literacy and Numeracy (NAPLAN)
- Social-Emotional Wellbeing (SEWB) as measured by the SEWB Survey designed and validated by ACER.

Selection of schools

The study was conducted in government schools in relatively disadvantaged communities in three regions in NSW. Three groups of schools were created to achieve a quasi-experimental design, with six schools offering TSR programs and a control group of four schools not offering TSR programs. The former were divided into two groups of three, with one offering the initial shorter program of six months and the other offering the longer program of 12 to 18 months. Students in Grades 5 and 6 were the subjects of study. The 10 participating schools were thus of three kinds:

1   three schools offering the initial six-month TSR program ('initial')
2   three schools offering the longer TSR program extending over 12 to 18 months ('longer-term')
3   four schools serving as a control group that were matched on key school community characteristics but were not participating in the TSR program ('non-participating').

Requirements for quasi-experimental research on the impact of the arts

Research on the impact of the arts has encompassed a broad range of both qualitative and quantitative methodologies (Brice Heath and Roach 1999; Catterall *et al.* 1999; Oreck *et al.* 1999; Stone *et al.* 1998; Upitis and Smithrim 2003; Vaughn 2002). The evidence for the transfer of learning within the arts to academic domains has created considerable debate. The argument that correlation between learning in the arts and academic gains does not present definitive evidence of causation has been raised (McCarthy *et al.* 2004). The academic gains identified in the association with the arts may have resulted from the higher SES of students that have an opportunity to study in the arts in comparison to the SES of students who lacked such opportunity (McCarthy *et al.* 2004). These arguments created the need for 'research that could offer "clean" evidence on the effects of the arts [that] demands one or more control or comparison groups with which individuals in arts "treatment" or "intervention" can be compared' (Brice Heath 2008: xi).

Reflection on the term 'clean evidence' indicated the need for a study of sufficient statistical power to identify differences between the treatment group and control group. The specific requirements for a quasi-experimental design for methodological investigation into the arts are the presence of a control group, the measurement of non-arts academic achievement, and instruction in the arts in general (Winner and Hetland 2000). Longitudinal data serve to clarify the role of the arts initiative on student outcomes.

The quasi-experimental approach of the Australian study incorporated longitudinal data. It was based in a region of low SES, 370 students participated which enabled sufficient statistical power for 'clean evidence', non-arts academic achievement was one of the measured outcomes, and instruction was in the arts in general (different applications of TSR for different schools) and a control group was employed (Brice Heath 2008: xi; McCarthy *et al.* 2004; Winner and Hetland 2000).

The quasi-experimental methodology required a well-matched control group for the schools that were participants in TSR. Since January 2010 information on demographics and performance of all schools in Australia was publicly accessible at an online website (My School) (http://myschool.edu.au) including performance on NAPLAN in which students across the country in Years 3, 5, 7 and 9 are tested in reading, writing, language conventions (spelling, grammar and punctuation) and numeracy. For a particular school, the website contains a descriptive statement written by the school, student background as indicated by the school's location on the Index of Community Socio-Educational Advantage (ICSEA), enrolment and performance of students at the school on NAPLAN, with an indication of how the school performed compared to 'statistically similar schools' and all schools, student attendance rate and, for secondary schools, Year 12 results and destinations of students after they leave school (ACARA 2011a). ICSEA is a measurement of SES which includes measures of school remoteness, and percentage of indigenous enrolments as illustrated in Table 5.1 (ACARA 2011c). ICSEA is scaled to a mean of 1,000 with a standard deviation of 100 (ACARA 2011c). In March 2011 an updated version of the online website

Table 5.1 Variables used in the construction of the ICSEA in 2009 and 2010

	ICSEA 1 2009 (My School)	ICSEA 2 2010 (My School 2)
Social-educational information	13 variables constructed from estimates based on Australian Bureau of Statistics census data	7 and 6 variables constructed from data supplied directly by parents for 71% and 29% of schools, respectively
Proportion of ATSI enrolments	The proportion of Aboriginal and Torres Strait Islander students enrolled in the school as indicated on school enrolment records	As for 2009
Accessibility/ Remoteness	The school's value on the Accessibility/ Remoteness Index of Australia	As for 2009
Proportion of disadvantaged LBOTE students	N/A	The proportion of students from LBOTE families having low school education levels as indicated in school enrolment records

Source: adapted from Barnes (2010)

My School 2 was released. Demographic data about the schools were gathered from the My School and My School 2 websites on ICSEA and enrolment. ICSEA 1 data collected from the My School website in 2010 enabled the choice of control schools, while ICSEA 2 data collected from My School 2 in 2011 provided a more accurate comparison of ICSEA between the experimental groups. The ICSEA 2 data collected from My School 2 was different from the ICSEA 1 data as shown in Table 5.1 (Barnes 2010). Not surprisingly, the inclusion of direct data from parents for the ICSEA 2 showed an increase in the predictive power of ICSEA for NAPLAN results from 59 percent to 68 percent (ACARA 2011c). The provision of detailed information through the My School website enabled the selection of a well-matched control group as described below.

Demographics of the cohorts

The research was conducted in government primary schools in three regions in Sydney that have some of the most disadvantaged communities in the country. Eight schools were participating in TSR program for Grades 5 and 6 students, four in the shorter-term program and four in the longer-term program. Each school was invited to participate in the study. One in each group declined so we proceeded with a total of six schools, three in each group. The control schools were chosen from 15 schools in the same region that did not participate in the TSR program and which provided the best match on ICSEA 2010 scores and enrolment. There were five such schools, four of which provided data within the time frame of the study. The names of the schools were changed to a pseudonym to protect the anonymity of the participants. The demographics of the three cohorts of schools, enrolment average and ICSEA average are summarised in Table 5.2. Weighted mean enrolments of the three groups were 439 (longer-term), 359 (initial) and 444 (non-participating).

Table 5.2 Demographics of the three cohorts involved in the study

Category	School (pseudonym)	Date of TSR commencement	Enrolment	ICSEA 1	ICSEA 2
Longer-term (n = 109)	Cooper Stone Public School	2009 semester 1	296	918	937
	Willow Brook Public School	2009 semester 1	493	907	886
	Margaret Park Public School	2009 semester 2	289	929	973
	Weighted mean		439	910	903
Initial (n = 140)	Curraburra Public School	2010 semester 1	340	819	827
	Alfield Public School	2010 semester 1	204	1100	1058
	Bonvilla Public School	2010 semester 1	330	992	990
	Weighted mean		359	905	903
Non-participating (n = 121)	Banksia Public School		479	955	959
	Docks Creek Public School		332	862	915
	Shornville Public School		477	813	867
	Pinlowe Public School		387	948	942
	Weighted mean		444	883	913

Weighted mean ICSEA 1 scores were 910 (longer-term), 905 (initial) and 883 (non-participating) for ICSEA. The ICSEA 2 scores provided an improved match between the cohorts, with those who had not participated in TSR having the highest ICSEA of 913, and the initial and longer-term cohorts having an ICSEA of 903. The slightly increased ICSEA for the non-participating group of schools would act as a slight bias towards the identification of higher outcomes in those who had not participated. The weighted mean in each instance takes account of the relative numbers of students in each school that participated in the study.

Research questions

1   What was the effect of the TSR program on (1) attendance, dropout, detention and suspension, (2) student achievement – literacy and numeracy (NAPLAN, school test results) and (3) student wellbeing?

2   What was the difference in the effects between the initial TSR program (6 months) and the longer-term TSR program (12–18 months) in the above-mentioned outcomes?

3   What were the stakeholders' (students, parents, teachers, and principals) perceptions of the effects of the TSR program?

4   What were the important pedagogies and processes of the TSR program that enabled its success?

Research hypotheses and statistical methods

1   There will be no difference between students in TSR and those not participating in TSR in attendance, dropout, detention and suspension, student achievement – literacy and numeracy (NAPLAN, school test results) and student wellbeing.

2   There will be no difference between students in the initial TSR program and

those in the longer-term TSR program in attendance, student achievement – literacy and numeracy (NAPLAN, school test results) and student wellbeing.

The above-stated null hypotheses were rejected for a pre-determined probability value (p value) of 0.05, which indicated that the result was unlikely to have occurred by chance. A p value of 0.05 indicated that there was a 95 percent chance that there was a difference between the cohorts. The lower the p value the less likely the result was to have occurred by chance. To enable simultaneous comparisons between the three groups, ANOVA (analysis of variance) was employed. ANOVA was used to determine if the means of the three groups were equal, and Bonferroni comparisons were used to determine what pairs of cohorts were driving the significance. The mean can be considered to describe the central location of the data, while the standard deviation showed the spread of the data. A 95 percent confidence showed an estimated range of values within a given cohort, in which the probability of observation of a value outside the 95 percent confidence interval was less than 5 percent.

Research participants and research activities

The characteristics of participants in each school are summarised in Table 5.3. The SEWB surveys were administered 'on location' by researchers from Educational Transformations staff. Collection was facilitated by the provision of a 'data collection guide' for each school.

Table 5.3 Characteristics of participants

Type of activity	Total participants (number, type)	Schools involved (number and type)	Participation strategy
Consent forms returned	370 students (Yrs 5 & 6)	10 primary schools	N/A
Survey completion	271 students (Yrs 5 & 6)	6 primary schools	Whole class/students withdrawn from class for Year 5/6
Case studies	4 principals 12 parents 8 teachers 20 students (Yr 5) 20 students (Yr 6)	4 primary schools	Each group interviewed separately Teachers interviewed individually Students withdrawn from TSR class time Parents interviewed at time that was convenient for them and the interviewers
Collection of school data	25 administrative staff teachers 10 principals	10 primary schools	
Total (combined activities)	370 students 25 administrative staff 4 principals 12 parents 8 teachers	10 primary schools	

Consent forms were distributed to 931 students in Grades 5 and 6. The percentage of the consent forms returned varied greatly with a maximum of 92 percent for Curraburra and a minimum of 16 percent for Pinlowe and Docks Creek, as shown in Table 5.4. Schools involved in the case studies were also chosen to participate in the SEWB survey, which enabled data triangulation across the study, as illustrated in Table 5.4.

Methodology for determining impact on student achievement

Data on gender, grade level, attendance, detentions and suspensions, grades and NAPLAN results were collected from 10 schools and categorised according to participation in TSR program. Longitudinal data on attendance were gathered from the My School 2 website which provided student attendance rates for 2008, 2009 and 2010. The student attendance rate was defined as the 'number of actual student days attended during the period' and was 'collected by schools and supplied for an agreed comparative period during the school year' (ACARA 2011b). The data on student attendance rates were collected for students in Grades 1 to 6 for those schools that participated in the research (ACARA 2011b). Attendance data were gathered from all schools who had a TSR program at their school for attendance on a TSR class day (Tuesday, Wednesday and Thursday) and for a day that was considered 'normal' during that same week. Data on attendance were gathered for Tuesday and Thursday of week 2 in term 3 for non-participating schools. For all schools excepting Curraburra the attendance data were gathered in the second week of term 3; for Curraburra due to extenuating circumstances the data were gathered in the third week.

The grades collected were from 2010 semester 1 reports and the number of dropouts, suspensions and behavioural incidences (detentions) were from throughout Semester 1 in 2010. The NAPLAN Grade 5 data for 2008, 2009 and 2010 were obtained from participating schools. The NAPLAN 2008 data were gathered from the non-participating schools and the schools from the longer-term cohort who had participated in TSR since semester 1 in 2009 (Cooper Stone and Willow Brook Public Schools). NAPLAN 2009 and 2010 data were gathered for all the participating schools. The Grade 5 results were of interest as they were for a year level that participated in TSR. Docks Creek Public School provided the 2010 and 2009 data without student names, and NAPLAN data for 16 students were randomly selected from both the 2009 and 2010 cohorts using Predictive Analytics Software (PASW), and incorporated into the cohort of students who had not participated in TSR. The provision of 16 students from Docks Creek Public School increased the student numbers in the non-participating cohort by eight for the 2009 and 2010 NAPLAN data analysis in comparison to the original cohort numbers as shown in Table 5.4.

Three groups of schools: (1) TSR – initial (six-month program), (2) TSR – longer-term program and (3) non-participating in TSR were compared to determine differences in students within or without the TSR program and also between the initial and longer-term programs. Each of the three cohorts of schools was composed of multiple schools as listed in Table 5.4. The initial and longer-term cohorts were comprised of three schools, while the non-participating in TSR cohort contained four schools. The data in Table 5.5 were collected from the My School website

Table 5.4 Level of involvement of schools in the study

Category of school	School (pseudonym)	Level of involvement*	Enrolment number	Estimated number of grade 5/6	Consent forms returned (%)	SEWB completed	Number of SEWB (completed totals per cohort)
Longer-term TSR (n = 109)	Willow Brook Public School	A+B+C+D	493	120	80/120 (66%)	78/120 (65%)	
	Cooper Stone Public School	A+B	296	66	19/66 (29%)		
	Margaret Park Public School	A+B+C+D	289	60	10/60 (17%)	11/60 (18%)	89
Initial TSR (n = 140)	Curraburra Public School	A+B+C+D	340	90	83/90 (92%)	74/90 (82%)	106
	Bonvilla School	A+B+C+D	330	88	37/88 (42%)	32/88 (36%)	
	Alfield Public School	A+B	204	55	20/55 (36%)		
Non-participating in TSR (n = 121)	Banksia Public School	A+B+C	479	120	37/120 (31%)	34/120 (28%)	76
	Shornville Public School	A+B+C	477	128	50/128 (39%)	42/128 (33%)	
	Docks Creek Public School	A+B	332	94	16/94 (17%)		
	Pinlowe Public School	A+B	387	110	18/110 (16%)		
	Total			931	370/931 (40%)	271	

Note: A denotes consent form distribution, B denotes collection data, C denotes SEWB survey and D denotes case study.

Table 5.5 Demographics of the three cohorts of schools for the study of impact on student achievement

TSR category	School (pseudonym)	Enrolments	ICSEA 1	ICSEA 2	Number of participating students	Percent of participation in cohort
Longer-term TSR	Cooper Stone East School	296	918	937	19	17.4
	Willow Brook Public School	493	907	886	80	73.4
	Margaret Park Public School	289	929	973	10	9.2
	Total participants for cohort				109	100
	Weighted mean	439	910	903		
Initial TSR	Curraburra Public School	410	819	827	83	59.3
	Alfield Public School	204	1100	1058	20	13
	Bonvilla Public School	330	992	990	37	26.4
	Total participants for cohort				140	100
	Weighted mean	359	905	903		
Non-participating in TSR	Banksia Public School	479	955	959	37	30.3
	Docks Creek Public School	332	862	915	16	13.1
	Shornville Public School	477	813	867	50	41
	Pinlowe Public School	387	948	942	18	15.6
	Total participants for cohort				121	100
	Weighted mean	444	883	913		
	Total participants in study				370	

(www.myschool.edu.au) and from individual schools. ICSEA was well matched between the three cohorts; the non-participating schools showed the highest weighted mean ICSEA 2 of 913, and 903 for both the initial and the longer-term as shown in Table 5.5.

The three cohorts were well matched in terms of gender and grade levels as illustrated in Tables 5.6 and 5.7, respectively, with no statistically significant difference in the distribution of gender or grade levels between the three cohorts (data not shown). Effect sizes were calculated using the equation described by Hattie (2009) (see Appendix).

Methodology for determining impact on student wellbeing

Three cohorts of schools: (1) TSR – initial (six-month program), (2) TSR – longer-term program and (3) non-participating in TSR, were surveyed to determine differences in students within or without the TSR program and also between the initial and

Table 5.6 Gender demographics according to TSR participation category

			Gender		Total
			Female	Male	
TSR participation category	Longer-term TSR	Count	57	52	109
		% within TSR category	52.3	47.7	100.0
		% of total	15.4	11	29.5
	Initial TSR	count	66	74	140
		% within TSR category	47.1	52.9	100.0
		% of total	17.8	20.0	37.8
	Non-participating in TSR	count	65	56	121
		% within TSR category	53.7	46.3	100.0
		% of total	17.6	15.1	32.7
Total		count	188	182	370
		% of total	50.8	49.2	100.0

Table 5.7 Demographics of students' grade level

			Grade of student		Total
			Grade 5	Grade 6	
TSR participation category	Longer-term TSR	Count	54	55	109
		% within TSR category	49.5	50.5	100.0
		% of total	16	19	29.5
	Initial TSR	count	81	59	140
		% within TSR category	57.9	42.1	100.0
		% of total	21.9	15.9	37.8
	Non-participating TSR	count	60	61	121
		% within TSR category	49.6	50.4	100.0
		% of total	16.2	16.5	32.7
Total		count	195	175	370
		% of total	52.7	47.3	100.0

longer-term programs. Each of the three cohorts of schools was comprised of two schools as shown in Table 5.8. ICSEA scores were well matched between the three cohorts; the non-participating schools had the highest weighted mean ICSEA 2 of 908, the initial 876, and the longer-term 896 as shown in Table 5.8.

The SEWB survey was developed and validated by the ACER. The SEWB survey was completed by students in Grades 5 and 6 in semester 2, term 1 (13–19 August 2010). Students were encouraged to ask the research staff and their classroom teachers for an explanation of any questions they could not comprehend. Extra time was

Table 5.8　Demographics of the individual schools and the three cohorts involved in the study of the impact on student wellbeing

TSR Category	School (pseudonym)	Date of TSR commencement	Enrolments	ICSEA 1	ICSEA 2	% of participation in SEWB
Longer-term	Willow Brook Public School	2009 semester 1	493	907	886	88
	Margaret Park Public School	2009 semester 2	289	929	973	12
		Weighted mean	468	909	896	100
Initial	Curraburra Public School	2010 semester 1	410	819	827	70
	Bonvilla School	2010 semester 1	330	992	990	30
		Weighted mean	386	870	876	100
Non-participating	Banksia Public School		479	955	959	45
	Shornville Public School		477	813	867	55
		Weighted mean	478	878	908	100

provided for students with low levels of literacy or LBOTE; no students exceeded an hour for the completion of the survey.

The SEWB of students from Grades 5 and 6 were not previously identified as statistically different (Bernard *et al.* 2007: 60); therefore, they were grouped together within this study to increase the power to detect differences between the three cohorts. The data provided in the report prepared by ACER specified the percentage of students in agreement for each statement in the survey according to gender and participation in TSR. The report also included the results of over 20,000 students in the SEWB, which provide an indication of trends in SEWB in Australia, and data on gender differences in responses to specific statements of SEWB. The gender demographics of the three cohorts and the SEWB controls are specified in Table 5.9. Over 20 percent of the SEWB controls were surveyed in NSW which was the site of the study. The SEWB control cohort was not considered to be a valid comparison group for the longer-term and initial TSR cohorts:

1　As the controls contained only 10 percent students from low SES and those students in Grade 6 from the top 10 percent of SES showed significantly higher SEWB when compared to students from the lowest 25 percent of SES (Bernard *et al.* 2007: 66).

2　The cohorts of schools involved in this study can be considered to have a low SES as our analysis revealed an ICSEA score that is lower than the mean of 1000. For example the initial TSR schools have a weighted mean ICSEA 2 of 876 as shown in Table 5.8, which is greater than one standard deviation of 100 below the national mean of 1000 and thus is in the lower 15.8 percent of the population.

Table 5.9   Demographic information of the cohorts involved in the study of impact on student wellbeing

Cohort	Gender				Gender not specified		Total count
	Boys		Girls		Count	Percent	
	Count	Percent	Count	Percent			
Longer-term TSR	33	37	45	50.6	11	12.4	89
Initial TSR	46	44	51	48	9	8.5	106
Non-participating TSR	30	39	35	46	11	14	76
SEWB controls (year 6)	1,198	60.4	784	39.6	—	—	1982
SEWB controls (all years)	11,640	56	8,638	41	633	3	20,911

The longer-term and initial TSR groups were compared to the non-participating in TSR which were sourced from a similar region and have similar ICSEA to the other cohorts as shown in Table 5.5. A significant difference was identified in survey results for boys and girls in Grades 5 and 6 in an Australia-wide survey of over 11,000 students (Bernard *et al.* 2007: 64), thus a separate analysis of boys and girls was considered important for the study. The percentage of girls and boys within the three cohorts were reasonably well matched with no more than five percent difference between the girls and just over six percent difference for the boys as shown in Table 5.9. The category of 'gender not specified' on Table 5.9 indicated that the student neglected to answer the gender section in the survey.

The data from the SEWB survey were analysed by ACER who provided a report of overall levels of SEWB and measures in seven levels of the SEWB construct. The data within the report provided by ACER were analysed to identify differences between the three cohorts of schools. Statistical analysis was performed on data provided by ACER on the SEWB survey responses; strongly disagree, disagree, agree and strongly agree were coded as a one, two, three and four, respectively. ANOVA was used to compare the means of the cohorts, with Bonferroni post hoc comparisons to determine which pairs drove the significance.

Methodology for case studies

The schools for the case studies were chosen for their involvement in TSR, two schools from the longer-term TSR cohort and two from the initial TSR cohort. The schools were chosen based on their improvement in NAPLAN from years 2008 to 2009 (data not shown). The schools chosen were Willow Brook and Margaret Park from the longer-term TSR and Bonvilla and Curraburra from the initial cohort. For each school the participation of two teachers, 10 students (five from Grade 5, five from Grade 6), principal and two parents was requested. Consent was then obtained from the participants in the case study, and individual schools organised the timing of the interviews. The case studies were completed in semester 2 of 2010 during the week of 24–31 August.

Notes were taken by the researchers at the time of the interviews and these were analysed for themes that were categorised according to the major foci of this study: engagement, TSR and academic engagement, TSR and social and behavioural impact and capacity building. Drafts for each case study were forwarded to the principals for their approval.

Summary

The need for well-designed quasi-experimental studies has been described in literature. The methodological approach of quasi-experimental design in the TSR project involved important elements such as longitudinal data, the participation of 370 students which enabled sufficient statistical power for 'clean evidence', non-arts academic achievement and in the arts in general (different applications of TSR for different schools) and a control group. Central to the design of the research was the use of data provided through the Australian government website My School, which enabled the selection of the control schools which best matched the schools with TSR programs in both ICSEA and enrolment numbers.

The length of time in arts programs was investigated through comparisons between three groups of schools: (1) longer-term TSR (12–18 months); (2) initial TSR (6 months); and (3) non-participating (control). Ten schools were involved in the study, with three schools from the longer-term and initial cohorts, and four from the control group. A total of 370 students from Grades 5 and 6 were involved, with over 100 students represented in each of the three cohorts. The data collected included gender, grade level, attendance, results in school reports and NAPLAN results. The SEWB survey was administered to a total of 271 students, in six schools, two from each of the three cohorts. To enable simultaneous comparisons between the three groups ANOVA was employed. ANOVA was used to determine if there was a statistically significant difference between the means of the three groups, and Bonferroni comparisons were used to determine what pairs of cohorts were driving the significance. The gender and grade level of the three groups were compared which ensured that the three cohorts were well matched. The influence of gender on each of the studied variables was examined and the results were considered for the final analysis. Effect sizes were calculated to determine the magnitude of the study outcomes. Case studies were conducted in four schools, two from each of the longer-term TSR and initial cohorts.

Significance

While the Australian study involved a relatively small number of schools it is profoundly significant for two reasons. First, it has been conducted against a background of extensive research in other countries that have yielded consistent findings, as summarised in Chapter 4 and extended in Chapters 6 and 7. Second, it was a very rare opportunity to study schools in matched settings that differed on a single factor only, namely, whether an innovative program in the arts was offered to students at the same level in primary schools. The settings were matched using a robust index, namely, the ICSEA, developed over several years for all schools in Australia, with the best iteration confirming that these schools in the same or neighbouring suburbs were indeed a good match.

The range of qualitative and quantitative methods employed in this research enabled us to examine the effect of the TSR programs on student outcomes of an academic and psychological nature in the highly disadvantaged settings in the western suburbs of Sydney in New South Wales, the results of which are reported in Chapters 6, 7 and 8.

6 Impact on student achievement

The starting point for Chapter 6 is a summary of findings from around the world in research on the impact of the arts on student achievement. This extends the review of research in Chapter 4. The major findings of the Australian study in the areas of student achievement (school tests, national tests) and student attendance are then reported. Comparisons are made between student performance in schools participating in the arts and those in matching schools that did not participate. Comparisons between the initial and longer-term arts programs provide evidence of the impact on student achievement and attendance, with the impact increasing the longer students are in the program.

Impact of the arts on student achievement

Involvement of students in the arts has been shown to increase academic achievement (Bamford 2006; Catterall *et al.* 1999; Wetter *et al.* 2009), IQ (Schellenberg 2006), attendance (Dreeszen *et al.* 1999), attitude to attendance (Brice Heath 2002; Upitis and Smithrim 2003), performance on standardised reading and verbal tests (Butzlaff 2002), verbal skills (Hetland and Winner 2001), reading for pleasure (Upitis and Smithrim 2003) and literacy (Bamford 2006; Hunter 2005; Spillane 2009). The findings of Catterall, Chapleau and Iwanaga were discussed in Chapter 4, they also found that students that engaged in the arts were seen to make positive academic development between 8th to 10th and 10th to 12th Grades (Catterall *et al.* 1999). Students of low SES involved in arts showed increased reading proficiency (Catterall *et al.* 1999). Improvement in literacy across multiple studies showed a range of 18–24 percent with an average of 22 percent improvement (Bamford 2006). Students in Grades 4 to 6 showed significantly improved grades in all subjects except physical education compared to students not practising music (Wetter *et al.* 2009). Students' involvements with extra-curricular music lessons were significantly correlated with reading for pleasure (Upitis and Smithrim 2003).

A meta-analysis of 80 reports identified a causal link between classroom drama and increased verbal skills which transferred to new materials (Hetland and Winner 2001). The above-mentioned gains in academic outcomes may be driven in part by changing attitudes towards school attendance. Upitis and Smithrim (2003) found that Grade 6 girls involved in Learning Through The Arts (LTTA) were significantly happier to come to school than similar students at schools without LTTA programs. LTTA involved professional artists who worked directly with the students after devising the curricula in conjunction with the classroom teachers (Upitis and Smithrim 2003). LTTA was a Canadian longitudinal study with a total sample size of 6,675, with students that spanned Grades 1 to 6 (Upitis and Smithrim 2003). Students from a low SES background involved in arts programs were three times more likely to win an award for school attendance (Brice Heath 2002).

Music instruction has been shown to significantly increase spatial-temporal reasoning skills (Hetland and Winner 2001), encourage mathematics reasoning (Vaughn 2002), improve numeracy (Hunter 2005; Spillane 2009) and significantly improve mathematics results (Bamford 2006; Catterall *et al.* 1999; Hunter 2005; Upitis and Smithrim 2003). Improvement in mathematics was identified in multiple studies and showed a range of 3–15 percent with an average of 6 percent improvement (Bamford 2006). Catterall *et al.* (1999) showed that students involved with instrumental music (middle and high school) had significantly higher levels of ability in mathematics by Grade 12. Students of low SES involved with music, when compared to peers of equivalent SES not involved with music, also showed significantly higher mathematics results (Catterall *et al.* 1999). The absolute differences in mathematics skills between students participating in instrumental music versus those not participating was found to increase significantly over time (Catterall *et al.* 1999). Analysis of LTTA initiatives revealed that there was a significantly higher mathematics achievement for Grade 6 students at LTTA schools than those at schools without arts programs (Upitis and Smithrim 2003). Mathematics skills and results were found to be significantly linked to music initiatives across multiple longitudinal studies.

Illustrative findings in the Australian study

In this section we summarise the key findings of the Australian research on the impact of programs offered by TSR in highly disadvantaged settings in the western suburbs of Sydney in New South Wales. The methodology was described in Chapter 5.

Impact on academic grades

The grades achieved by students were assigned a numerical value of 5, 4, 3, 2 and 1 for A, B, C, D and E, respectively. There was no statistically significant difference in the academic grades for females and males (data not shown). The percentage of females and males according to TSR participation category were well matched with a maximum difference of 5 percent more girls/5 percent fewer boys in the non-participating in TSR cohort in comparison to the initial TSR cohort as shown in Table 5.6. The academic subjects of English, mathematics, science and technology and human society were placed into one group and the means of those participating in TSR (initial and longer-term TSR) were compared with ANOVA to those students who had not participated in TSR as shown in Figure 6.1. The individual

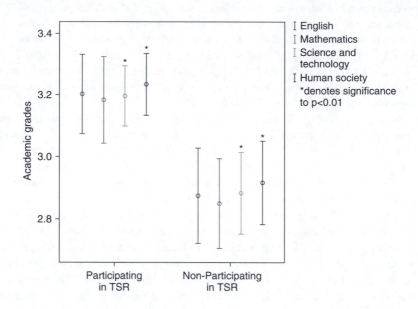

Figure 6.1 The 95 percent confidence intervals for academic grades for individual subjects
according to TSR participation status

academic subjects were compared with ANOVA for students with TSR and without.
Effect sizes were calculated to obtain a measure of the magnitude of the differences
in student outcomes. The formula for the calculation of the effect sizes is contained
in the Appendix. Effect size (d) describes the magnitude of study outcomes (Hattie
2009). An effect size of 1.0 is equivalent to an increase in one standard deviation and
can be 'typically associated with advancing children's achievement by two or three
years or improving the rate of learning by 50 percent' (Hattie 2009: 9). An effect size
of above d = 0.4 was described as within the 'zone of desired effects', which can be
described as real-world difference in achievement (Hattie 2009).

The 95 percent confidence intervals are indicated by the vertical lines which showed
the predicted range of 95 percent of the students' grades, while the circles indicated the
mean grades of the cohorts (A, B, C, D, E were assigned the numerical values of 5, 4,
3, 2 and 1, respectively) as shown in Figure 6.1. Students who had participated in TSR
(initial and longer-term TSR) showed significantly higher academic grades (English,
mathematics, science and technology and human society) in comparison to those
students who had not participated in TSR as shown in Figure 6.1. The effect size of d
= 0.46 for the difference in science and technology grades falls within Hattie's zone
of desired effects, while d = 0.34 for human society would be considered medium in
size (Hattie 2009).

The percentage of students with A or B grade in English was highest for the longer-
term TSR cohort, intermediate for the initial TSR cohort and lowest for the non-
participating in TSR cohort as illustrated in Figure 6.2.

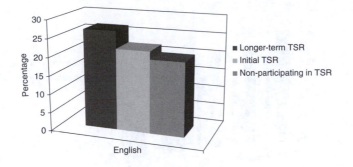

Figure 6.2 Percentage of students with a grade of A or B in English according to TSR participation category

Impact on national test scores in literacy

The Year 5 NAPLAN results were reported in bands from three to eight, band three indicates students below the national minimum, band four indicates students are at the national minimum and students in bands five to eight are above the national minimum (ACARA 2010b). To calculate the percentage of students below, at and above the national minimum standard, bands from five through to eight were assigned a numerical value of 5, while the other bands retained their original values of 3 and 4.

The 2008 NAPLAN comparisons provide baseline data for the longer-term TSR cohort, as they were not participating in TSR in 2008. No significant statistical differences were found between the longer-term and non-participating cohorts for the literacy domains in 2008 as illustrated in Figures 6.3 and 6.4. The percentage of students above the national minimum for the baseline results of Year 5 2008 NAPLAN was lower in the longer-term TSR for the majority of the literacy domains

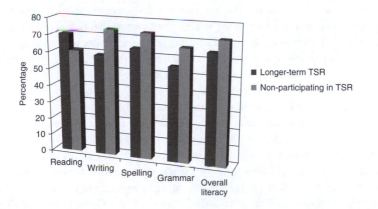

Figure 6.3 Percentage of students above the national minimum for the literacy domains in Year 5 NAPLAN 2008 results according to TSR participation category (baseline data are for longer-term TSR)

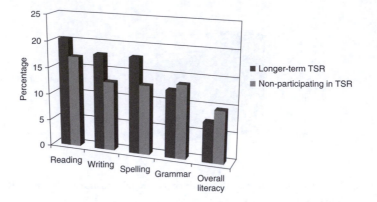

Figure 6.4   Percentage of students below the national minimum for the literacy domains in Year 5 NAPLAN 2008 results according to TSR participation category (baseline data are for longer-term TSR)

(writing, spelling, grammar and punctuation and overall literacy) in comparison to those students who had not participated in TSR. These data show that before the TSR had begun, the longer-term cohort had a lower percentage of students above the national minimum in four of the five literacy domains in comparison to the control group (non-participating).

The comparison of the percentage of students below the national minimum for the literacy domains shows that prior to participation in the TSR the longer-term cohort showed a higher percentage of students below the national minimum for reading, writing and spelling in comparison to the non-participating cohort as illustrated in Figure 6.4. These data suggest that although there were no significant differences between the cohorts for the baseline data, generally the TSR longer-term cohort prior to participation had lower student results in literacy.

The comparison of Year 5 2009 NAPLAN bands showed a higher mean for all the literacy domains for the longer-term TSR cohort in comparison to those students who had not participated in TSR as shown in Figure 6.5 and Table 6.1. The longer-term TSR cohort showed significantly higher results for reading, and overall literacy in comparison to those who had not participated in TSR, as shown in Table 6.1. The effect sizes for reading ($d = 0.79$), writing ($d = 0.46$) and overall literacy ($d = 0.77$) were within the 'zone of desired effects' which can be considered to be real-world differences in achievement (Hattie 2009).

The percentage of students above the national minimum in Year 5 NAPLAN 2009 results were higher in the longer-term TSR for all the literacy domains in comparison to those students who had not participated in TSR as shown in Figure 6.5. The percentage of students below the national minimum standard was lower for the longer-term TSR for writing, spelling and grammar and punctuation, and overall literacy in comparison to the non-participating in TSR as shown in Figure 6.7.

The comparison of Year 5 2009 NAPLAN bands provided baseline data for the initial TSR cohort as it had not commenced its TSR program. Those students who

Table 6.1 Descriptive statistics for the Year 5 2009 NAPLAN bands for literacy domains according to TSR participation category (baseline data are for initial TSR)

		N	Mean	Std. Deviation	Significance	Effect size
Reading	Longer-term TSR	44	6.2727	1.24571	p = 0.0002*	0.79
	Initial TSR	48	5.1250	1.24840	p = 0.00005**	
	Non-participating in TSR	60	5.2667	1.21943		
	Total	152	5.5132	1.32218	p = 0.00001	
Writing	Longer-term TSR	44	6.0682	1.10806	p = 0.067	0.46
	Initial TSR	48	5.3125	1.22312	p = 0.008**	
	Non-participating in TSR	59	5.5254	1.19418		
	Total	151	5.6159	1.21029	p = 0.008	
Spelling	Longer-term TSR	44	6.2273	1.17856		0.34
	Initial TSR	48	5.7500	1.39146		
	Non-participating in TSR	59	5.8305	1.13187		
	Total	151	5.9205	1.24109	p = 0.142	
Grammar	Longer-term TSR	44	6.0909	1.27258		0.36
	Initial TSR	48	5.0833	1.45622	p = 0.001**	
	Non-participating in TSR	59	5.6441	1.22844		
	Total	151	5.5960	1.36713	p = 0.002	
Literacy	Longer-term TSR	38	6.3947	1.02771	p = 0.008*	0.77
	Initial TSR	48	5.3958	1.18033	p = 0.0001**	
	Non-participating in TSR	31	5.5806	1.02548		
	Total	117	5.7692	1.16991	p = 0.0001	

Notes

* denotes Bonferroni post hoc comparison to non-participating in TSR with significance to p<0.01

** denotes Bonferroni post hoc comparison to longer-term in TSR with significance to p<0.01

did not participate in TSR achieved a higher mean for all the literacy domains for the longer-term cohort in comparison to the initial (baseline data) students prior to their participation in the program as shown in Table 6.1. The longer-term TSR

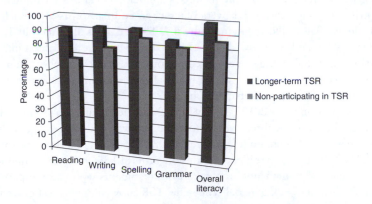

Figure 6.5 Percentage of students above the national minimum for the literacy domains in Year 5 NAPLAN 2009 results according to TSR participation category

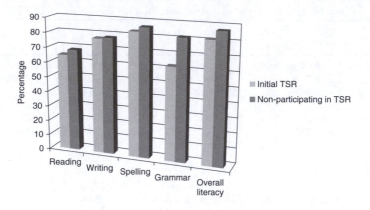

Figure 6.6   Percentage of students above the national minimum for the literacy domains in Year
5 NAPLAN 2009 results according to TSR participation category (baseline data are
for initial TSR)

cohort showed significantly higher results for reading, writing, spelling, grammar
and punctuation and overall literacy in comparison to the initial TSR (prior to their
participation in TSR), with p values that indicated a less than one percent chance that
there was no difference between the longer-term and initial TSR NAPLAN results as
illustrated in Table 6.1.

Comparison of the NAPLAN 2009 results provided baseline data for the initial
cohort. The percentage of students above the national minimum in Year 5 NAPLAN
2009 results was higher in students who had not participated in TSR for all the literacy
domains in comparison to the initial TSR cohort prior to their participation in TSR
as illustrated in Figure 6.6. The non-participating in TSR cohort showed a lower
percentage of students below the national minimum standard for writing, spelling,
grammar and punctuation, and overall literacy in comparison to the baseline data
for the initial TSR as illustrated in Figure 6.7. These data as illustrated in Table 6.1,
and Figures 6.6 and 6.7 show that prior to participation in TSR the initial cohort
was significantly below the literacy outcomes of the longer-term cohort, and showed
a lower percentage of students above national minimum in all literacy domains in
comparison to the non-participating cohort.

The comparison of the 2010 Year 5 NAPLAN literacy results showed no significant
differences between the three cohorts (data not shown). The percentage of students
above the national minimum (bands five to eight) for the literacy domains for Year 5
NAPLAN 2010 results were higher for the longer-term TSR cohort in writing, spelling
and grammar and punctuation in comparison to students who had not participated
in TSR as illustrated in Figure 6.8. The initial TSR showed the highest percentage of
students above the national minimum for spelling, and showed a higher percentage of
students in writing above the national minimum level in comparison to students who
had not participated in TSR as shown in Figure 6.8.

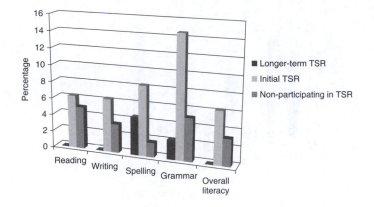

Figure 6.7 Percentage of students below the national minimum for the literacy domains in Year 5 NAPLAN 2009 results according to TSR participation category (baseline data are for initial TSR)

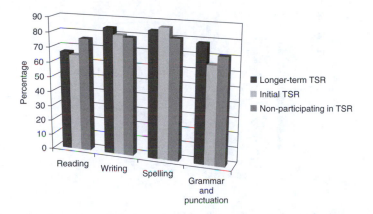

Figure 6.8 Percentage of students above the national minimum for the literacy domains in Year 5 NAPLAN 2010 results according to TSR participation category

The percentage of students below the national minimum standard in 2010 was lower for the longer-term TSR and initial TSR for writing, spelling and grammar and punctuation in comparison to students who had not participated in TSR as illustrated in Figure 6.9.

The comparison of the percentage of students below the national minimum for grammar and punctuation showed a similar level of students below the national minimum for the baseline comparisons in 2008 between the longer-term prior to their participation in TSR and those that had not participated in TSR. The baseline data for the initial cohort showed the highest percentage of students below the national minimum for grammar and punctuation, prior to participation in TSR in comparison to the longer-term TSR students and those who had not participated as shown in the

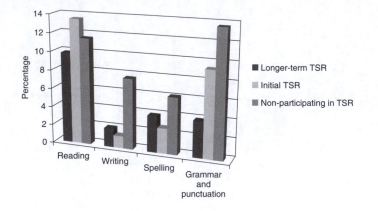

Figure 6.9 Percentage of students below the national minimum for the literacy domains in Year 5 NAPLAN 2010 results according to TSR participation category

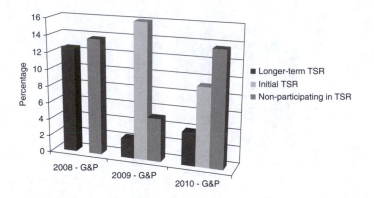

Figure 6.10 Percentage of students below the national minimum for grammar and punctuation (G&P) in Year 5 NAPLAN 2008, 2009 and 2010 results according to TSR participation category

2009 data set in Figure 6.10. The 2010 results show the lowest percentage of students below the national minimum in grammar and punctuation in the longer-term TSR cohort, intermediate for the initial and highest for those who have not participated in TSR. These data are illustrated in Figure 6.10. They suggest that interaction of students with TSR leads to a reduced percentage of students below the national minimum for the literacy domain of grammar and punctuation.

Impact on attendance

Attendance and absence at school were assigned a numerical value of one and zero, respectively. ANOVA was employed to detect differences between the means of the three cohorts with Bonferroni post hoc comparisons to determine the pairs of data driving the overall significance. There was no statistically significant difference in the attendance for females and males; therefore, female and male students were considered together. Students' attendance on the TSR day and 'normal day' did not show statistically significant variance within the individual cohorts, although statistical significance was identified through comparison between the three cohorts. The weighted percentage of student attendance rate was calculated from the data collected from the My School website.

The students from the longer-term TSR showed the highest level of attendance, with an intermediate level for the initial TSR cohort and lowest for students who had not participated in TSR as shown in Figure 6.11. The longer-term TSR and the initial TSR cohorts showed significantly higher attendance in comparison to non-participating in TSR cohort.

The longer-term TSR cohort showed significantly higher attendance on a TSR class day, in comparison to those who had not participated in TSR as shown in Figure 6.12. The percentage of students who were absent on a day that their school had participated in TSR was lowest for the longer-term TSR cohort, slightly higher for the initial TSR in comparison to the non-participating in TSR on a 'normal day'. In comparison to the students who had not participated in TSR there was a difference of over 7 percent more students present in the longer-term and initial TSR cohorts.

The comparisons of the student attendance rates showed an equal percentage of students absent in 2008 for the longer-term prior to their participation in TSR, and those students who formed the comparison group (non-participating in TSR), and higher rate of absence for the initial cohort prior to their participation in TSR as illustrated in Figure 6.13. The longer-term cohort (after 12 months of involvement with TSR) showed the lowest percentage of students absent in 2010, with the initial

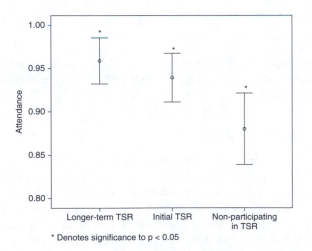

Figure 6.11　The 95 percent confidence intervals for attendance according to TSR participation category

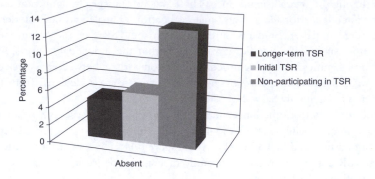

Figure 6.12   Percentage of students absent on a TSR day according to TSR participation category

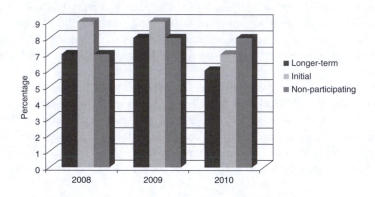

Figure 6.13   Student absence rate according to TSR participation category and year

cohort (after 6 months of TSR) at an intermediate level and the highest percentage of students absent was observed for those students who had not participated in TSR as shown in Figure 6.13.

Summary of illustrative findings

The key findings of the study in student achievement and attendance are illustrated in Table 6.2. The calculation of an effect size provided a measurement of magnitude of the study outcomes, which was translated into gain in time. The effect size of d = 0.79 was equivalent to a gain of at least one year in reading and literacy. The difference in grades was seen as an impact of about half of one year in science and technology. The difference in absenteeism on a TSR day represents 65 percent less absenteeism with participation in longer-term TSR in comparison to those that have not participated.

Table 6.2 Summary table of illustrative findings

Indicator of student performance	Longer-term TSR	Initial-TSR	Non-participating in TSR	Gain in time
Reading	d = 0.79 (p = 0.0002)			At least one year in reading and literacy achievement
Overall literacy	d = 0.77 (p = 0.0008)			
Academic grades	d = 0.13 (p = 0.022)			
Science and technology	d = 0.46 (p = 0.0001)			Lift in achievement by about ½ a year in science and technology
Attendance percent absent on TSR day	4.6	5.7	13.2	

Students that participated in TSR showed significantly higher grades in their academic subjects (English, mathematics, science and technology and human society) in comparison to those who had not participated in TSR. Grades in science and technology and human society were significantly higher for students who had participated in TSR in comparison to those who had not participated in TSR. A previous study identified similar results for students who had practised music with increased grades for academic subjects (Wetter *et al.* 2009). The effect sizes of TSR on the increased academic grades, science and technology grades and human society showed effect sizes of 0.13, 0.46 and 0.34, respectively, which were similar to the findings of Winner and Cooper of increased academic achievement (d = 0.10) for students who had studied the arts (Winner and Cooper 2000).

NAPLAN 2008 provided the baseline data for the longer-term group. There was no significant difference between scores for Grade 5 for longer-term and non-participating schools. In fact, a higher percentage of students in the latter were above the national minimum than those in the former for four of the five domains. The analysis of the Year 5 NAPLAN 2009 data for longer-term TSR schools in comparison to non-participating schools shows significantly higher results for reading, writing, spelling, grammar and punctuation and overall literacy. The 2009 results were relevant to this study as they present the point at which the students from the longer-term cohort would have participated in the program for 5 months. The effect sizes for the increased band scores for the Year 5 NAPLAN 2009 were 0.79, 0.46, 0.34, 0.36 and 0.77 for reading, writing, spelling, grammar and punctuation and overall literacy, respectively. The percentages of students above the national minimum remained higher in the Year 5 2010 NAPLAN for the longer-term TSR for writing, spelling and grammar and punctuation in comparison to students who had not participated in TSR.

The initial TSR showed in the baseline data of 2009 Year 5 NAPLAN a lower percentage of students above the national minimum in reading, writing, spelling, grammar and punctuation and overall literacy in comparison to non-participating in TSR cohorts. The results of the 2010 NAPLAN showed improvement for the initial TSR with a higher percentage of students above the national minimum level in spelling and writing in comparison to the students who had not participated in TSR. A similar pattern was observed in the initial TSR for the students below the national minimum standard. These data indicate gains in literacy for the initial TSR cohort.

Attendance was significantly higher for the longer-term TSR and initial TSR cohorts in comparison to the non-participating in TSR. The attendance rate of students in 2010 showed the lowest percentage of absence for the longer-term TSR, at an intermediate level for the initial TSR and highest for those schools that had not participated in TSR. Previous studies have identified similar effects on attendance (Dreeszen *et al.* 1999) and attitude to attendance (Upitis and Smithrim 2003). The higher attendance of the longer-term and initial TSR cohorts could have positively influenced the students' grades and NAPLAN results.

As the same effect sizes observed in literacy in the longer-term TSR in the 2009 NAPLAN results were not observed in 2010 NAPLAN when an additional school was incorporated into the longer-term cohort, a multi-factorial model in which other dependent factors play a part should be considered rather than a causation model. Increased performance across multiple disciplines as observed in this study has been previously identified, indicating that engagement with music encourages 'general cognitive or intellectual functions' (Wetter *et al.* 2009: 372). TSR can be thought of as working 'alongside a range of other initiatives and relationships specific to local contexts' (Hughes 2005: 19). Hughes described the influence on music programs on disengaged students:

> Those with poor educational experiences need to be engaged in a range of ways, indeed sometimes creative activities can be the first step to addressing needs in a wider sense. They have proved to be effective in engaging disaffected learners and encouraging participation in other learning and skills activities.
>
> (Hughes 2005: 20)

Summary

The influence of music programs on reading, literacy and numeracy have been observed in other studies. Baseline measurements of the NAPLAN results in 2008 showed no significant differences between the longer-term cohort (prior to participation in TSR) and those who had not participated in TSR. NAPLAN 2009 provided the baseline data for the initial group for which we see the same pattern. Significantly higher Year 5 NAPLAN 2009 results for the longer-term TSR cohort were observed in reading, writing, spelling, grammar and punctuation and overall literacy ($p < 0.01$), with the largest effect size of d = 0.79 for reading, which was within the 'zone of desired effects' for educational research and equivalent to a gain in achievement of at least a year. The comparison of the Year 5 2010 NAPLAN results showed lower percentages of students below the minimum national level for the longer-term TSR and initial TSR cohorts in writing, spelling and grammar and punctuation in comparison to those students who had not participated in TSR.

Significantly higher academic grades were observed for students who had participated in TSR in comparison to those who had not participated in TSR. The largest effect size was observed for science and technology grades, of d = 0.46 which was equivalent to a gain of half a year in achievement. The achievement of higher English grades in students who participated in TSR triangulates with the NAPLAN Literacy results in this study. Attendance was significantly higher for the longer-term cohort on a TSR day, with the initial cohort at intermediate level and the non-participating cohort with the lowest level of attendance on a normal day. The observed increased attendance may have contributed to the observed increased student achievement.

In summary, those students in the TSR achieved higher academic grades, literacy results and attendance than those students that did not participate in TSR. These findings were particularly apparent for the longer-term TSR cohort, who showed the highest levels of achievement in literacy and attendance in comparison to both the initial and non-participating cohorts. These gains in attendance and academic outcomes may account for the high levels of SEWB reported in Chapter 7.

Significance

The impact of participation in the arts reported above is astonishing given that students were engaged for no longer than one hour per week. Indeed, we did not expect to find differences on the scale that has been documented. As described in Chapter 5, we began (as we should) with the hypothesis that there would be no difference. Given that we were studying students in matched schools, the findings have important implications for policy and practice, as set out in Chapter 10. For example, the evidence that gains in learning were as much as one year demands attention. For many, the obvious reason is that students tend to come to school in larger numbers on the days that the TSR program is offered. Clearly, students are unlikely to learn in the areas that were tested if they are not at school. Findings in relation to attendance are especially noteworthy. We have applied the most stringent tests to form our conclusions drawing, in particular, on the internationally recognised work of John Hattie, Professor and Director of the Melbourne Education Research Institute at the University of Melbourne.

7   Impact on student wellbeing

The starting point for Chapter 7 is a summary of findings from around the world on the impacts of the arts on psychological and behavioural indicators. This extends the research background in preceding chapters. The SEWB survey, which was employed in this study, was designed and validated by ACER. The survey was administered to 271 students, to two schools from each of three cohorts. Findings in relation to the six levels of SEWB are presented.

As we demonstrate in the pages that follow, student SEWB was influenced by participation in TSR program, with the longer-term cohort showing the highest percentage of students at the highest level of overall SEWB, the initial TSR at an intermediate level and those who had not participated having no students at the highest level. Significantly different responses to statements related to stress and depression were identified for male and female students respectively, who participated in TSR in comparison to those who did not.

Impact of the arts on psychological and behavioural indicators

Participation in arts programs was found to increase various psychological indicators such as resilience (Oreck et al. 1999), self-regulation (Hunter 2005; Oreck et al. 1999), self-esteem (Brice Heath and Roach 1999; Hunter 2005; Upitis and Smithrim 2003), self-efficacy (Catterall and Peppler 2007), identity (Oreck et al. 1999), self-concept (Catterall et al. 1999) and motivation (Bamford 2006; Catterall et al. 1999; Hunter 2005) and the ability to experience flow (completely focused motivation) (Oreck et al. 1999). The findings of a study of the influence of creative arts programs on self-efficacy (Catterall and Peppler 2007) were detailed in Chapter 4. Student learning in the arts was described as: (1) independent and intrinsically motivating, (2) fostering learning for understanding and (3) transforming student characterisations of learning barriers into 'challenges' to be solved (Bamford 2006: 108). Students from a low SES background who were involved with performing showed an increase in self-concept and motivation from Years 8 to 10, peaking at Year 12 compared to students who were not involved in arts programs (Catterall et al. 1999). The qualities of resilience, self-regulation, identity and the ability to experience flow observed within 26 case studies 'correlated and interact reciprocally, each having the effect of strengthening the other' (Oreck et al. 1999: 70).

The 'high-demand high-risk' atmosphere of rehearsal and performance encourages the growth of 'skills and capacities rooted in their personal recognition of themselves as competent, creative, and productive individuals' (Brice Heath and Roach 1999: 29). Self-esteem showed increases of about 15 percent (as measured by questions regarding: (1) feels good about him/herself, (2) feels she/he is a person of worth, (3) is able to do things as well as others and (4) on the whole is satisfied with self) in the arts group compared to the NELS: 88 controls (not participating in arts group) (Brice Heath and Roach 1999: 30). The observed difference in self-esteem becomes particularly relevant when it is considered that students in arts programs were about twice as likely as those that were not to be in situations that exacerbate feelings of insecurity and uncertainty such as parental relationship change, frequent moves, and parents losing or starting a job and going on or off welfare (Brice Heath and Roach 1999). In Australia, Saubern (2010) described the impact of the TSR program on students' self-esteem:

> The light in the faces of the children, teachers and assistants as they rehearse a song that they've written themselves, about themselves, is a wonderful sight to see. It's a flash of that rare and precious sense of achievement, of having done something good.
>
> (Saubern 2010: 14)

Improvement in the behavioural indicators of empathy (Catterall *et al.* 1999; Hunter 2005), tolerance (Catterall *et al.* 1999), cooperation (Hunter 2005), skills of collaboration (Hunter 2005), and communication skills (Hunter 2005) were observed in students who actively participated in various arts programs. Sustained student involvement in theatre arts was found to be significantly related to increased tolerance and empathy to others (measured through the question 'Is it ok to make a racist remark?') in Grade 10 students compared with 'no drama' students with similarly low SES backgrounds (Catterall *et al.* 1999: 15). A student in the previously described LTTA (Chapter 6) program described the changes they perceived within themselves: 'The arts taught us how to bring out inner feelings, how to cooperate, listen, and express ourselves through movement' (Grade 6 student) (Upitis and Smithrim 2003: 19).

Impact on student wellbeing

The SEWB survey was employed for the measurement of the student psychological indicators that include resilience, attitudes, engagement and coping skills (Bernard *et al.* 2007). The SEWB survey allows the determination of six distinct levels of student SEWB, ranging from the lowest to the highest levels which were described as 'social and emotional indicators that students at each level are likely to display' (Australian Council for Educational Research 2010: 11; Bernard *et al.* 2007). The overall SEWB was determined by considering both the presence of positive elements and the absence of the negative elements as outlined in Table 7.1.

There are several categories of social and emotional factors that influence students'

Table 7.1 Overall SEWB

Presence of positive indicators of social and emotional well-being:	*Absence of negative indicators of social and emotional well-being:*
The young person generally appears to . . .	The young person generally does not appear to . . .
• have positive self-esteem (likes him/herself) • volunteer to make his/her community a better place • like being in school • get along with classmates including those who are different • get along with teachers • be interested in helping others • participate in a wide range of activities • relate positively to family • feel like he/she belongs in school • make responsible choices to stay out of trouble • feel safe and free from physical harm	• engage in unhealthy behaviour (alcohol, drugs) • have significant periods of time when he/she feels down • act impulsively • be lonely or a loner • under-achieve in one or more areas of schoolwork • be very stressed • act dishonestly (lie, cheat or steal) • worry too much about what others think of him/her • lose his/her temper

Source: Adapted from Australian Council for Educational Research 2010: 7–8

wellbeing which include (Australian Council for Educational Research 2010: 11; Bernard *et al.* 2007):

• resilience – rational attitudes, coping skills
• positive social skills and values
• positive work management and engagement skills – learning capabilities including work confidence, persistence, organisation, cooperation.

The above aspects of SEWB can be considered to be internal qualities found within individual students. Environmental factors including community, home and school have also been identified to influence students' SEWB.

The five components of the SEWB construct relevant to this study were described as follows:

Indicators of SEWB
This category includes students' self-perceptions of the presence of their positive emotions and behaviours (e.g. happy, get along with others, participated) and the absence of negative emotions and behaviours (e.g. do not take drugs, not feeling hopeless, not feeling stressed).

Indicators of resilience
This category includes students' self-perceptions of their emotional capabilities/coping skills and positive, rational attitudes (e.g. not putting yourself down when you do not understand something, believing you have what it takes to be successful).

Indicators of positive social skills and values
This category includes students' self-perceptions of their social capabilities, such as friendship making, solving conflicts, understanding how people feel, willingness to follow rules, and important social values (e.g. respect, caring, honesty, responsibility and good citizenship).

Indicators of positive work management and engagement skills
This category includes students' self-perceptions of their learning capabilities, such as work confidence (e.g. raising hand to answer a difficult question), persistence, organisation (e.g. planning time) and work cooperation.

Indicators of positive school life
This category includes students' perceptions of the positive actions of teachers, including teachers caring about students, helping students be successful, discussing values and social and emotional skills and values, as well as involving students in decisions about classroom rules and interesting school activities.

> (Australian Council for Educational Research 2010: 11)

The higher the numerical value of the overall SEWB the higher the students' self-perception of SEWB. Table 7.2 shows the descriptions of the SEWB levels of student self-perception.

The variability of the characteristics of students at various levels of SEWB was described:

> Students assigned to a given level of SEWB are likely to be characterised by many but not necessarily all of the social emotional characteristics that define that level. Students are also likely to endorse all the statements at the levels below their nominated level. For example, students at Level 2 on the SEWB scale are likely to endorse the statements at that level. Students at Level 5 are likely to endorse the statements at Level 5, more likely to endorse the statements at Level 4 and extremely likely to endorse the statements at Level 2.
>
> (Australian Council for Educational Research 2010: 11)

Impact on overall social and emotional wellbeing

The percentage of students at the highest levels of overall SEWB (levels 5 and 6) was highest for the longer-term TSR, at an intermediate level for initial TSR, and lowest for those who had not participated in TSR as illustrated in Figure 7.1. The longer-term TSR cohort shows a higher percentage of students at the overall SEWB levels of 6 and 5, in comparison to students in the initial or the non-participating TSR cohorts. The initial TSR cohort shows an intermediate level of percentage of students at levels 5 and 6 of SEWB which is below and above the percentages of students for the longer-term TSR and the non-participating TSR, respectively. These data suggest that the longer schools have been involved in TSR the higher the percentage of students at the two highest levels of SEWB as shown in Figure 7.1 and Table 7.2.

Table 7.2 Descriptions of the six levels of SEWB

Level	SEWB levels of student self-perception: SEWB
6	Students are highly likely to demonstrate a full range of positive indicators (emotional, social and behavioural) of SEWB in different areas of their lives. They are unlikely to experience behavioural, emotional or interpersonal difficulties and are likely to achieve to the best of their ability. They are also likely to often experience a range of positive emotions (e.g. enthusiasm and energy, curiosity in the way things are, hopeful about future, love of learning).
5	Students are likely to display most positive indicators of SEWB in many areas of their lives. Emotionally, they are not likely to feel very stressed, worry too much and to lose their temper a lot. Socially, they are likely to volunteer to do things to make their school and community safer. Educationally, they are likely to perceive that they are doing their best in their schoolwork.
4	Students are likely to display many positive indicators of SEWB. Emotionally, students are likely to feel they now belong in school and they are not likely to have felt very helpless and down for extended periods. However, they are still likely to get stressed, worry a lot and lose their temper. Behaviourally, they are not likely to be mean to others or to get in trouble. Socially, they are likely to participate in many activities inside and outside of school but they are not likely to volunteer. Educationally, they are not likely to be doing their best in their schoolwork.
3	Students are likely to display some positive indicators of SEWB and a few negative indicators. Emotionally they are likely to feel safe and they are not likely to feel lonely. Behaviourally, they are no longer likely to yell (younger children). However they are still likely to get into trouble and be mean to others. Socially, they are likely to be getting along with members of their family and teachers and they are likely to help others who are unhappy. However, they are not likely to participate in a range of activities. Educationally, they are likely to be doing well in school, however they are not likely to be doing their best in their schoolwork.
2	Students are likely to display few positive indicators of SEWB and a large number of negative indicators. Emotionally, students are likely to feel happy and like the kind of person that they are. However, students are likely to feel lonely, very down and hopeless for a week or more, lose their temper, worry a lot and feel unsafe. Behaviourally, most are not likely to drink excessively or use drugs. However, they are likely to be mean to others, and to break things. Socially, students are likely to perceive themselves as getting along with most of their classmates. However, they are likely to have difficulty getting along with members of their family as well as teachers and they do not like to help people who seem unhappy.
1	Students are not at all likely to display indicators of positive SEWB (e.g. do not like themselves, are not happy, do not get along with classmates, do not like engaging in play, do not enjoy meeting new people, do not believe that it is important to treat everyone with respect, do not want to do their best in school). They are very likely to display many negative social and emotional indicators (e.g. take drugs, drink too much alcohol). They may also be likely to display other negative indicators of SEWB not surveyed (e.g. suicidal ideation, sleep difficulties, eating disorders).

Source: Adapted from Australian Council for Educational Research 2010: 20

Impact on overall resilience, attitudes and coping skills

The percentage of students at the highest levels of resilience (levels 6/5) shows a gradual decrease from the highest level of 28.1 percent for the longer-term TSR students, to an intermediate level of 19.8 percent for the initial TSR students and the

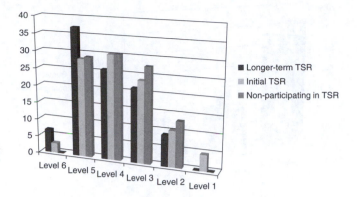

Figure 7.1 Comparison of percentage distribution of overall SEWB according to TSR participation category

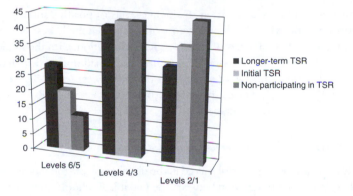

Figure 7.2 Comparison of the percentage distribution of student resilience according to TSR
participation category

lowest level 11.8 percent for the non-participating in TSR students, which represents
a change of about 8 percent between each cohort. The percentage of students at the
lowest levels of resilience (levels 2/1) shows a gradual increase from longer-term
TSR at the lowest percentage, intermediate percentage for the initial TSR and highest
for those who have not participated in TSR. These findings, illustrated in Figure 7.2
indicated that increased duration of the TSR at a school is associated with higher level
of resilience within the student cohort.

Impact on social skills and values

The longer-term TSR cohort showed the highest percentage of students at levels
6 and 5 of overall positive social orientation as shown in Figure 7.3. Relatively large
differences were observed in the distribution of students in the various levels between
the two initial schools, thus both schools were analysed separately. Curraburra showed

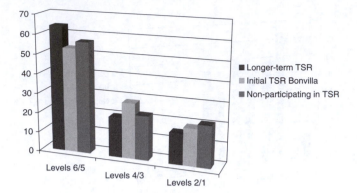

Figure 7.3 Comparison of percentage distribution of overall positive social orientation according to TSR participation category

a decreased percentage of students at the higher levels of positive social orientation in comparison to Bonvilla. The longer-term cohort showed the lowest percentage of students at the two lowest levels of positive social orientation, with the initial school Bonvilla at an intermediate level and those schools who had not participated in TSR showed the highest percentage of students at the two lowest levels. These findings, illustrated in Figure 7.3, indicated that long-term involvement in TSR was associated with higher positive social orientation.

Impact on overall work management and engagement

Relatively large differences were observed in the distribution of students at the various levels of positive work orientation between the two initial schools, thus both schools were analysed separately. Curraburra showed a decreased percentage of students at the higher levels of positive work management in comparison to Bonvilla. The longer-term TSR cohort showed the highest percentage of students at levels 5 and 6 of positive work orientation, the initial TSR schools showed the highest level of students at the middle levels of 4 and 3. Bonvilla showed the lowest percentage of students at the bottom two levels of positive work orientation, the longer-term TSR was slightly higher and the non-participating in TSR showed the highest percentage of students at levels 1 and 2 as illustrated in Figure 7.4. These findings indicated a relationship between longer-term TSR and higher percentages of students in the top two levels of positive work orientation.

Impact on school life

The percentage of students for the highest levels of positive school indicators was highest for the longer-term TSR, at an intermediate level for the initial TSR and lowest for the non-participating in TSR, as shown in Figure 7.5. These data indicate an influence of the TSR on positive school indicators.

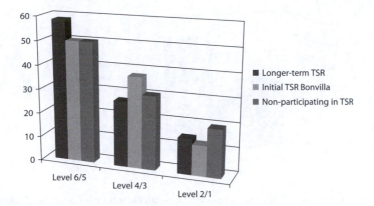

Figure 7.4   Comparison of percentage distribution of overall positive work orientation according to TSR participation category

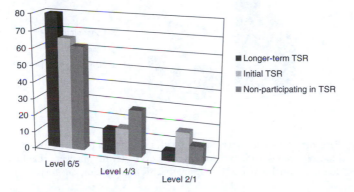

Figure 7.5   Comparison of percentage distribution of overall positive school indicators according to TSR participation category

Impact on indicators of social and emotional wellbeing

Male students who participated in TSR showed significantly reduced agreement to the statement 'I feel stressed' in comparison to students who had not participated in TSR as illustrated in Figure 7.6.

The boys in the longer-term TSR had the lowest percentage of agreement with the statement 'During the past six months, I have felt so hopeless and down almost every day for one week that I have stopped doing my usual activities'. At an intermediate level were the initial TSR cohort and then at the highest level were the non-participating in TSR. The girls in the longer-term TSR showed the lowest percentage who agreed with the above statement. At an intermediate level was the non-participating in TSR and the highest level was for the initial TSR. These findings, illustrated in Figure 7.7,

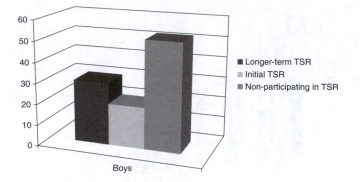

Figure 7.6 Percentage of boys who agreed with the statement 'I feel very stressed' according to TSR participation category

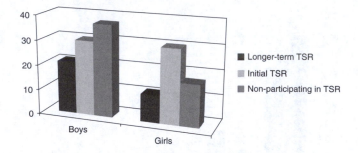

Figure 7.7 Percentage of students who agreed with the statement 'During the past six months, I have felt so hopeless and down almost every day for one week that I have stopped doing my usual activities' according to TSR participation category

suggest that increased length of time in TSR is associated with reduced depression in boys and that the longer-term TSR program is associated with a significantly reduced depression in girls.

The longer-term TSR cohort had the highest percentage of students who agreed with the statement 'I get along with most of my teachers', the initial TSR program showed an intermediate level below and above the longer-term TSR and non-participating in TSR, respectively. These findings, as summarised in Figure 7.8 and Table 7.3, suggest that the longer students were associated with TSR the greater their perceived ability to get along with their teachers.

The percentage of students who agreed with the statement 'I get into too much trouble' was highest in those schools that did not participate in TSR, intermediate in the initial TSR and lowest for longer-term TSR, as illustrated in Figure 7.9 and Table 7.3. These data indicate a positive relationship between length of time in TSR and improved behaviour.

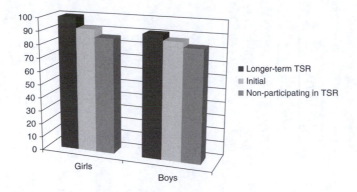

Figure 7.8 Percentage of students who agreed with the statement 'I get along with most of my teachers' according to gender and TSR participation category (Vaughan, Harris and Caldwell 2011: 24)

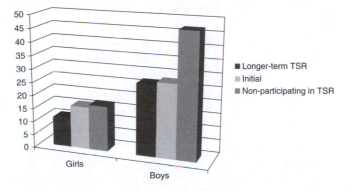

Figure 7.9 Percentage of students who agreed with the statement 'I get into too much trouble' according to gender and TSR participation category (Vaughan, Harris and Caldwell 2011: 24)

The percentage of boys who agreed with the statement 'When I do badly at school-work I think I'm a failure' was lowest for the longer-term TSR schools, intermediate for the initial TSR and highest for the non-participating TSR schools. The observed increased lack of confidence after a bad result for boys who did not participate in TSR indicates a positive relationship between participation in TSR and positive work orientation, as illustrated in Table 7.3.

The percentage of girls who agreed with the statement 'I feel confident when doing difficult schoolwork' was highest for the longer-term TSR, slightly lower for the initial TSR and lowest for those girls who had not participated in TSR. These findings, as illustrated by Table 7.3, showed that a higher percentage of girls who had participated in TSR programs were confident when doing difficult homework in comparison to those girls who had not participated.

Table 7.3 Summary of the findings of the SEWB study for the statement categories of behaviour, social skills and self-esteem

Statement categories and statements	Component of SEWB	Percentage difference of students who agreed with the statement in comparison to those students who had not participated in TSR			
		TSR participation category			
		Longer-term TSR		Initial TSR	
		Boys (n=33)	Girls (n=45)	Boys (n=46)	Girls (n=51)
Behaviour					
I lose my temper a lot	Overall SEWB	↓11		↓22	
I have difficulty controlling myself when I get angry	Resilience	↓12		↓22	
When I get angry, I act without thinking	Resilience	↓25		↓34	
I have difficulty calming down quickly when I get very upset	Resilience	↓10	↓12	↓12	↓15
I am sometimes quite mean to other people	Overall SEWB	↓27	↓17	↓27	↑4
I get into too much trouble	Overall SEWB	↓20	↓6	↓19	↓1
I can't stand having to behave well and follow the rules	Social Orientation	↓28		↓2	
I can be trusted to do what I say I am going to do	Social Orientation	↑7	↑4	↑6	↑6
Social skills					
I feel lonely	Overall SEWB	↓12		↓7	
I get along with most of my teachers	Overall SEWB	↑8	↑14	↑1	
I think that someone who treats me unfairly is a bad person and that it is OK to hurt them back	Social Orientation	↓23		↓14	↑6
I am good at understanding how other people feel	Social Orientation	↑5	↑7	↑9	
I try to make sure that everyone has a fair chance to win, even if it means that I lose	Social Orientation	↑15	↑11	0	↓15
I try hard not to say or do things that hurt other people's feelings	Social Orientation	↑19	↑6	↑6	↓3

Table 7.3 continued

Self-esteem / confidence

I like the kind of person I am	Overall SEWB	↑5	
When I do badly in my schoolwork, I think 'I'm a failure'	Resilience	↓20	↑9	↓3
When I don't understand something I'm learning, I think that 'I really don't have what it takes to be successful'	Work Orientation	↓8		↓8
I feel confident when doing difficult schoolwork	Work Orientation	↑11		↑4 ↓5 ↑9

Note

→ indicates a reduced percentage agreement to the statement in comparison to the non-participating in TSR cohort

↑ indicates an increased percentage agreement to the statement in comparison to the non-participating in TSR cohort

The percentage of girls who agreed with the statement 'I feel safe and free from danger' was greatest for the longer-term TSR, at an intermediate level for the initial TSR and lowest for those girls who had not participated in TSR, as shown in Table 7.4. 8 percent more boys agreed with the statement that 'I feel safe and free from danger' in the longer-term TSR in comparison to those in the non-participating cohort. These findings suggest that participation in the longer-term TSR may contribute to feelings of safety.

The percentage of girls who agreed with the statement 'I am someone who loves to learn' was highest for the longer-term TSR; at an intermediate level for the initial TSR and lowest for those girls who had not participated in TSR. These findings, as illustrated in Table 7.3, suggest a positive relationship between the length of time in TSR for girls and their love of learning.

The percentage of boys who agreed with the statement 'I can't stand having to behave well and follow the rules' was lowest for the longer-term TSR, with a difference of 28 percent in comparison to the non-participating in TSR cohort. These findings, as illustrated in Table 7.4 show that longer-term participation in TSR for boys is related to substantially lower dissatisfaction with school rules.

The percentage of boys who agreed with the statement 'There are things that I study in my classes that interest me' was highest for the longer-term TSR cohort, lower for the initial TSR cohort and lowest for the non-participating in TSR cohort. The percentage of boys who agreed with the statement 'Teachers remind students about the importance of doing their best in their schoolwork' was higher for the longer-term TSR and initial TSR cohorts in comparison to the non-participating in TSR cohort, as shown in Table 7.4. The findings illustrated by Table 7.4 indicate that the involvement of boys in TSR was related to increased school engagement in comparison to boys who had not participated in TSR.

The survey responses that showed differences between the three cohorts were categorised into behaviour, social skills, self-esteem, confidence, worry, depression, self-expression and teacher–student relationships. The category of behaviour contained a large proportion of responses about anger control or impulsivity. The boys who participated in TSR self-reported a decreased lack of control in anger. Empathy was measured in the response to the statements 'I try to make sure that everyone has a fair chance to win, even if it means that I lose' and 'I try hard not to say or do things that hurt other people's feelings'. Boys in the longer-term TSR showed an increased agreement of 15 and 19 percent and boys in the initial TSR showed an increased agreement of 9 and 6 percent for the former and latter statements, respectively, in comparison to those boys who had not participated in TSR. Longer-term TSR students showed improved student–teacher relationships. These data showed the perceived influence of the TSR on different aspects of SEWB as shown in Tables 7.3 and 7.4.

Summary

The longer-term TSR showed the highest percentage of students at levels 5 and 6 in overall SEWB with a difference of 12.7 percent and 14.9 percent in comparison to the

Table 7.4 Summary of the findings of the SEWB for the statement categories of worry/depression, self-expression and teacher–student relationships

Statement categories and statements	Component of SEWB	Percentage difference of students who agreed with the statement in comparison to those students who had not participated in TSR			
		TSR participation category			
		Longer-term TSR		Initial TSR	
		Boys (n = 33)	Girls (n = 45)	Boys (n = 46)	Girls (n = 51)
Worry/depression					
I worry too much about my schoolwork or what others think of me	Overall SEWB	↓17	↓7	↑1	↑3
During the past six months, I have felt so hopeless and down almost every day for one week that I have stopped doing my usual activities	Overall SEWB	↓16	↓6*	↓7	↑13
I have difficulty controlling how depressed I get	Resilience	↓15	↓25	↓14	↓19
I have a hard time controlling how worried I get	Resilience	↓17		↓9	
I feel very stressed	Overall SEWB	↓22*		↓32*	
I feel safe and free from danger	Overall SEWB	↑8	↑5	↓3	↑2
In school, I am learning about different feelings people can have and how I can cope with stress	School indicators	↓12		↓1	
Self-expression					
It is hard for me to describe how I feel deep down	Resilience	↓25		↓6	
I shouldn't have to do schoolwork that is boring	Work orientation	↓29		↓21	
There are things that I study in my classes that interest me	School indicators	↑15		↑1	
I am someone who loves to learn	Overall SEWB	↑5		↑1	
Teacher–student relationships					
Teachers remind students about the importance of doing their best in their schoolwork	School indicators	↑11		↑13	
Most of my teachers go out of their way to help us appreciate people from different cultural backgrounds	School indicators	↑10	↑11	↑4	↑9

Table 7.4 Continued

Most of my teachers include activities and class discussions that allow students from different backgrounds to contribute and share with their class their own ideas and experiences	School Indicators	↑12	↑12	↑10	↑5
My teachers try hard to be nice to me	School Indicators	↑10		↓7	
I have a teacher who cares about me	School Indicators	↑7	↑11	↓8	↑9

Note
↓ indicates a reduced percentage agreement to the statement in comparison to the non-partcipating in TSR cohort
↑ indicates an increased percentage agreement to the statement in comparison to the non-particpating in TSR cohort
* indicates significantly different (p<0.05) agreement with the statement in comparison to the non-participating in TSR cohort

initial and non-participating TSR, respectively. Comparisons of indicators of SEWB, resilience, positive social skills and positive work management and engagement skills showed that the longer-term TSR showed the highest percentage of students at levels 5 and 6, with the highest percentage difference observed for resilience at 8 and 16 percent in comparison to the initial TSR and non-participating in TSR, respectively. The longer-term TSR schools showed an 8 percent increase in the percentage of students at the two highest levels of positive work orientation in comparison to the non-participating in TSR schools. The initial cohort school, Bonvilla, showed a lower percentage of students in the lowest two levels of positive work orientation and engagement, with a difference of 7 percent in comparison to the non-participating in TSR cohort. The initial TSR showed a higher percentage of students at levels 5 and 6 for overall SEWB, indicators of SEWB and resilience, with the highest percentage difference for resilience with 8 percent in comparison to those schools who did not participate in TSR. Comparison of levels 1 and 2 of resilience showed the lowest percentage of students in the longer-term TSR, intermediate level for the initial TSR and lowest for the non-participating in TSR. In summary, students who participated in TSR had higher overall SEWB and resilience, which showed the greatest magnitude of difference in the longer-term TSR in comparison to those schools who had not participated in TSR.

The distribution of positive school indicators showed the highest percentage of students from the longer-term TSR cohort at levels 5 and 6, with an intermediate percentage for the initial TSR and the lowest for the non-participating in TSR which indicated an influence of TSR on positive school indictors. These findings indicate that the TSR may positively influence students' perceptions of school life, with a stronger effect observed for the longer-term TSR.

Categories of responses to the SEWB survey that showed differences between the three cohorts were behaviour, social skills, self-esteem, confidence, worry, depression, self-expression and teacher–student relationships. The category of behaviour contained a large proportion of responses about anger control or impulsivity. The boys who participated in TSR self-reported a decreased lack of control in anger. This finding is of particular interest considering the relationship between impulsivity and early-onset offenders described in Chapter 4. Longer-term TSR students showed improved student–teacher relationships. Male students who participated in TSR showed statistically significant lower agreement with the statement 'I feel stressed' in comparison to male students who had not participated in TSR. Female students in the longer-term TSR showed statistically significant lower agreement to a statement related to depression in comparison to female students who had not participated in TSR. The analysis of student responses to the various statements in the SEWB survey indicated that how the TSR had apparently influenced SEWB within the students was through decreased lack of control in anger, decreased stress and worry, increased self-esteem and confidence, increased positive teacher–student relationships, increased social skills and increased self-expression. Previous studies have shown improvement in resilience, self-regulation, self-esteem, identity, self-concept, tolerance and cooperation observed in students who actively participated in various arts programs. These data indicate that students who participated in the TSR showed higher levels of overall SEWB, with large differences observed in resilience and that the longer the duration of the TSR the larger the effect on SEWB. Processes and pedagogies that account for these impacts are described by key stakeholders involved in the case studies reported in Chapter 8.

Significance

Consistent with the findings on student achievement and attendance reported in Chapter 6, it is striking that such dramatic differences were found on measures of social and emotional wellbeing on the basis of one hour per week in arts education. We expect the reader will wish to be reassured that the two set of schools (participating and non-participating) were indeed matched sets. Referring again to the methodology in Chapter 5 may provide this reassurance. As for Chapter 7, the findings demand the attention of policymakers and practitioners who are often at their wits' end to know what to do in their efforts to assure student wellbeing on indicators like those in ACER's SEWB survey. There are many strategies but foremost should be to ensure that well-designed programs in arts education are delivered in a balanced curriculum and a holistic view of learning.

8   Studies of schools where arts interventions have succeeded

Chapter 8 begins with an account of key features of successful arts interventions and their impact on educational and psychological outcomes. This extends the research background contained in previous chapters.

The four case studies of schools offering the TSR program were conducted in semester 2 in 2010 in two longer-term schools (Willow Brook and Margaret Park) and two initial schools (Bonvilla and Curraburra). Information was drawn from interviews conducted at each school with: the principal; approximately 10 students, five from Year 5 and five from Year 6; two teachers, one from Year 5 and one from Year 6; and two parents. We were particularly interested in stakeholders' perceptions of the influence of TSR on students' outcomes and processes and pedagogies that account for the impact. The key findings are summarised in Table 8.1.

The findings are discussed within the framework of similar studies in different nations. Illustrative findings for student outcomes were increased confidence of teachers and students, improved behaviour of students and a positive influence on student attendance. Processes and pedagogies identified as important for the program were kinetic, performative and creative elements and the full engagement of classroom teachers in the program. These findings are discussed in the pages that follow.

Studies of schools where arts interventions have succeeded

According to Russell-Bowie (2010), the percentage of pre-service primary teachers confident in music teaching was lowest for teachers from Sydney (39 percent) and the United States (37 percent) in comparison to their counterparts in Ireland (63 percent), and South Africa (52 percent). A study of teachers' attitudes toward, and the use of, arts in teaching in the United States from urban, suburban and rural schools led to a recommendation that teachers need ongoing support for their own creative and artistic development (Oreck 2004). The confidence of primary teachers in England was seen to increase through the Voices Foundation Primer which involved interaction with music specialists, enabling staff to develop 'strategies, ideas and skills during the course of the year' (Rogers *et al*. 2008: 495). A teacher using the Voices Foundation Primer described their increased confidence in teaching music:

> Before Voices Foundation I was not doing much National Curriculum music. I did some listening but not much teaching of musical skills. This has all changed. Through the training I now feel really confident. The kids really enjoy it.
>
> (Rogers *et al.* 2008: 488)

Along with the observed increased confidence of teachers through involvement in arts interventions, increased student confidence was also reported. In-depth ethnographic investigations of 124 youth-based organisations in the United States, 48 of which involved the arts, led to the following statement which described the influence on students' confidence (Brice Heath and Roach 1999; Brice Heath 2002):

> Through their involvement in effective youth-based arts organizations, young people cultivate talents and dispositions they bring into their . . . association with such high-demand high-risk places. Once there, the intensity of these groups builds and sustains a host of skills and capacities rooted in their personal recognition of themselves as competent, creative, and productive individuals.
>
> (Brice Heath and Roach 1999: 29)

Stakeholders involved in arts programs have reported increased attendance on days in which the students had their class in the arts (Bryce *et al.* 2004; Upitis and Smithrim 2003). Students of the Boys' Business program in an Australia study reported increased attendance on music class days (Bryce *et al.* 2004). Over a quarter of the 50 Canadian teachers interviewed who participated in the previously described LTTA programs (Chapter 6) reported that the students were generally less likely to be absent on days when artists were at the school (Upitis and Smithrim 2003).

Increased attendance may influence the academic achievement of students. Qualitative evidence has shown a perceived influence of arts programs on students' academic achievement in Australia and the United States (Bryce *et al.* 2004; Oreck *et al.* 1999). The influence of increased student confidence on improvement in reading achievement in a New York City public school was described by a teacher who formed part of a longitudinal multiple-case study:

> She went from the bottom reading group in the fourth grade to the top in grade five . . . She seemed to feel better about herself. Somehow she got the message that she was special and a good person. I honestly don't think this would have happened if it weren't for the music program.
>
> (Oreck *et al.* 1999: 67)

Social and behavioural benefits through participation in the arts have been identified in Australian and Canadian schools (Hunter 2005; Upitis and Smithrim 2003) and were reported in Chapter 7. A student involved in LTTA expressed the social and behavioural benefits of their participation in the arts: 'Arts are important to meet new people, make friends, stay out of trouble, and be with a "good group"' (Grade 6 student) (Upitis and Smithrim 2003: 20).

The role of school culture and teacher beliefs associated with the arts has been identified as important to the ability of teachers to successfully engage in arts initiatives and arts education (Garvis and Pendergast 2010; Oreck 2004). The bifurcation of disciplines, which has influenced the value placed on the arts, was discussed in Chapter 1. The relationship between school culture and teacher beliefs was described by Garvis and Pendergast in the Australian context:

> School culture may place greater value on some subjects than others. The relatively low status of music and arts education in comparison to subjects such as mathematics, language and science in some schools may also contribute to negative teacher beliefs of their individual and collective efficacy.
>
> (Garvis and Pendergast 2010: 9)

In the United States, the influence of teachers' experience and evidence of efficacy of arts on their participation in arts in their classrooms was described by Oreck: 'Teachers who have seen specific academic and behavioural improvement appear to have the strongest commitment to using the arts on a regular basis' (Oreck 2004: 67) and 'Teachers who have evidence that artistic approaches aid student learning are more able to justify the time spent on the arts and to articulate the benefits to students and parents' (Oreck 2004: 66). The above studies indicated that teachers need to have evidence of the impact of the arts either from direct practice or academic studies, and to be in a school culture that places high value on the arts, to enable their full practice of arts in their classrooms (Garvis and Pendergast 2010; Oreck 2004).

Student participation in the arts has been shown to encourage student self-expression (Burton *et al.* 2002). Student self-expression was identified as more prevalent in teacher descriptions of students from arts-rich schools in comparison to those in arts-poor schools in the United States (Burton *et al.* 2002). Self-expression may be influenced by the creative elements within arts initiatives. The importance of the development of creativity for the economy of the twenty-first century and successful learning were discussed in Chapter 1 (Florida 2005) and Chapter 2 (Cisco 2008; MCEETYA 2008). Increased creativity was found in students in visual arts programs in the United States as detailed in Chapter 4 (Catterall and Peppler 2007). The rationale in the draft of the National Curriculum for the arts in Australia emphasised the need for arts education to 'creatively engage' young Australians (ACARA 2010a). An artist described the role they played in the encouragement of creativity in the LTTA in Canada: '[I'm a] catalyst – energiser – creative spark plug. I brought to both the teachers and students the reality that creativity enhances all of our lives in a myriad of ways' (Upitis and Smithrim 2003: 34).

Case study of Willow Brook Public School

Willow Brook Public School serves approximately 490 students. The school's catchment area is rated as being within the bottom two quartiles on the ICSEA, with 57 percent of residents living in public housing. Students come from a diverse range of cultural backgrounds, including between 35 and 40 percent of students from Pacific Islander backgrounds, for many of whom English is not their first language.

There was an air of excitement and passion throughout Willow Brook when they were asked to describe their experiences of TSR. Staff and students alike spoke of the program and the TA, who had worked with the school, with great enthusiasm. Both TSR programs that have been run at the school offered all students the opportunity to try something new. The programs and performance groups, including the Drumbeat group and choirs, which have developed alongside TSR, have helped to uncover some of the musical talents of the students, which may not have otherwise been recognised. The programs have been particularly successful in highlighting the skills of some students, who may not shine in the academic or sporting arenas.

One of the key areas of success within the program, described by both staff and students, was the ability of the TAs to engage and encourage all students. The talent of the current TA was described as 'captivating'. A number of students reported that they had initially been a little bit nervous about participating and performing in front of their peers but after the first few weeks, the students had reached the consensus that TSR was 'amazing'. The students reported that the TA was able to focus on particular students who might be a little shy, nervous, or tend not to participate in class activities, and encourage them to join in and enjoy the choral activities. They said that she had high expectations in terms of student participation but made everyone feel that it was 'okay to make mistakes the first time you try'.

The program and, particularly, the performance groups, have provided students with new opportunities to work together and perform in front of their peers and the broader community. Students involved in the Drumbeat program reported that the regular in-school performances helped them to get used to performing in front of people, so that they can relax and enjoy their performances outside the school. Students in the Drumbeat performance group and choir have performed for small audiences within the community, at regional education week celebrations and at the TSR concerts, allowing them to see the outcomes of TSR programs at other schools. The most exciting opportunity offered to selected students within the Drumbeat performance group was to travel to Melbourne and perform in front of a large audience, including key political and media figures. For most of the students who performed, the fully funded trip represented their first flight and their first trip to Melbourne. For those students who performed, this trip seemed to be one of the highlights of their time at Willow Brook.

The TSR programs, in particular, have been described as being highly engaging for students and have helped them to stay more engaged and focused in other classes. Teachers at Willow Brook reported that the TA has managed to ensure that the goals of TSR lessons are clearly defined and designed to progressively develop students' understanding of music theory and practice.

This learning 'in a fun way' has developed students' confidence in a range of areas, including performance in front of their peers. The experience of performance, both in front of peers and in the wider community, was reported to increase student confidence, to make them feel special and to give them pride in their achievements.

Witnessing the fun and opportunities that the students in the performance groups were having, their friends and younger students in the school reported that they weren't scared to try out for the groups and looked forward to having the same opportunities.

Teachers, parents and students all reported their belief that TSR had made some difference to student attendance rates, particularly on performance days. All of the students involved in the interviews for this case study reported that they would make sure that they came to school on the days that their classes participated in TSR.

Following on from the successful 2009 Drumbeat program, the school has established performance groups which involved a number of students, particularly boys in Grades 5 and 6. Staff worked with the teacher responsible for the Drumbeat performance group to select students who would benefit the most from their involvement. In a number of cases, this has included students who have been previously recognised to have issues with their behaviour or anger management. Of the three students in the Drumbeat performance group who participated in the interviews for this case study, two admitted that prior to joining the group they had bullied other students, had issues with managing their anger and, generally, had spent a considerable amount of time 'in trouble'. All students acknowledged that the behaviour of these two students, while not perfect, had improved considerably since they had been involved in Drumbeat.

Students found their participation in the program and in the groups to be highly rewarding in terms of self-expression and reducing their levels of anger. The percussion group, in particular, provided a positive physical outlet for student energy. Students reported that being involved in the music programs helps them to express their feelings and to stop feeling angry or sad. They indicated that TSR helps people to find their voice and develop strengths in areas that they hadn't recognised strengths before.

The acting principal of Willow Brook described the TSR programs within the school as the result of 'pure collaboration'. He reported that he had been impressed with the willingness of TSR to work with staff and students to devise programs that met their needs and to offer ongoing support to ensure the sustainability of the programs. Prior to observation and participation in the 2009 Drumbeat program, under the leadership of the TA, teachers at Willow Brook had voiced their desire to be 'up-skilled' in the performing arts. Following their participation in TSR Drumbeat program in 2009, however, two Willow Brook teachers worked with the TA to write a sustainable percussion program that was tailored to the needs of the school.

A Grade 6 teacher, who was involved in the development of the ongoing school percussion program, reported that TSR had provided ongoing support for all teachers. Teachers were provided with a CD of the songs that were used in the percussion program. The recordings were described as an invaluable tool to support teachers by giving them an understanding of what the songs should sound like. The school also worked with TSR to develop a DVD recording of a choral lesson that is being used for professional learning and marketing purposes by both parties. Teachers indicated that this recording, like the CD of the percussion, would help them to develop their own knowledge of the music and techniques used by TAs before they deliver the program to their classrooms.

The music programs within the school draw support from two other invaluable sources. The first is the Drumbeat group, particularly those Grade 6 boys who have been involved in the percussion performance group since 2009. This group of boys has been given the opportunity to collaboratively lead music classes in their own classrooms. As indicated above, the Drumbeat group includes a diverse range of students, including some who had been identified as having issues with behaviour and/or anger management. The boys involved, however, reported that these leadership roles encouraged them and made them feel proud of the skills that they had developed.

The second source of support for the music programs, which is currently being developed by the school, involves parents and the wider school community. Students' participation in the performance groups is actively supported by parents, grandparents and other family members through a high level of attendance at all student performances and through participation. One parent reported that the community support for the school's music programs has helped to create new social networks among parents. Regular attendance at student performances and participation in the community choir offer a new way to bring members of this very diverse community together and to demonstrate their support for their children and the school.

Summary of findings at Willow Brook Public School

Students and staff of Willow Brook showed a real appreciation of the opportunities that TSR provided. In addition to providing students with a music program that they might not have otherwise been able to access, TSR provided them with an opportunity to demonstrate their talents, to perform in front of their peers and their community and, for some students, a significant grant gave them an opportunity to travel and perform in Melbourne. The students' enthusiasm for TSR was palpable, with some of the Grade 6 students bemoaning the fact that they would not have the support of their TA next year, once they moved on to high school. Support and encouragement for everyone to do their best were evident throughout the school. The students reported that their TA supported the talents of all students; it didn't matter if they were not the best singers or drummers, as long as they gave it their best try. In the words of one student, 'She expects us to give 100 percent but not 200 percent'.

The staff members at Willow Brook had taken advantage of all of the professional learning opportunities offered by TSR in order to create an engaging and sustainable music program within their school. Following the success of Drumbeat, the staff have been able to develop their own percussion-based program, which incorporates students' cultural knowledge, creativity and skills and enables students to act as mentors for their teachers and peers. The second year of TSR has enabled staff to be involved in and observe a vocal program and to support a student and community choir. Working within a diverse community, involving a number of community members that face a range of disadvantages, the staff, parents and students have embraced all of the opportunities that TSR can provide for schools. TSR has provided a significant addition to the vibrant, enthusiastic and supportive environment of Willow Brook.

Case study of Margaret Park Primary School

Margaret Park Primary School is a small school serving less than 300 students. The school serves a mid-to-low SES community with approximately 8 percent indigenous students and 35 percent of students from a LBOTE. While facing a relatively high level of student mobility (around 30 percent), it has a group of highly dedicated parents who actively support school programs.

The first TSR program at Margaret Park was initiated mid-way through 2009, with a focus on activities to build students' confidence, social skills and self-esteem. Following a staff evaluation, a TSR program for 2010 was tailored to meet staff requests for a stronger focus on music instruction and developing their skills in the subject area.

The 2010 TSR program was described in glowing terms by school staff, students and parents alike. All members of the school community highlighted the fun inherent in the music program and, in particular, the effective management of the program by the TA. It was evident during interviews that the TA's approach and skills were integral to the success of TSR. Although this was the second TSR program run at Margaret Park, it was apparent that the music- and performance-focused program offered in 2010 was deemed to be far more successful than the initial program for two primary reasons. First, when TSR was implemented in 2009, there was an overlap between the social development programs that it offered to Margaret Park students and those that were already in place within the school. The second reason offered for the outstanding success of the 2010 TSR program was the skill of the TA in providing stimulating, personalised and fun learning opportunities for both students and teachers.

The teachers stated that the TA was able to get all students actively involved in classes, circulating the instruments so that everyone had an opportunity to play the favoured djembes (an instrument). The students involved in these interviews reported that the TA allowed them to have fun and make a lot of noise within the TSR program, while also giving them 'learning for life', including reading and performing music. All of the students interviewed indicated that they enjoyed the performative aspect of TSR and all but one of these students had applied their TSR learning to playing other instruments in their free time. Aside from one student who found the music theory 'boring', the students all reported that the TA made the learning fun and provided them with the opportunity to explore music.

The kinetic quality of practical percussion lessons was embraced by almost all of the students in the school. The students described the physicality of the percussion lessons as 'fun' and allowing them to get their high energy levels 'out of their system'. The only critique of the program that was raised by the students was that they would have liked more opportunities to use their creativity and learning to develop their own songs. They did report, however, that they felt a strong sense of accomplishment when they were able to put together the different elements that they had learned, including percussion, vocals and dance movements, to form a performance piece. The students indicated that their ability to perform the songs that they had learned in TSR made them feel happy and 'good about themselves'.

An increased confidence of students at Margaret Park was described by the principal, several teachers and a parent. The safe environment created by the TA in the 2010 program enabled students to take risks through performance both within and beyond the classroom. The performance component of the 2010 program extended beyond the classroom doors to the school community in assembly, performances in old-age homes and larger-scale performances within the community. The risk-taking involved within the performance aspect of the 2010 TSR program was described as encouraging students to develop their confidence. A teacher reported that students who were previously described as shy, were seen to 'come out of their shell' through their participation in the 2010 TSR program. The principal described the TSR as having an influence on building the self-esteem of the students and acting as a 'vehicle' to encourage students to try new things.

The theoretical component of the TSR involved cross-curriculum links to mathematics. Students reported that the TA integrated mathematical concepts within the 2010 TSR classes, such as fractions in the study of musical notation. The program, including cross-curriculum links, was perceived by both the teaching staff and students as fun and influenced positive emotions in the students. One student described after TSR class she felt she was more focused, as if she had just begun her school day. Another student described the way TSR class had an impact on her in her statement that it 'made you feel good, made you feel happy'. A teacher described how the students were never late on the day of their TSR class. The TSR class was perceived as an outlet for creative energy for students.

The teachers indicated that the risk-taking involved in performance in front of their peers in the TSR program had boosted the confidence of many of their students. They stated that the playful nature of the 2010 TSR program encouraged all students to participate in performances both inside and out of the classroom without fear of judgement or reprisal from their classmates. All of the school staff said that TSR had given their students the confidence to try new things and follow their interests.

While the school encourages a range of group activities, the collaborative work that takes place within the TSR program and performance groups has given students new social avenues to develop friendships. Some of the boys involved in the percussion performance group had developed new friendships with others from the group.

While the school had some teachers with strong knowledge and skills in music, each of the three teaching staff interviewed for this case study reported that prior to their participation in TSR they had not felt confident in leading music instruction within their own classrooms. They all indicated that they had a store of musical instruments in their classrooms that had been 'gathering dust' prior to the 2010 TSR program. Through their involvement in TSR and the erection of a new school hall, the school has created a designated music room to support a sustainable music program within the school.

The TA for the 2010 TSR program was described as having the pedagogical knowledge and skills to scaffold an effective learning program for both students and teachers. By using repetition, reframing and revisiting ideas throughout the weekly classes, the TA gave students and staff the skills to read and perform musical pieces.

All of the teachers interviewed for this case study greatly appreciated the learning support provided by the TA, who gave them notes and recordings of the songs that they had learned in the program. The teachers reported that after being actively involved in the running of the TSR they would now feel comfortable in replicating this style of class, particularly the use of percussion instruments and allowing their students the space to perform.

Summary of findings from Margaret Park Primary School

TSR offered students a safe environment to explore their creativity and perform in front of their peers. The participants indicated that TSR provided students with a focus for their energies and a sense of accomplishment and confidence through the acquisition of new skills. The various levels of performance events, from group performances in class, performances in school and large-scale public performances, provides students and staff with avenues to showcase their new skills.

TSR performances facilitate risk-taking in a safe environment, which can encourage students to try new things and build their capacity in other areas of school life. Teachers at Margaret Park reported an increase in confidence in some students, particularly those students who weren't catered for within the traditional school curriculum. TSR offered these students new avenues of self-expression and the confidence to pursue new activities. It was noted that this is particularly relevant for students in the middle years, who are about to make the transition into high school.

Prior to the implementation of TSR, a number of teachers at Margaret Park lacked confidence and skills to develop and sustain quality music instruction. Their observation of and participation in TSR, particularly in the more recent music-based program, has encouraged teachers to incorporate new approaches to music education into their teaching. TSR has helped the school to identify and overcome limitations, specifically with regards to time and facilities, to the development of a sustainable music program.

Case study of Bonvilla Primary School

Bonvilla Primary School is a medium-sized school which caters to 330 students. It is located within a region of low to medium SES, with 92 percent of students from homes with a LBOTE. There is a high diversity of language backgrounds within the LBOTE student population. Bonvilla Primary School provides an inclusive environment that supports a diverse student population which includes classes for students with special learning needs.

TSR began at Bonvilla Primary School in semester 1 of 2010, with a drumming program which was focused on students from Grades 5 and 6 and students with special learning needs. The drumming program involved body percussion, beat box and drumming on a range of percussion instruments. A choir program was implemented by the TA in semester 2 of 2010 which involved the same groups of students. The same TA was employed for both the drumming and choir programs.

The TSR program was described in highly complimentary terms by the staff and students at Bonvilla Primary School. The principal reported that he thought the program was engaging and the students described the program as fun and energising. Both teachers involved in this case study reported that the majority of their students were engaged by the TSR program. They described how the TA showed positive behaviour management skills. One teacher reported that she would have valued a discussion of her role in behaviour management in the TSR program prior to its commencement. The principal reported that the TA was able to vary her pedagogical approach to engage all students including those with special learning needs.

The TSR program was described as creative by the students, principal and one teacher at Bonvilla Primary School. Many students reported that TSR classes were fun and they particularly enjoyed the kinetic aspects of the classes such as the body percussion and drumming. The beat box lessons incorporated into the drumming program were also highly favoured by the students. Many students reported that their favourite element of the class was their creation of new rhythms on the drums. These new rhythms were then played to the class forming one aspect of performance within the TSR program. The students performed at various levels including the class level, at a school assembly, at a multicultural festival and at a concert in the region. The performative aspect of the TSR was reported by students, a teacher and the principal to be a highlight for members of the school community and was described as providing the students with a 'destination' for their efforts in TSR classes.

Involvement in TSR classes was reported by parents, teachers and students as increasing the confidence of some students. The performative aspect of TSR classes was reported to be integral to the confidence building of the students. Confidence gained in the TSR program was thought to contribute to improved academic achievement of some students. One student described how the confidence she had gained from her participation in TSR had contributed to her improvement in English, as she now felt more confident to read aloud to her class. TSR was described by one teacher as being especially effective in building the confidence of students who did not possess strong verbal skills. One parent indicated her son had gained confidence through involvement in the TSR program that had contributed in part to his improvement in mathematics.

Members of the school community described the strong musical focus that TSR had brought to the school. TSR encouraged self-expression for students within a novel context for the school. One teacher and one student described how TSR acted to 'refresh and renew' the students. The majority of students interviewed (90 percent) reported that their attendance had improved on TSR classroom days in comparison to normal school days. This finding on attendance was in contrast to the other members of the school community who did not perceive an effect of TSR on attendance.

Involvement in TSR was reported by the school community to have a substantial impact on the behaviour of some students. The principal described how Grades 5 and 6 students were at a crucial age for the establishment of self and he thought that their involvement in TSR encouraged a greater level of maturity and mutual respect. Teachers identified students they thought could benefit from playing a key role within the music program, some of whom had previously been identified as having behavioural difficulties. The principal indicated that some of the boys who participated in the drumming group showed a reduction in suspensions after their engagement with TSR.

The TA encouraged new groups of students to work together as reported by a teacher and parent. Some students described how they worked better in groups and had made new friends since their involvement with TSR. The formation of new friendships was reported by a student to be encouraged by the new skills developed in the TSR program. One parent described how TSR had encouraged her daughter to learn to deal with different people. The quality of the performance of the students at a concert in the region was reported as 'magnificent' and 'unbelievable' by school staff and indicated the influence of the TSR on students' ability for cooperative work.

The principal reported that the drumming program had continued after Semester 1 under the direction of his teachers. One teacher described how her involvement in TSR had provided her with the capacity to implement a drumming program within her class for 2011 and described how the provision of professional development within the TSR program would increase her capacity for the implementation of music programs. A teacher described how the students of the current TSR program could mentor younger students in developing their skills which would enable the expansion of music programs within Bonvilla Primary School. One parent reported that her daughter became so enthusiastic about the beat boxing technique that she was currently teaching her siblings the method.

Summary of findings at Bonvilla Primary School

The TSR program implemented at Bonvilla in 2010 provided an inclusive environment which was described as highly engaging and fun. The participants of the program enjoyed the kinetic learning they experienced through the drumming program. TSR offered the students of Bonvilla a positive environment in which to express their creativity.

The confidence of some students was reported to increase with their engagement in the TSR program. The students at Bonvilla were provided with multiple performance opportunities within the classroom and larger-scale performances, which were described as important to building student confidence. The confidence that some of the students gained from their participation in TSR was reported to positively contribute to academic outcomes. The interviewed students felt that TSR had affected their attendance although this opinion was not supported by all members of the school community.

Involvement in the TSR was reported by the school community to have a substantial impact on the behaviour of some students, including a reduction in suspensions. The collegial environment created by the TA improved the ability of the students to work within groups. The deconstruction of gender stereotypes was facilitated by the involvement of the students with TSR.

The capacity of teachers to implement sustainable musical programs was encouraged by TSR. Further professional development for TSR would facilitate the longevity of music programs at Bonvilla.

Case study of Curraburra Primary School

Curraburra Primary School is a kindergarten to Grade 6 primary school that enrolled 410 students. The school community faces a range of disadvantages, including almost 90 percent of the community being rated in the lowest quartile in ICSEA, the measure of SES used by ACARA. Research has recognised the local area as having high levels of disadvantage, with over 97 percent of houses in the area being public housing. Curraburra Primary School serves a community with high levels of cultural diversity, including approximately 55 percent of students from homes with LBOTE. Six classes include small numbers of between 9 to 15 students with special learning needs, including two early intervention classes.

Initially, the school was provided with two TAs, who delivered programs to different grade levels on different days of the week. While one TA quickly established a successful program that engaged and was embraced by students, the other faced issues with illness and was not able to provide a consistent program throughout the semester. After extensive consultation with TSR, Curraburra now has one TA who offers her consistent, engaging program over two days throughout the school.

Over the seven months since TSR was established, students had been involved in a range of activities, including a percussion program, which involved drumming, playing instruments, body percussion and beat boxing, and some dancing. At the time of this case study, students had begun a drama program, which gave them extensive opportunities to improvise and perform in front of their peers. This highly successful program was described by teachers as being engaging for all students, particularly those activities that involved performance in front of their peers. The students reported that some of the girls were a little shy when the class began but that the TA gave everyone a lot of opportunities to get involved. They indicated that once everyone became involved for the first time, they realised how much fun it was to act and perform and so they got over their nerves and it 'brought us out of our shell'.

In-class performances were described as involving a lot of laughter, although students were quick to clarify that the laughter was because they were all having fun and not because they were laughing at anyone. They indicated that it was considered as important to show respect for one another in TSR and throughout the school. The TA managed to establish a safe and supportive environment where all students felt free to express themselves and display their talents. Students were able to create and develop their own ideas. This included a rap about the cultural diversity and friendships within their school, which was performed at a local concert.

The fast-paced nature of TSR classrooms, in which the TA spends 10–15 minutes on each activity, helped to engage students. One teacher reported that this format was particularly beneficial for her students with special learning needs, who sometimes found it difficult to sustain concentration on a particular activity for extended periods. The TA used a range of approaches and pedagogic tools to scaffold student learning and encourage participation from all students. She was described as a brilliant and energetic facilitator who has managed to develop strong connections with the students of Curraburra.

All teachers interviewed for this case study reported that they were sceptical at first about the inclusion of TSR within their already full teaching load. While they recognised the potential value of music and performing arts, they initially viewed the performing arts program as just another thing that would take time away from their literacy and numeracy teaching. Once they began observing the program, however, these teachers reported that they were able to see the value of the program, which engaged students who were often difficult to engage.

One teacher, who led a small class of students with mild intellectual disabilities, said that her students' participation in the TSR music program had highlighted the link between music and language. While she indicated that TSR might not have been the only source of influence, she stated that she had noticed a change in students' reading aloud. She suggested that the percussion work and focus on tempo might have helped her students to understand the importance of tempo in reading.

The percussion, dancing and drama programs run by TSR have encouraged students to work together in small groups and in whole-class activities. The range of activities offered within each class also assisted the TA in the encouragement of all students to participate in at least some of the activities. Students reported that the TA chose groups in TSR classes and so they often worked with students in their class that they might not know very well. One teacher offered a specific example of two students who would previously argue in the classroom but developed a friendship by rehearsing and performing a dance together for TSR.

Staff indicated that the TSR program has encouraged students to draw on the knowledge and skills from their cultural backgrounds and to bring their knowledge of music and dance from outside the school into the school program. This has led to a number of positive interactions between students, who were encouraged to demonstrate their knowledge and skills by their peers.

As noted previously, the primary focus of teaching at Curraburra is on literacy and numeracy. As such, it took time to convince the teaching staff of the value of the program. The persistence shown by the school and TSR, however, has paid off. They have been able to tailor programs specifically to the needs of Curraburra students. Once they established a consistent program across the school, all staff recognised the value of the program. Despite the early difficulties, TSR is valued throughout the school.

Teachers reported that observation and participation in TSR classes have benefitted them in a number of ways. One teacher in particular indicated that the program had given her more confidence in leading performing arts programs in her own classroom and had highlighted the range of music and dance facilities within the school of which she had previously not been aware.

Summary of findings at Curraburra Primary School

TSR provides a high-quality tailored performing arts program, the likes of which the school would not otherwise have been able to afford. Teachers observing TSR have recognised the benefits that these programs have provided for their students, who have been given the opportunity to express themselves and demonstrate skills that might not be seen in a traditional classroom setting. These observations have provided teachers with both the impetus and skills to sustain these types of performing arts programs.

One of the most important aspects of TSR observed within the school was the enjoyment and enthusiasm that it created among the students. All students interviewed for the case study indicated that they found the program to be fun and that they liked participating in dancing classes, dramatic improvisations and percussion performances both within and outside of the school. The teachers described the TA as brilliant, enthusiastic and able to sustain the engagement of all students, including those with behavioural issues or intellectual disabilities. While there are many factors that can be associated with changes in student attendance, academic performance and behaviour, a number of staff members reported that they had noticed changes in each of these areas since the establishment of TSR in the school.

Comparative analysis of findings

Teacher confidence and capacity building

Increased confidence was a key theme in the case studies, both of the teachers and students, as summarised in Table 8.1. Teachers at Curraburra, Margaret Park and Willow Brook reported increased confidence in teaching music programs through their involvement in TSR. Staff in the longer-term TSR schools described their music programs as sustainable, while some teachers at the initial schools identified a need for increased professional development. The interaction for the teachers with the TA at the longer-term schools enabled increased confidence of the teachers to provide a sustainable music program through their regular observation and participation in TSR classes. A similar increased teacher confidence has been described for teachers involved with the Voices Foundation Primer (Rogers *et al.* 2008) based in England, and teachers from the United States described a need for ongoing support to aid their creative development as teachers (Oreck 2004).

The increased confidence the teachers involved with the longer-term TSR reported increased skills in teaching the arts as shown in Table 8.1 which may have encouraged capacity building of those schools. Capacity building is considered a key goal within the organisational framework of TSR (2011b). The TAs that were aligned with the goal of capacity building provided resources to achieve this goal. TAs provided recordings of songs and audio visual recordings which were reported to encourage the sustainability of the music programs. The 'provision of resources' from the TA encouraged the sustainability of the program and thus helped to encourage 'the simple practical objectives of giving every child, in every school, in every hamlet, village, town and city, in every state and country around the world, the opportunity to engage immediately with music' (Jorgensen 2003: 211–12, cited in Finney 2003).

Student confidence, attendance and academic achievement

Increased student confidence was reported in Margaret Park, Bonvilla and Willow Brook. The risk-taking involved in performance in Bonvilla and Margaret Park was

Table 8.1 Summary of the findings of the case studies

Themes	School (pseudonym)				
	Longer-term TSR Willow Brook	Margaret Park	Initial TSR Bonvilla	Curraburra	
Engagement	All students engaged and encouraged. Program drew on cultural knowledge of students.	All students actively engaged. Stimulating, personalised and fun learning opportunities.	Students engaged. Program fun, creative and energising.	All students engaged. Program fun and creative within a safe and supportive environment. Program drew on cultural knowledge of students.	
TSR and students academic engagement	Increased student confidence. Increased attendance on TSR day.	Increased student confidence. Increased self-esteem. Increased punctuality on TSR days.	Increased student confidence. Some contribution to academic gains. Students reported increased attendance on TSR days.	Some contribution to improvement in students' ability to read aloud. Increased attendance.	
TSR and impact on students' social skills and behaviour	Improved behaviour and reduction in levels of anger and sadness. Facilitated students' self-expression.	Students feel happier and 'good about themselves'. Developed new friendships.	Greater level of maturity and respect in some students. Developed new friendships. Facilitated students' self-expression.	Developed new friendships. Burn off energy.	
Capacity building	Increased confidence and skills in teaching performing arts. Sustainable music program supported by parents and wider community and draws on cultural capital of community members. Programs tailored to needs of the school.	Increased confidence and skills in teaching music. Increased for leading performing arts classes. Sustainable music program developed.	Increased skills in teaching music for a teacher.	Increased confidence for leading performing arts classes for a teacher. Programs tailored to the needs of the students.	

considered to be linked to increased confidence of the students. TSR was described as having a positive influence on student attendance in all schools involved in the case study. Stakeholders at Bonvilla and Willow Brook described how they thought that the attendance of students improved on TSR class day. Stakeholders involved in arts programs in Australia and the United States have reported a perceived increased attendance on days in which the students had their class in the arts (Bryce *et al.* 2004; Upitis and Smithrim 2003).

The increased attendance noted by stakeholders may have influenced the student's academic achievement. The confidence gained from involvement in TSR was reported by staff and students at Bonvilla to influence the academic achievement of students. For example, a student from Bonvilla explained that the confidence gained through interaction with TSR was transferred to her ability to read aloud, and a teacher at Curraburra reported a similar finding with her description of students showing increased ability to read aloud after their involvement with TSR. Staff from Willow Brook reported that students were more engaged and focused in other classes due to their involvement in TSR. Qualitative evidence has shown a perceived influence of arts programs on students' academic achievement (Bryce *et al.* 2004; Oreck *et al.* 1999).

Consistent with previous research that found that academic achievement can also be influenced by students' perceived social efficacy (Bandura *et al.* 1996), changes in student behaviour were noted in response to the TSR program. The students and staff at the longer-term TSR school, Willow Brook, reported that the students' involvement with TSR had resulted in decreased anger, decreased sadness and reduced the frequency with which they got into trouble. The behaviour of students at Bonvilla was also thought to have improved through their involvement with TSR. The formation of new friendships was reported to be facilitated by TSR in Bonvilla, Curraburra and Margaret Park. Qualitative evidence of social and behavioural benefits through participation in the arts has been identified in Australian and Canadian schools (Hunter 2005; Upitis and Smithrim 2003).

Processes and pedagogies of TSR

The majority of stakeholders interviewed in the case studies described how all students were engaged by the TSR classes. TAs with strong pedagogical skills enabled sequential lesson design at Willow Brook and Margaret Park. The use of fast-paced activities with 10 to 15 minutes for each activity was reported to encourage the engagement of students with special needs in Curraburra. The use of cross-curriculum links to mathematics was reported in Margaret Park, with fractions used for a study of music notation. The various processes and pedagogies described above provided a non-prescriptive approach to arts education which responded to specific needs of the individual schools and enabled 'content . . . derived in relation to local environments, culture and resources' (Bamford 2009: 52). The TSR program drew on the cultural knowledge of students and parents as illustrated in Table 8.1. The impact of TSR on refugee backgrounds was examined through a qualitative multiple-case study approach which also identified the use of student cultural knowledge within the TSR classes (Grossman and Sonn 2010). Bamford described the role of cultural context within the teaching of the arts: 'More than any other subject, the arts (itself a broad category) reflect unique cultural circumstances, and consequently, so does the teaching of the subject' (Bamford 2009: 51).

The role of school culture and teacher beliefs associated with the arts has been identified as important to the ability of teachers to successfully engage in arts initiatives and arts education (Garvis and Pendergast 2010; Oreck 2004). The uptake of the TSR program by teachers and students was seen to vary depending on the teacher's understanding of the benefits of the program. Those teachers who had previous positive experiences at other schools, or knew of the program, reported full class participation or engagement. In contrast those teachers that did not perceive benefits of the TSR program for their students reported reduced participation from their class. Some of the teachers at Curraburra showed initial hesitation for the incorporation of TSR into their teaching schedule due to constraints on time (partially caused through demands on teaching literacy and numeracy). Through their interaction with TSR their valuing of the arts increased, as they saw their students' increased engagement in arts classes. This outcome was described by Oreck (2004) for teachers in the United States as mentioned at the beginning of this chapter.

The majority of teachers did not describe any difficulties with the inclusion of the TA within their classroom. One teacher reported that they would have liked the TA to initiate a conversation about their role in behaviour management. TAs' involvement in behaviour management was not mentioned by other teachers. Burnaford (2003) described the role of TAs in behaviour management as perceived through observation of teaching artists in Chicago:

> For almost all artists in my experience, teachers assume the role of disciplinarians while artists are present. Being 'the heavy' is not fun, especially when it is essentially divorced from the teaching. All good teachers know that behaviour management (another interesting language choice in the profession) is best addressed as part of a larger set of values, teaching strategy repertoire, and curriculum design approaches that are student-responsive. Teaching Artists, if they remain a vital presence in classrooms, will be more and more accountable for managing behaviour for themselves as part of a professional role. It will most likely be part of the essential preparation – and may thus free the teacher to be more of a partner in a co-teaching relationship.
>
> (Burnaford 2003: 170)

The inclusion of a behavioural management element to the certification of TAs, or the encouragement of TAs to discuss their role in behaviour management within the classroom may, be beneficial to encourage improved TA and teacher relationships and classroom management.

The involvement of students in responsible roles was seen to encourage increased behavioural regulation for some students. There were in some classes 'students as teachers' who taught both peers and teachers. In some cases 'at risk' students were placed in positions of leadership within the program. The use of students as resources with the program was described by Brice Heath and Roach (1999):

As the evidence accumulated, it became clear that the ethos of these organizations and their easy inclusion of young people in responsible roles make rich environments of challenge, practice, trial and error, and extraordinary expectations and achievements. An ethos that sees young people as resources cascades through organizational structure as well as moments of hilarious play and concentrated work.

(Brice Heath and Roach 1999: 22)

The kinetic elements in the classes such as body percussion and drumming were favoured by the students at Margaret Park and Bonvilla. These kinetic elements were thought to be important for student stress release. These types of kinetic elements could be considered to engage the bodily-kinaesthetic intelligence mentioned in Chapter 1 (Gardner 2006). The ability of students to 'learn and enjoy through movement' was reported by an artist involved with the LTTA (Upitis and Smithrim 2003: 19). An English student who was part of an ethnographic study of one hour weekly music lessons of one class of Year 8 students (12–13 years old) described the importance of movement in his arts classes (Finney 2003):

Your body can show how you are thinking, what you are thinking, the way you are quite basically, the person you are. Your personality, who you are. If you can. Things like music can help express that. It's just a way of getting it out of your body. Most lessons are sit. You're just quietly sitting down answering questions out of a text book. And really kids of our age prefer to be doing something else. Practising something on the keyboard like we do in music or something different like in drama. Acting out. I suppose art's different even though it's still on paper. Because it's still another expression. I suppose that's why they're called expressive arts. (Brian)

(Finney 2003: 6)

An element of the 'expressive arts' (Finney 2003: 6) described above is the use of creativity to foster self-expression. The inclusion of creativity in the TSR classrooms was another pedagogy that was important to the success of the program. The stakeholders reported creative elements such as the composition of new rhythms on the drums, drama improvisation and the construction of a rap about cultural diversity within the TSR classes. These creative elements were thought to encourage student self-expression. The facilitation of student self-expression through TSR was reported at Bonvilla and Willow Brook. Increased self-expression through the arts and the importance of creativity has been identified in literature (ACARA 2010a; Burton *et al.* 2002; Catterall and Peppler 2007; Cisco 2008; Florida 2005; Upitis and Smithrim 2003).

In addition to kinetic and creative processes the element of fun was identified as important to the success of the program. Three of the case study schools reported the importance of the element of fun within the programs. The students at Curraburra described how the fun they had within their class produced laughter. Fun was identified as a guiding principle for planning the instructional program of arts in Singaporean schools, which was thought 'to engage and motivate students in the learning of art' (Ministry of Education Singapore 2008: 7). The element of fun through 'moments of hilarious play' was identified as important to the 'ethos' of youth-based organisations in the United States (Brice Heath and Roach 1999: 22).

Alongside an element of fun, performance was also identified as a crucial pedagogy in the classes. Performance occurred at all schools at various levels, including class, community and large-scale performance to enable maximum impact on the confidence of the students through risk-taking. The principal at Bonvilla described how the performance acted as a destination for the TSR class efforts. Performance has been identified as an important pedagogy for the arts (Bamford 2009; Stone *et al.* 1998). A study of the arts and cultural education in Iceland identified 10 quality indicators of arts education which included 'opportunities for public performance, exhibition and/ or presentation' (Bamford 2009: 52).

Summary

Four case studies were conducted in schools that participated in TSR, with two schools from each of the longer-term and initial cohorts. Principals, parents, teachers and students involved in the program were interviewed to ascertain their perception of TSR on student outcomes and elements important for the success of the program.

In summary, the confidence of students was reported to have increased through TSR classes and the performative aspects of the program. The behaviour of students showed improvement, through decreased anger, decreased stress and worry and increased self-expression, which were verified by the findings of the SEWB survey reported in Chapter 7. The confidence gained from TSR was described as 'spilling over' to other areas such as academic studies. TSR was found to increase the confidence of teachers to teach music with staff at the longer-term schools describing how TSR enabled sustainable music programs. TSR was reported to encourage increased attendance.

The pedagogy and processes employed by the various TAs was found to vary and reflect the specific needs of the schools and students involved. For teachers and their classes, engagement with TSR was seen to vary depending on teachers' perceived efficacy of arts education. The inclusion of the culture of the students was seen to be important to the program. Kinetic, creative and performance aspects of the program were important to students' stress release, expression and confidence, respectively.

Significance

If, as concluded in the first McKinsey report, the quality of a system cannot exceed the quality of its teachers, the attention of policymakers and practitioners should be focused on the quality of teaching provided in the TSR programs, with impressive outcomes reported in Chapters 6 to 8. In the final analysis, the effects described in Chapter 6 (student achievement and attendance) and Chapter 7 (student social and emotional wellbeing) must be attributed in large measure to the qualities of the TAs placed in schools by TSR, many of whom do not have formal teaching qualifications – they are professionals in their fields of artistic endeavour. There was evidence of a 'spill-over' effect, raising the level of knowledge and skill of staff at the school. There are important implications here for partnerships between schools and specialist non-profit organisations like TSR, but also for initial teacher education and ongoing professional development of staff who will be expected to deliver the Australian Curriculum (see Chapter 1). These implications are examined more closely in Chapter 10.

9 Turning around schools through engagement in the arts

One of the most remarkable findings in the research reported in Chapters 5 to 8 is that engagement in the arts has apparently added as much as one year to the learning of upper primary students. This exceeds the impact of most other factors that can lead to improvement on this scale. While participation in the arts is a worthy endeavour in its own right, its impact on learning in other areas can be attributed in part to higher rates of attendance, greater motivation and improved sense of wellbeing. The significance of the Australian study is magnified many times over because the findings are consistent with virtually every other study in the same field elsewhere around the world. The implications for policymakers are taken up in Chapter 10 but in Chapter 9 we address the question: 'Why has engagement in the arts not featured more prominently in efforts in many countries to turn around the performance of schools?' The search for the secrets of success in turning around schools may be easier than often seems the case.

We address three themes in Chapter 9. The first raises the possibility of the arts playing an important role in also turning around secondary schools. We illustrate by describing how this has been achieved in two secondary schools, one in England (Morpeth School), the other in Australia (Dandenong High School (DHS)), where major investments in the arts is a feature of efforts to transform the schools. The second theme considers in more detail the role of the non-profit and philanthropic sectors in supporting the arts as well as the role of business. This is a contentious area since some proponents of public education argue that this kind of support lets governments 'off the hook'; it is government that should be the sole provider, including funder, of public schools. A framework from the International Project to Frame the Transformation of Schools is adopted to explore the issue. Finally, we venture into new and possibly surprising territory by suggesting that restoring or extending the arts may, in fact, constitute an example of 'disruptive innovation' such has been the sidelining or curtailment of the arts in many jurisdictions. 'Disruptive innovation' is normally seen as a characteristic of computers and Web 2.0, and there can be few who would argue with that, but placing the arts in this category is an altogether different matter.

Turning around secondary schools

The Australian study reported in Chapters 5 to 8 was conducted at the upper levels of primary (elementary) schools in highly disadvantaged settings in Western Sydney.

Case studies of four schools were summarised in Chapter 8. However, the extended review of research contained in previous chapters included summaries of studies in secondary schools in several countries. In this section of Chapter 9 we include brief accounts of the role of the arts in helping to turn around two secondary schools, one in England and the other in Australia, in settings that are comparable with those in which the Australian research in primary schools was conducted. It is important to note that a focus on the arts was just one of the factors associated with the turnaround. The schools are excellent examples of a range of factors that came together to achieve such an outcome, including outstanding leadership; a coherent set of values; well-established links with the wider community, including organisations in the arts; and, of course, top-class teaching. Brian Caldwell has visited both schools and is thus able to provide a first-hand account that confirms their achievement, which has also been recognised by the selection of both schools for visits by national and state leaders.

Morpeth School (England)

Morpeth School is located in Bethnal Green, East London, in the Local Authority of Tower Hamlets. It enrols about 1,200 students with more than half having a Bangladeshi background, about one third white English and the remainder from a variety of backgrounds, including African, Caribbean, Chinese and Turkish. In May 2011 the school celebrated its centenary, and in 2009 it was identified by Ofsted as one of 12 Outstanding Schools in England that were 'achieving against the odds'. The percentage of students achieving five A*–C grades at GCSE, including English and maths (the main indicator of performance used by English schools), rose from 26 percent in 2001 to 54 percent in 2008, a figure which put the school above the national average. Given the high levels of deprivation in the school's catchment area this was a remarkable turnaround. It has gone from being one of the least popular schools of choice in its community to the most popular, with three applicants for every place. Until 2009 the school had only students aged 11–16 but in that year it joined with two other local schools to set up a sixth form.

Morpeth's success has been marked by visits from former prime ministers Blair and Brown as well as the Queen and a recent Ofsted report described the leadership and the quality of teaching as 'outstanding'. Headteacher (Principal) Sir Alasdair Macdonald, has led the school for almost 20 years and was knighted in 2007 for Services to Education.

Morpeth is one of about 325 secondary schools in England offering a specialisation in the arts – art, drama, media studies, music and photography. The school feels that the arts have been crucial in the development of the school. It is frequently in the arts that many of their pupils first experience success and use this as a platform. In addition, it is through the arts that the school has established its identity and it is the arts which, in many ways, provide the 'soul' of the school.

There is extensive community engagement in the school's performing arts program and up to 400 students are involved in the music department's extra-curricular offering, for which there are three full-time teachers and 20 part-time peripatetic teachers. In addition to a new performing arts building (costing £1.8

million, raised by the school and opened in October 2007 by film director Danny Boyle, the parent of a former student), there has been extensive refurbishment of the school's facilities including recording studios and a high tech music technology suite. The school is close to the Barbican Arts complex enabling links with visiting artists including Winton Marsalis. In 2009 the school Jazz Group were guests at the Lincoln Jazz Centre in New York. The school places considerable emphasis on residential experience and students travel widely in and beyond Europe. Aside from the New York visit recent trips have included Iceland, Spain, France and Belgium.

The school has a high national profile in another area – table tennis. There is mass participation in table tennis with several hundred young people from both Morpeth and local primaries participating on a regular basis, but there is also elite performance. On several occasions the school has reached national finals. The school sees both music and table tennis as opportunities for the students to realise that excellence can be achieved. The school believes it is important for the students' confidence and self-esteem to be among the best in their chosen activities. This is a principle consistent with a theme in Sir Ken Robinson's *The Element* that calls for schools to create such opportunities to enable students to be 'in their element' (Robinson 2009). The school also provides a base for parents to engage in their own learning. For example, up to 100 have English lessons every week conducted along with other programs, in temporary facilities at the rear of the school. A class, for example, might include women from Bangladesh, Somalia and Turkey with the instructor from another country. Many of these parents are enabled through this program to provide support for their children.

Another strand of Morpeth's strategy for raising attainment involves links with the world of business. In the early 1990s Morpeth was one of the first schools to establish a close partnership with a bank in the City of London. A range of programs developed from this, including a very strong business mentoring project. There are currently over 100 young people with a business mentor. The mentoring sessions take place both in school and in the City of London and transport to these sessions is provided through funds donated by businesses and charities.

In addition to this program, the school also sees former students as crucial in role modelling and raising aspirations. These former students are 'employed' by the school in a variety of ways – as academic mentors, as individual tutors, as sports coaches and as foreign language assistants.

Dandenong High School (Australia)

DHS opened in 1919 in the City of Dandenong, a suburb in the south-east of Melbourne. It is one of the oldest state high schools in Victoria and the oldest school, public or private, in Melbourne's outer east. The community has changed dramatically over the years, from a grazing and timber economy in the nineteenth century and, up until the Second World War, retaining the rural character of a close-knit country town. The post-war years were marked by an extraordinary industrial boom and large migration from Europe. It is now a major regional centre with large retail shopping complexes and is one of the most ethnically mixed communities in Australia.

DHS served 1,995 students from Years 7 to 12 in 2011, with 78 different languages spoken at home and with families coming from 80 countries. In 2011, the countries of origin of the 10 largest national groups were Australia (881), Afghanistan (301), India (108), Sri Lanka (99), New Zealand (84), China (53), Sudan (49), Bosnia and Herzegovina (34), Pakistan (24) and Philippines (24). Apart from the challenging socio-economic circumstances of most of its students and the wider community, the school must address particular needs such as the relatively large numbers of girls from Afghanistan who have had little or no previous schooling, and students from war-torn Sudan who have experienced violence and lack of schooling on a devastating scale.

DHS was one of three schools in close proximity that were amalgamated in 2007, coming together on two of the three sites, with most students and programs located on the traditional site of DHS, which retained its name. Enrolments were in steep decline in the other two schools whose buildings were generally derelict. Learning outcomes were of serious concern. A master plan was prepared in 2007, with a major feature being the building of seven new sub-schools (houses), each accommodating up to 300 students, at a cost exceeding $20 million. These were fully operational in 2011, offering a pedagogy that reflected a high level of collaborative effort on the part of students and teachers. While there is wide interest in the approach, this particular design/configuration presently has no counterpart in a secondary school in Victoria but it is closer in its vision to a school in Auckland, New Zealand, based on a Maori house model. According to architect Richard Leonard, 'that model fosters social relationship between students as well as staff, where there's a high level of interaction' (cited in Crafti 2011).

Part of the master plan was a performing arts centre, with a theatrette accommodating 350 students at a time, adjacent to a large sports facility available for community use. Funding of $10 million was included in the state budget for 2011–12 with the centre to be opened in 2013. Income from community use of the sports facility will contribute to the cost of the theatrette. The master plan provides for the further development of a visual arts facility on another part of the campus.

Apart from the intrinsic value of learning in the performing arts (music, choral, dance, drama), the initiative is an important strategy for increasing the engagement of students. Many of the national groups love to participate in these activities and the centre will increase the scope of the program. Attendance on days when they are offered is higher than on days when they are not, reflecting a similar pattern reported in earlier chapters for the TSR program at upper primary in disadvantaged communities in Western Sydney. The same is true in respect to participation in the sports program. For some groups of students, for example, Pacific Islanders, the combination of sports and the arts ensures a powerful engagement in the life of the school that would likely be absent if these specialisms were not offered. In a recent interview for a local newspaper a Year 8 boy with a Pacific Islander background declared that 'I like everything about my school'.

It is noteworthy that the current dance program is strong, including among boys. The choral program is thriving, with about 50 students from each of the seven houses performing for the community on most Monday nights. A major development in 2011 was the decision of Opera Australia, the country's leading opera company, to fund up to 25 students to write and perform their own operas. DHS is one of only 29 schools in Australia to receive such support, which is funded by a private philanthropist.

Despite its extraordinary cultural diversity and the potential for inter-racial clashes, there is a remarkable 'calmness' about the school. Older students help defuse conflicts among younger students, and parents and others in the community act promptly if there are signs of trouble. Measures of student wellbeing are higher than might be expected in such a context. Parent and student surveys provide evidence of a generally high level of satisfaction.

Martin Culkin has been principal of DHS since 2000 and became principal of the amalgamated school in 2007. He has oversight of the further developments under the expanded autonomy granted to principals from 2011 in a system that already has a high level of self-management. He noted that '2011 will be a pivotal year for the school as it strives to achieve the objectives of greater student engagement, true collaboration, enhanced educational opportunities and consolidation as one school from three former schools'.

The outstanding progress of the school was recognised in early 2011 with a visit by the premier of Victoria and two visits by the minister for education, all within six months of the election of the Coalition government in November 2010.

National and international comparisons

There are remarkable similarities between Morpeth and Dandenong. Both serve ethnically mixed communities that have dramatically changed their character in recent times. The success of both schools has been recognised by visits from leaders of the nation and state, respectively. Each has developed an ethos of relative calmness due in part to the engagement of parents and others in their communities. Above all, in the context of this book, they have selected the arts as an important means of engaging their students.

As noted above, Morpeth is one of about 325 secondary schools in England with a specialisation in the arts. In Victoria, as elsewhere in Australia, relatively few schools declare or are funded for such a specialisation. As reported for Victoria by Tarica (2011) 'among state secondary schools there are pockets of excellence. University High, Blackburn High, McKinnon Secondary College and Hamilton Secondary College are among those that have impressive performing arts programs, but they are the exception rather than the norm'. There is also the Victorian College of the Arts Secondary School (VCASS), a state high school that operates in a partnership with the University of Melbourne. It is located in the same precinct as the Victorian College of the Arts, which is a department of the University of Melbourne. VCASS specialises in dance and music and is the provider of academic programs for Gymnastics Victoria, Diving Victoria and the National Institute of Circus Arts. Senior students spend half of the week in academic studies and the other half in their chosen arts discipline.

As described in Chapter 1, the draft outline for a national curriculum in the arts in Australia acknowledges the importance of the 'creative industries'. It is noteworthy that Australia has one state secondary school that explicitly addresses the needs of students in this field. It is one of three 'state academies' in Queensland. The

Queensland academies are selective entry state high schools for students in years 10 to 12. They have been operating since 2007 as the Queensland Academy for Science, Mathematics and Technology (QASMT); the Queensland Academy for Creative Industries (QACI), and the Queensland Academy for Health Sciences (QAHS). QASMT is partnered with the University of Queensland, QACI with Queensland University of Technology (QUT), and QAHS with Griffith University (GU). All three academies exclusively offer the International Baccalaureate (IB) Diploma Program.

Built at a cost of $40 million, there is no counterpart to the style and scale of the QACI building in state education in Australia. It is located in the creative industries precinct of QUT and maintains a networked association with the only other school world-wide that can be matched, namely, the School of the Arts in Singapore (SOTA) which also offers the IB Diploma:

> With a vision to identify and groom future generations of artists and creative professionals to be leaders in all fields, SOTA builds on Singapore's unique strengths, including her multicultural Asian diversity and globally connected networks to synergise talents and resources.
>
> (School of the Arts Singapore 2011)

Social capital in support of the arts

Can programs in the arts like those under consideration in this book be offered without the support of entities other than government, especially in the state (public) sector of schooling under conditions of budget cutbacks or constraints? After all, the success of specialist schools in the arts in England is likely due in large part to partnerships with the philanthropic or corporate sector. This is now a deeply embedded characteristic of state secondary schools in England. The schools in the research reported in Chapters 5 to 8 were supported by TSR, a non-profit organisation, which is funded by private philanthropy although it draws some public funding. A major contributor is the Macquarie Group Foundation which also funded the research reported in these chapters. There have been major funding cutbacks in the United States where the level of this kind of support falls somewhere between the low of Australia and the high of England.

This is a contentious topic. After all, those committed to public schooling argue that the state should provide the resources to ensure that the agreed curriculum is offered in all settings. The reality is that they do not. On the other hand, even if there is commitment to public schooling, there is a strong case that the resources of the entire community, especially in specialist fields like the arts, should complement the support of the state. It is this kind of community support that may be necessary if not a pre-requisite to turning around struggling schools.

Framework for analysis

In this section of Chapter 9 we explore these kinds of partnership, sponsorship or support in the arts in schools. We frame our analysis by drawing on the concept of 'social capital', broadly defined, as set out by Caldwell and Harris in *Why Not the Best Schools?* (Caldwell and Harris 2008) on the basis of their research in the International Project to Frame the Transformation of Schools, described in more detail in Chapter 2.

The purpose of the International Project to Frame the Transformation of Schools was to explore how schools that had been transformed or had sustained high performance had built strength in each of four kinds of capital and aligned them through effective governance to secure success for their students:

- *Intellectual capital* refers to the level of knowledge and skill of those who work in or for the school.
- *Social capital* refers to the strength of formal and informal partnerships and networks involving the school and all individuals, agencies, organisations and institutions that have the potential to support and be supported by the school.
- *Spiritual capital* refers to the strength of moral purpose and the degree of coherence among values, beliefs and attitudes about life and learning (for some schools, spiritual capital has a foundation in religion; in other schools, spiritual capital may refer to ethics and values shared by members of the school and its community).
- *Financial capital* refers to the money available to support the school.
- *Governance* is the process through which the school builds its intellectual, social, financial and spiritual capital and aligns them to achieve its goals.

There were two stages. The first called for a review of literature on the four kinds of capital and how they are aligned through effective governance. An outcome of this review was the identification of 10 indicators for each form of capital and for governance. The second called for case studies in five secondary schools in each of six countries: Australia, China, England, Finland, the United States and Wales (the Australian component also included a primary school and a network of primary and secondary schools). The project was carried out by Melbourne-based Educational Transformations with different components conducted by international partners with funding from the Australian government and the Welsh Assembly government.

According to the Merriam-Webster online dictionary, capital refers to 'accumulated goods devoted to the production of other goods' or 'a store of useful assets or advantages'. Social capital, for example, may be viewed as 'accumulated goods' ('the strength of formal and informal partnerships and networks involving the school and all individuals, agencies, organisations and institutions that have the potential to support and be supported by the school') devoted to the 'production of other goods' (state-of-the-art curriculum and pedagogy leading to 'success for all students in all settings'). High levels of capital in each of the four domains constitute 'a store of useful assets or advantages'.

Indicators were devised for each kind of capital and of governance. They served as a guide to researchers in each of the six countries in the selection of schools and to help build a common understanding of what was meant by each concept (intellectual capital, social capital, spiritual capital, financial capital and governance). The indicators of social capital are relevant to the kinds of partnership, sponsorship or support associated with programs in the arts:

1   There is a high level of alignment between the expectations of parents and other key stakeholders and the mission, vision, goals, policies, plans and programs of the school.
2   There is extensive and active engagement of parents and others in the community in the educational program of the school.
3   Parents and others in the community serve on the governing body of the school or contribute in other ways to the decision-making process.
4   Parents and others in the community are advocates of the school and are prepared to take up its cause in challenging circumstances.
5   The school draws cash or in-kind support from individuals, organisations, agencies and institutions in the public and private sectors, in education and other fields, including business and industry, philanthropists and social entrepreneurs.
6   The school accepts that support from the community has a reciprocal obligation for the school to contribute to the building of community.
7   The school draws from and contributes to networks to share knowledge, address problems and pool resources.
8   Partnerships have been developed and sustained to the extent that each partner gains from the arrangement.
9   Resources, both financial and human, have been allocated by the school to building partnerships that provide mutual support.
10 The school is co-located with or located near other services in the community and these services are utilised in support of the school.

(Caldwell and Harris 2008: 185)

Developments in Australia

The Australian government through its Department of Education, Employment and Workplace Relations, commissioned a report on connections between business and schools. This was an outcome of a recommendation at the Australia 2020 Summit in 2008 that called for Australia's top 200 companies to make a contribution to education. The Business-School Connection Roundtable was established with leaders from the business sector. There were extensive consultations throughout the country and surveys were conducted to determine the extent of current and past associations. It was clear that partnerships were more numerous than generally understood. Recommendations for strengthening and extending engagement were made. The report (Business-School Connections Roundtable 2011) described such engagement in terms of transformation and the support of the wider community, consistent with several of the indicators of social capital:

> Our education system has embarked on a bold transformation to ensure that all our young people have access to a high quality 21st century education, regardless of where they live, their gender, cultural background or socio-economic status.

In combination with the development of a national curriculum, physical infrastructure, new technology and other reforms, school-based partnerships – with business and the wider community – promise to deliver effective outcomes for our young people. Such partnerships have flourished over the past two decades. In many cases, business involvement in education has seen marked increases in the quality and extent of engagement of students, parents and whole communities in their schools. Nevertheless, there is much to be done to ensure that all schools can benefit from business connections.

As the world has become more complex, so have the community's expectations of schooling. Contributing to this is a growing recognition that educating our young people is the responsibility of the entire community, not just schools. This has led to an increasing focus on schools developing partnerships with the broader community – including parents, community organisations, businesses, and other education institutions.

(Business-School Connections Roundtable 2011: 1)

This is, indeed, a social capital view of business-school connections rather than an ideological one that may in the past be construed as 'the privatisation of public education'.

Several of the recommendations were concerned with building the capacities of schools to engage with business. It was acknowledged that many schools lack experience, confidence and know-how. This is where an organisation like the Specialist Schools and Academies Trust has filled a similar need in England since it has helped broker partnerships for more than 3,000 schools, including those in the arts. The Roundtable report contained few references to arts-related support hence the significance of the work of the Macquarie Group Foundation on behalf of TSR.

There is also a need in Australia for a more systematic approach to the philanthropic support of schools, an area only partly addressed in the Roundtable report. There is a need, for example, to study the impact of philanthropic support on school outcomes. This kind of work got under way in 2011 in a partnership of ACER through its Tender Bridge project and the Ian Potter Foundation:

As a new research project, Leading Learning in Education and Philanthropy (LLEAP) aims to address these issues by exploring whether the full potential of funding and partnerships available to Australian schools is being achieved. The project aims to find ways to improve the quality of grant seeking and grant making in Australia, with a focus on identifying better ways for the philanthropy and education sectors to connect and collaborate.

(Anderson 2011: 56)

The research reported in Chapters 5 to 8 makes a contribution to understanding the connection between philanthropy and education in the arts, although there is a blurring of roles of foundations supported by business, such as the Macquarie Group Foundation, and a non-profit entity, such as TSR, which provides a service without charge to the public school sector. Resources are only now being created to assist foundations target their support (see, for example, Brown 2010).

Developments in the United States

There is impressive support for schools from the business and philanthropic sectors in the United States and some of this is directed to schools that specialise in the arts. The United States is often held up as the international benchmark for support from these sectors. Interestingly, however, it seems that there is a need for greater coherence and more targeted arrangements that align with national priorities in education.

In January 2011, 900 bankers, entrepreneurs and experts in education policy met at the Education Innovation Forum in a White House initiative to 'revolutionise education' and 're-imagine learning'. Participants were responding to President Barack Obama's State of the Union address in the same month that described his administration's commitment to 'finding new strategies for leveraging change in the nation's schools' (Toch 2011: 68). In a broader perspective on the initiative, Koch drew attention to the shift in recent decades from the 1980s, when the major stakeholders and protagonists were professionals in the education sector, including organisations representing the interests of teachers and school boards, through the 1990s when several entrepreneurs were involved in creating new 'school designs', to the turn of the century and beyond and the growing interest in charter schools:

> The movement was led by a new generation of socially conscious entrepreneurs drawn to public education by the opportunity to help the nation's many disadvantaged students. Freed from school bureaucracies and union contracts by charter school laws and committed to the campaign for greater accountability in education, they sought to create a new, performance-driven brand for public schooling.
>
> (Toch 2011: 68)

Contributors to the effort include the Wallace Family Foundation and the Bill and Melinda Gates Foundation.

While significant funds and high levels of expertise have been brought to bear, work to date has been targeted mainly in major cities. There is evidence of impact on a project-by-project basis but there has been no large-scale research on broad impact across the schools sector. A case can be made that the focus on cities, disadvantaged students and charter schools has been associated with, or a major contributor to, the narrowing of the curriculum and the unrelenting focus on testing that has been the subject of so many critical comments. Will this also be the case in Australia and other countries that look to the United States in designing the school reform effort?

A movement that was pioneered in the United States has commenced in Australia and England in the form of the Teach for America (TFA) initiative. A 'summit' in Washington DC of current and past participants in the program attracted 11,000, with four foundations committing $100 million to a TFA endowment. TFA draws outstanding graduates who commit to a period of service in mostly challenging circumstances with limited initial teacher preparation. Evidence to date suggests that only a small minority have contributed to the teaching of the arts.

Specialist secondary schools in England

There are approximately 325 specialist arts colleges in the state or aided sector in England. Descriptions of specialist schools in England are contained in Chapter 2. Information provided to the authors by the Specialist Schools and Academies Trust revealed that these receive cash or in-kind support from 248 sponsors. Of these, 76 are clearly identifiable as foundations, trusts, churches, charities or guilds. Businesses with an international profile that provide support include Aldi, BAA including its airports at Heathrow and Gatwick, British Airways, British Telecom (BT), Cisco Systems, Hewlett Packard, HSBC (various branches), Microsoft, Rolls Royce and Sharp Electronics. These are not arts industries though they support arts education in many specialist arts colleges. Other noteworthy sponsors include the Duchy of Cornwall administered by the Prince of Wales, Weston Cricket Club and Walsall Football Club. Guild support includes the Worshipful Company of Fishmongers.

Education in the arts as 'disruptive innovation'

We conclude the chapter by canvassing a paradox, namely, that strengthening or re-introducing the arts in school education may be an example of 'disruptive innovation' which some observers believe is the key to the transformation of schools.

Christensen, Johnson and Horn (2008) did much to popularise the idea of 'disruptive innovation' in *Disruptive Class*. Christensen and Horn updated their work in an interview reported in *Phi Delta Kappan* (Richardson 2011):

> A disruptive innovation is an innovation that transforms the complicated, expensive services and products into things that are so simple and affordable that you and I can use them. [Christensen]
>
> (Richardson 2011: 32)

> A bit of misreading of the book [Christensen *et al.* 2008] is that disruptive innovations are good and sustaining innovations are bad. What we want is a system that does both. We want a robust system that is always creating sustaining innovations that will drive products to market and make them better and serve people better. That also leaves room over time for disruptions to come in and change things. [Horn]
>
> (Richardson 2011: 34)

Leadbeater and Wong incorporated the idea of 'disruptive innovation' in their Innovation Grid, as illustrated in Figure 9.1.

The elements were described in these terms:

- *Improve* schools through better facilities, teachers and leadership.
- *Supplement* schools by working with families and communities.

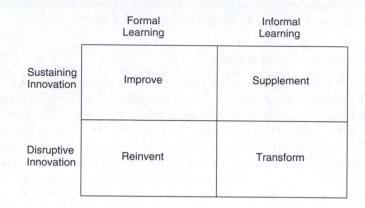

Figure 9.1 The Innovation Grid (Leadbeater and Wong 2010: 4)

- *Reinvent* schools to create an education better fit for the time.
- *Transform* schools by making it available in radically new ways.

The particular innovations reported by Leadbeater and Wong are disruptive to the extent that they involve radically different forms of schooling or learning and new arrangements that gave rise to alternative schools, with most of their illustrations from developing countries. They described how these emerge:

> A band of disruptive innovators is emerging within school systems in many parts of the developing world. Yet radical innovation rarely comes from the mainstream. Most often it comes from renegades, mavericks, and outsiders working in the margins.
>
> (Leadbeater and Wong 2010: 4)

Where does this sit with the proposition that education in the arts may be an instance of 'disruptive innovation'? We set this alongside the prevailing view that it is the advent of computers that is the 'disruptive innovation'. In Australia, according to TSR, there are 700,000 primary students who do not learn through the arts (2011a). In England, despite the development of an arts specialism in secondary schools, there is a case that the arts have been sidelined in the primary school. It is the arts that are under pressure with budget cutbacks in the United States. The unrelenting focus on literacy and numeracy and preoccupation with national tests has apparently had the same effect in these countries. The introduction or re-introduction of significant programs in the arts can therefore be considered 'disruptive' in these policy and budgetary contexts. Moreover, a driving force may be what Leadbeater and Wong described (above) as 'a band of disruptive innovators' or 'renegades, mavericks and outsiders working at the margins' (Leadbeater and Wong 2010: 4).

Who has been responsible for sidelining or cutting back in the arts? Notwithstanding, for example, the inclusion of the arts in the new Australian Curriculum, or its inclusion in existing curriculums in England and the United States, it is governments that are mandating the narrow focus that must take a large part of the blame. One could argue that parents have also contributed to this narrow focus since high-stakes testing has been politically popular. After all, who can argue with the proposition that students should be tested against standards and that high standards in literacy and numeracy are essential. These explanations are consistent with the way Leadbeater and Wong explained the lack of disruptive innovation in education:

> Disruptive innovation in education is too weak because state regulation, teacher union power, parental conservatism, and political micromanagement create high barriers to new entry. Creating diverse new ways for people to learn is still too difficult. Disruptive innovation needs more support and encouragement.
>
> (Leadbeater and Wong 2010: 4)

Significance

We conclude that there is a lack of alignment between what the evidence shows is the impact of the arts on learning, and efforts being made, especially in Australia, England and the United States, to turn around the performance of schools. Even though there has been significant progress in recent years, it is only now that the need for more coherent and better targeted support of the non-profit, philanthropic and business sectors has been recognised. This sets the stage for a well-defined agenda for policymakers and our purpose in Chapter 10 is to provide recommendations.

10   A policy agenda

We drew attention in Chapter 1 to the pernicious effects on arts education of a narrow focus on high-stakes testing and posed two questions. What if the curtailment of arts education not only robs students of the intrinsic benefit of an artistic experience but further reduces the performance of students in literacy and numeracy? Moreover, what will it mean to a nation if such a cut-back increases the gap between high- and low-performing students on these same tests and decreases the life chances of students, even to the extent of increasing the probability they may subsequently be involved in crime or other anti-social behaviour? Our purpose in *Transforming Education through the Arts* was to critically examine these issues and provide evidence that Australia and similar nations will benefit from greater rather than lesser engagement in the arts in school education.

The centre-piece of the book is a study of the impact of an arts program on attendance, achievement, and social and emotional wellbeing of students in highly disadvantaged settings in the outer suburbs of Australia's largest city (Sydney). The program was offered by a non-profit organisation, TSR with this research supported by philanthropy (Macquarie Group Foundation). Conducted in 2010, the study was a rare example of 'quasi-experimental' research, for we were able to compare outcomes for students in a matched set of schools where the program was not offered.

Limitations of the research

Before summarising the most significant findings it is important to acknowledge the limitations of the Australian research. The schools involved in the study were located in particular communities in a small number of regions in the system of government (public) schools in Western Sydney, NSW. On their own, the findings cannot be generalised to other schools in similar settings, either in these regions or other regions in NSW or elsewhere in Australia. There can be no assurance that schools that choose to participate in TSR will experience the same impact. Nevertheless, the outcomes in the current study warrant the most serious attention.

There are other limitations which arise from the selection of schools. It was not possible to achieve a perfect match of schools that are participating and not participating in TSR. However, there is a very good match. While there may be a range of factors that contribute to patterns in the findings, a major distinguishing factor is participation in a TSR program. A key resource in achieving the match was the ICSEA score of schools in the study. ICSEA was developed by ACARA. We were able to achieve a close match of scores on the ICSEA for the two sets of schools in the study. While ICSEA is contentious and changes were made in 2010, it was the most transparent of SES-type indicators at the time of the study.

There is of course a need for more research and variations in the research design. Before and after studies will be helpful, but were not possible in the investigation reported in Chapters 5 to 8. Longitudinal data enabled comparisons of the three groups of schools, prior to their participation in the TSR program, which revealed lower percentages of students above the national minimum for the majority of the literacy domains in the initial and longer-term TSR cohorts, in comparison to the non-participating cohort. Similar patterns were seen for attendance, indicating a bias in the research for higher achievement and attendance to be found in the non-participating cohort. Deeper case studies that look more closely at particular pedagogies employed by the TSR and their TAs will be helpful.

Overall, and subject to these limitations, the findings support the efficacy of TSR programs. Policymakers at all levels should encourage participation as one of many strategies to help close the gap in achievement of high- and low-performing students.

Significance of the research and related studies

While the Australian study has the limitations set out above, the importance of the findings is magnified many times over because they are similar to the findings of related studies in other settings as these were summarised in several chapters. Indeed, the findings of related studies provide the context for reporting the outcomes of the Australian study (see Chapters 4, 6, 7 and 8). Given the case for the arts and evidence of their sidelining set out in Chapter 1, we concluded each chapter with what we considered to be the most significant findings that have implications for policy and practice, and these are summarised below.

As reported in Chapter 1, for many centuries the arts have been at the centre of education and society in a holistic view of human development. In more recent times there has been a bifurcation of endeavour that has led to the arts being sidelined when the curriculum has narrowed or there has been a need to cut public expenditure. This is despite evidence of the contribution the arts make to national creativity and to the wellbeing of the individual citizen. The social and economic costs will be high in nations that have succumbed under these circumstances.

There has been consistent advocacy of a holistic view of education, the desirability of connectedness in the curriculum, and an expanded role for the arts. The so-called twenty-first-century skills emphasise creativity and innovation for which the importance of the arts should be assumed (Chapter 2). However, there is a disjunction between what has been advocated and what lies at centre-stage in the reform agenda in many countries. It is disconcerting that progress is slow and that a holistic view of learning has been impaired, despite a consensus among those whose business it is to make connections between education, economy and society. It is profoundly disappointing that neither the first nor the second McKinsey report could find much evidence that these connections were being made (Chapter 3).

Who has been responsible for sidelining or cutting back in the arts? Notwithstanding, for example, the inclusion of the arts in the new Australian Curriculum, or its inclusion in existing curricula in England and the United States, it is governments that are mandating the narrow focus that must take a large part of the blame. One could argue that parents have also contributed to this narrow focus since high-stakes testing has been politically popular. After all, who can argue with the proposition that students should be tested against standards and that high standards in literacy and numeracy are essential.

We concluded in Chapter 3 that there is a lack of alignment between what the evidence shows is the impact of the arts on learning and efforts being made, especially in Australia, England and the United States, to turn around the performance of schools. Even though there has been significant progress in recent years, it is only now that the need for more coherent and better targeted support of the non-profit, philanthropic and business sectors has been recognised, a line of argument that was taken up and extended in Chapter 9.

It is rare to find such consistent evidence in support of particular approaches in curriculum and pedagogy as we found in a comprehensive review of research that was reported in Chapters 4, 6 and 7, especially where that evidence applies to improving the life chances of students in highly disadvantaged settings (Chapter 4). There are examples of structures, processes and techniques (a more accurate description in some instances would be fads) that have been implemented nation-wide or system-wide that may have had a marginal impact, or an early impact that subsequently flat-lines, but on the evidence before us, initiatives in arts education do not fall into this category.

The findings in the Australian TSR study are particularly striking in their consistency (Chapters 6, 7 and 8). Schools participating in TSR programs outperform those that are not participating on most indicators selected for investigation on the basis of previous research. Those in the longer-term program tend to outperform those in the initial program. The impact is striking given that students were engaged for no longer than one hour per week. For example, the evidence that gains in learning were as much as one year demands attention. For many, the obvious reason is that students tend to come to school in larger numbers on the days that the program is offered, in comparison to those schools that are not participating in TSR. Clearly, students are unlikely to learn in the areas that were tested if they are not at school. Furthermore, it is noteworthy that dramatic differences were found on measures of social and emotional wellbeing on the basis of one hour per week in arts education.

If, as concluded in the first McKinsey report, the quality of a system cannot exceed the quality of its teachers, the attention of policymakers and practitioners should be focused on the quality of teaching provided in TSR programs, which must be attributed in large measure to the qualities of the TAs placed in schools by TSR, many of whom do not have formal teaching qualifications – they are professionals in their fields of artistic endeavour.

In Chapter 9 we canvassed the proposition that, unexpectedly and perhaps paradoxically, education in the arts may be an instance of 'disruptive innovation'. We set this alongside the prevailing view that it is the advent of computers that is the 'disruptive innovation'. In Australia, according to TSR, there are 700,000 primary students who do not learn through the arts (TSR 2011a). In England, while there is an arts specialisation in 325 specialist secondary arts colleges, there is evidence that the arts have been sidelined in primary schools. It is the arts that are under pressure with budget cutbacks in the United States. The unrelenting focus on literacy and numeracy and preoccupation with standardised tests has apparently had the same effect in these countries. The introduction or re-introduction of significant programs in the arts may therefore be considered 'disruptive' in these policy and budgetary contexts.

Overall, we contend that a major design flaw has opened up in these and comparable nations and that school education, especially in the public sector, is at risk unless corrective action is taken as a matter of urgency.

Residualisation in the public sector through sidelining of the arts

The sidelining of the arts reported in Chapters 1 and 3 appears to be more evident in public (state) schools than in private (non-state) schools, and more so in public schools in highly disadvantaged settings than in their counterparts in more affluent communities. An explanation lies in the fact that large numbers of private schools have, at least in the eyes of parents, a more holistic view of the curriculum and have well-developed programs in the arts that have withstood the narrowing effect of high-stakes testing. There are notable exceptions, of course, especially for public schools of long standing or where the arts are a 'protected' specialisation. An associated reason that takes account of socio-economic status in the public sector as well as in the private sector is that these schools have more financial resources to draw on or higher levels of social capital from which they can secure support for the arts.

An outcome for public schools in many settings is a further loss of students to the private sector, a trend that has continued unabated in Australia, for example, where high-stakes national testing and efforts to build capacity in literacy and numeracy with a high level of transparency on the My School website appear to have had little effect, if the balance of students in the public and private sectors is an indicator. The same trend is also evident in England but not to the same extent because publicly funded school choice options do not exist to the same extent as in Australia. Private schools in England receive no public funding; all private schools in Australia receive public funding on a sliding scale according to their capacity to raise their own funds. While observers in the United States such as Diane Ravitch report the same narrowing of curriculum, it has been generally possible to hold the line, so to speak, and the richness of the student experience continues to prevail in many schools and school systems. Apart from that, there are few options other than charter schools for parents in the United States since all faith-based schools are constitutionally barred from public funding.

If a longer historical view is taken, there is a persuasive narrative that takes the following form. Faith and reason became separated after the Enlightenment. In education this meant a strict separation of Church and State in school education. In Australia, for example, the late nineteenth century saw the creation of free, compulsory and secular state schools. Church schools were initially not publicly funded and the state sector was dominant, leaving relatively small numbers of independent church schools operating along the lines of English private ('public') schools and diocesan Catholic schools. Now, more than a century-and-a-quarter later, energised by ever-increasing public funding, the private or non-government sector is strong to the point that the majority of secondary students in the Australian Capital Territory (ACT) are now in private schools and, in the largest capital cities such as Melbourne and Sydney, the majority of upper secondary students (Grades 10, 11 and 12) are also in private schools.

There are many explanations that need not be canvassed here but one is that an increasing number of parents value private schooling, which in Australia may be a reflection of the better outcomes in those schools compared to those in the state system (Marks 2009). Marks reported that accounting for prior achievement and socio-economic background of students resulted in 'value added' of between 5 percent and 9 percent for Australian private school students. These findings do not hold true internationally with public schools showing an advantage of 12 score points on average (for OECD countries) over private schools (Program for International Student Assessment 2007), which may be a reflection of private school funding differences internationally. Along with de-zoning or choice within the public sector, there is evidence of the 'residualisation' of public schools in many communities.

In his insightful foreword to Robyn Ewing's comprehensive review of the place of the arts in Australian education (Ewing 2010) Professor John O'Toole, Lead Writer for The Arts in the Australian Curriculum, cited in several chapters, and Foundation Chair of Arts Education at the University of Melbourne, provided a supporting narrative in commenting on the emerging Australian Curriculum:

> Comparing this latest government curriculum with Australia's first, in Victoria in 1872, is revealing. Then as now, a debate raged in the United Kingdom and Australia about 'the basics', and whether breadth and depth in education were opposite or complementary – the latter claim led by a man who was both an Inspector of Schools and an artist, poet Matthew Arnold [who wrote that] 'Intelligent reading . . . when children . . . possess it they owe it not to the assiduity with which they have been taught reading and nothing but reading, but . . . far more to the civilising and refining influences'.
>
> The Victorian Education Act's founding fathers may have been aware of Arnold's words, but they weren't overly concerned with the exact curriculum – they were so cock-a-hoop with their victory in getting legislation for a secular education system passed in 1872 that they hardly bothered about what actually got taught, just so long as it didn't include religion. The Act relegated the curriculum itself to less than half a page, in an appendix, with a curriculum based on seven-and-a-bit subjects. These were Reading, Writing, Arithmetic, Grammar,

Geography, Drill and where practicable Gymnastics; and additionally, for girls, sewing and needlework. There was nothing creative in this list of subjects, and the Arts were not at all part of the package – for even the needlework wasn't there for its aesthetic qualities.

(O'Toole 2010: v)

This narrative can be extended with the bifurcation of science and the arts described in Chapter 1, or more generally in terms of issues addressed in this book, a bifurcation based on a sidelining of the arts and a focus on other areas of the curriculum, especially but not exclusively, on literacy and numeracy arising from national high-stakes testing. This lies at the heart of the mis-alignment described in Chapter 3. The outcome of these two 'separations' – faith and reason on the one hand, and the arts and other areas of the curriculum on the other – is the further residualisation of public education, with the effect most evident in disadvantaged settings where resources, both social and financial, are insufficient to stem the flow of students to public schools in other communities or to the private sector. This is a devastating development given that espoused public policy is to build the public sector and reduce disparities in achievement. In developing this narrative we acknowledge that secular state schools may have as powerful a values base as faith-based schools. This is consistent with the broad view of spiritual capital described by Caldwell and Harris (2008) and reported in Chapter 9. Spiritual capital refers to the strength of moral purpose and the degree of coherence among values, beliefs and attitudes about life and learning (for some schools, spiritual capital has a foundation in religion; in other schools, spiritual capital may refer to ethics and values shared by members of the school and its community).

The best efforts at school improvement are confounded by the separations described above. Contrasting initiatives in neighbouring regions in the state system of education in Victoria are noteworthy. The Northern Metropolitan Region in Melbourne includes some of the state's most disadvantaged communities. For several years there has been a steady drift of students from many schools in these communities to state schools in neighbouring suburbs or to the private sector. Achievement levels were of serious concern. Enrolments in many schools had fallen dramatically and many school buildings were crumbling. The region was the focus of a major 'regeneration' effort and a reforming principal, Wayne Craig was appointed regional director to transform the region. Millions of dollars were invested. World-class scholars were enlisted to help build capacity across all schools in an impressive array of professional development programs. These included David Hopkins, who served successive Secretaries of State for Education in England and is expert in school improvement (Hopkins 2007), and John Munro from the Graduate School of Education at the University of Melbourne. Hopkins, Craig and Munro and other contributors documented the effort in a well-written account in *Powerful Learning: A Strategy for Systematic Educational Improvement* (Hopkins *et al.* 2011). Evidence is provided of improvement on state and national tests but the upward trajectory is gentle rather than steep. Driving this work was 'an integrated school improvement model' that brings together the best of strategies for improvement, with 'powerful learning' focused on students who were literate, numerate and curious. It is fair to ask if this is an adequate conceptualisation of 'powerful learning', not because these capacities are unimportant and ought not to be included but whether they fall far short in respect to twenty-first-century skills, and the capacities that are nurtured through the arts.

Hopkins and Craig (2011: 37) offered a 'coda' for powerful learning which is impeccable in its alignment with themes in this book. For powerful learning:

> It is not just an accurate description of a strategy that focuses directly on enhancing the learning of all students in the region; it is also an idea that is capturing the imagination of teachers, parents and young people around the world. It is an idea that has its roots in the best practice of the teaching profession, and it has the potential to make every young person's learning experience stretching, creative, fun and successful. It reflects the current drive to tailor schooling to individual need, interest and aptitude, so making it increasingly personalised.
>
> (Hopkins and Craig 2011: 37)

However, the concept of 'curiosity' goes nowhere near far enough to capture the breadth of curriculum and the diversity of pedagogy that will embrace the arts, that the evidence reported throughout this book suggests will make a dramatic contribution to improvement in literacy and numeracy through higher levels of engagement and enhanced social and emotional wellbeing.

There is a fascinating contrast between these well-intentioned and modestly successful initiatives in the Northern Metropolitan Region, as described by Hopkins, Craig and Munro, and efforts to build the capacity of school leaders in the neighbouring Eastern Metropolitan Region. This region contains a larger proportion of students from more advantaged communities although there are pockets of disadvantage. While priorities are also placed on improvement in literacy and numeracy, school leaders have received copies of Yong Zhao's *Catching Up or Leading the Way: American Education in the Age of Globalization* (Zhao 2009) which rejects the kind of high-stakes testing that now characterises the Australian scene and concludes, as cited in Chapter 3:

> As we enter a new world rapidly changed by globalisation and technology, we need to change course. Instead of instilling fear in the public about the rise of other countries, bureaucratising education with bean-counting policies, demoralizing educators through dubious accountability measures, homogenising school curriculum, and turning children into test takers, we should inform the public about the possibilities brought about by globalisation, encourage educational innovations, inspire educators with genuine support, diversify and decentralise curriculum, and educate children as confident, unique, and well-rounded human beings.
>
> (Zhao 2009: 198)

These contrasting perspectives on building capacity for system change in neighbouring regions in the public school system in Victoria are consistent with the theme of this section of Chapter 10, namely, rather than marginal or transitory improvement in areas of high-stakes testing, sidelining the arts is likely to lead to a flat-lining of achievement, leaving more affluent parts of the system and private schooling with a comparative advantage. Correcting this design flaw is a matter of urgency in Australia and other systems or nations that have invested so much in a narrow approach. We turn our attention to a policy framework through which this urgency can be addressed.

Recommendations for policy and practice

In Chapter 1 we cited the work of UNESCO in the area of the arts in education. UNESCO considers education in the arts to be a universal human right, implying that its absence or sidelining is a breach of the Convention on the Rights of the Child. A 'road map for arts education' was prepared at the First World Conference on Arts Education held in Lisbon in March 2006 (UNESCO 2006) and this contained 79 recommendations with a focus on: (1) educators, parents, artists and directors of schools and educational institutions, government ministries and policy makers (15 recommendations); (2) government ministries and policymakers (29 recommendations); and (3) UNESCO and other intergovernmental and non-governmental organisations (35 recommendations). A sample of 24 recommendations for (1) and (2) are contained in Table 10.1. Each is consistent with findings of research reported in this book and responds positively to the issues raised in various accounts of existing policy and practice. Recommendations in Table 10.1 represent about 30 percent of all recommendations and the full set is relevant, hence we recommend action on all.

There's something about the arts

Some readers may question the focus on the arts in this book as though we were not giving due weight to other areas of the curriculum where a contribution to economy and society is made and the passions of students can be fulfilled. This is not the case. We reiterate at this point that there are many areas where a case can be made that they have also been sidelined. At the same time we acknowledge that due attention has been given to different areas of specialisation in some jurisdictions. The specialist schools movement at the secondary level in England is a good example, as introduced in Chapter 2 and addressed in various places throughout the book. These different areas are profoundly important and student engagement in learning across the curriculum can be enhanced if, for example, one is passionate about history or sport or technology.

There is, however, something special about the arts that warrants particular attention in a book largely devoted to the topic. Apart from the substantial body of research that supports their inclusion and challenges any attempt at sidelining the field, there is the issue raised in Chapter 1 that the bifurcation of the arts and science has been one of the great 'separations' for a long period of time. More than that is the connection between 'the arts' and 'the spirit' that is fundamental to the human condition. Attention was drawn to this connection in May 2011 when reports were

Table 10.1 Sample recommendations for policymakers and practitioners in UNESCO report 2006

Focus	Type of action	Sample recommendations
Educators, parents, artists, and directors of schools and educational institutions	Advocacy, support and education	1. Raise public awareness and promote the value and social impact of arts education, creating a demand for arts education and skilled arts educators 2. Provide leadership, support and assistance for teaching and learning in and through the arts 3. Promote active participation in, and accessibility to, the arts for all children, as a core component of education
	Partnerships and cooperation	1. Encourage active and sustainable partnerships between educational contexts (formal and non-formal) and the wider community 2. Facilitate participation in learning contexts by local arts practitioners and the inclusion of local art forms and techniques in learning processes in order to strengthen local cultures and identity 3. Facilitate cooperation between schools and parents, community organisations and institutions, and mobilise local resources within communities to develop arts education programs, so as to enable communities to share transmitting cultural values and local art forms
	Implementation, evaluation and knowledge-sharing	1. Implement and evaluate collaborative school–community projects that are based on the principles of inclusive cooperation, integration and relevance 2. Encourage effective documentation and sharing of knowledge between teachers 3. Share information and evidence with stakeholders, including governments, communities, the media, NGOs and the private sector
Government ministries and policymakers	Recognition	1. Recognise the role of arts education in preparing audiences and different sectors of the public to appreciate artistic manifestations 2. Acknowledge the importance of developing an arts education policy which articulates the links between communities, educational and social institutions and the world of work 3. Recognise the value of successful locally developed, culturally relevant arts education practices and projects. Recognise that future projects should replicate the successful practices implemented so far
	Policy development	1. Translate the growing understanding of the importance of arts education into the commitment of resources sufficient to translate principles into action, in order to create a greater awareness of the benefits of arts and creativity for all and support for the implementation of a new vision for arts and learning

Table 10.1 Continued

Focus	Type of action	Sample recommendations
		2. Design policies for national and regional research in the area of arts education, taking into account the specificities of ancestral cultures as well as vulnerable population groups
		3. Encourage development of strategies for implementation and monitoring, so as to ensure the quality of arts education
	Education, implementation and support	1. Make professional education for artists and teachers available to enhance the quality of Arts Education delivery and, where they don't exist, set up arts education departments in universities
		2. Make education of arts teachers a new priority within the education system, enabling them to contribute more effectively to the process of learning and cultural development, and make sensitisation to the arts a part of the training of all teachers and of education actors
		3. Make trained teachers and artists available in educational institutions and non-formal settings in order to permit and foster the growth and promotion of arts education
	Partnerships and cooperation	1. Promote partnerships among all concerned ministries and governmental organisations to develop coherent and sustainable arts education policies and strategies
		2. Encourage government officials at every level to join forces with educators, artists, NGOs, lobby groups, members of the business community, the labour movement and members of civil society to create specific advocacy action plans and messages
		3. Encourage the active involvement in education of arts and cultural institutions, foundations, media, industry, and members of the private sector
	Research and knowledge-sharing	1. Develop a complete databank of human and material arts education resources and make this available to all educational institutions, including via the Internet
		2. Ensure dissemination of information about arts education, implementation and follow-up by Ministries of Education and Culture
		3. Encourage the creation of collections and inventories of works of art that enrich Arts Education

Source: selected from UNESCO 2006.

published on the research of Professor Semir Zeki, a neurobiologist at the Institute of Cognitive Neuroscience, Department of Anatomy at University College London. As Peter Craven, an Australian literary and cultural critic observed:

What an extraordinary thing it is that scientific experiments in London have proved that the experience in art can give great pleasure. Or rather, how extraordinary it is that scientific labour and research funding has been expended to tell us what we have always known and should not have been in danger of forgetting.

(Craven 2011: 15)

Craven was referring to research by Zeki who scanned the brains of volunteers as they looked at 28 pictures including *The Birth of Venus* by Sandro Botticelli and *La Grenouillère* by Claude Monet. Under the headline 'Viewing art gives the same pleasure as being in love', The *Telegraph*'s science correspondent Richard Alleyne quotes Zeki: 'There have been very significant new advances in our understanding of what happens in our brains when we look at works of art'; 'Essentially, the feel-good centres are stimulated, similar to the states of love and desire' (Alleyne 2011).

Several responses can be made to these reports. First, if we accept the findings, they affirm the fundamental connections between the arts, in this instance art, and the human spirit. Second, it should be acknowledged that at the time of writing the research was the subject of peer review, as it should be. Third, even though this may be the case, it is important to point out that Zeki has been researching the area for several decades and has published widely in refereed books by leading publishing houses (Zeki 1993, 1999).

Bridging the gap

The Summary Report of the TSR research reported in Chapters 5 to 8 was entitled *Bridging the Gap in School Achievement through the Arts* (Vaughan *et al.* 2011). The idea of 'bridging the gap' may also be employed to address the gap between science and the arts, as illustrated in the research of Semir Zeki reported above.

Richard Florida's construction of a Global Creativity Index reported in Chapter 1 accommodated the capacities that can be nurtured through the arts. We noted that 'while Florida was considering creativity in general terms, he developed several carefully specified and highly regarded indices which measured capacities that are developed through the arts, notably tolerance, which included values and self-expression'. It is therefore disappointing that recent studies that led to various indices of innovation assume that it is technology alone that drives innovation. For example, the Intelligence Unit at *The Economist* published its rankings of the 'world's most innovative countries' in 2009 (*The Economist* 2009). There is an assumption throughout that technology is the driver. To some extent this is understandable given that the report was sponsored by Cisco, but it contrasts with Cisco's view of twenty-first-century skills that should be nurtured in schools, as cited in Chapter 2 (Cisco 2008).

Japan is the top-ranking nation in the 2009 ratings ahead of Switzerland, Finland, the United States and Sweden; the United Kingdom is 18th and Australia 21st. With technology the key driver, the United Kingdom and the United States are expected to slide down the list by 2013. The report concludes that 'under the Obama administration in the United States, the focus on long-term investments in such areas as environmental technology and education as set forth in the economic recovery plan may at least help slow the decline' (*The Economist* 2009: 10). It remains to be seen whether investments in education will be at the expense of areas of the curriculum where creativity and innovation are nurtured, and these include the arts. On present indications the prognosis is not good given the focus on high-stakes testing with the dysfunctions reported in Chapters 1 and 3.

The good news is that the links between technology and the arts are being recognised by curriculum designers and good progress is being made. Southcott and Crawford (2011: 122) report that: 'Since the 1980s, all areas in Australian school curriculum have been influenced by information and computing technology (ICT) and music has been no exception. In the past twenty years there has been rapid, almost overwhelming expansion of the use of technology in school music programs'. While this may be the case, serious concerns have been raised about the place of music in schools and these were reported in Chapter 1. Moreover, there is a gap in understanding of those developing an ICT curriculum and those developing a music curriculum, with this extending to other studies in the arts (Southcott and Crawford 2011: 131).

Reversing the effects of disruptive change

A major theme of this book is that there has been a major disruption in efforts to design an education that matches the needs of the individual, society and economy in the twenty-first century. Every configuration of knowledge and skill that are required in the years ahead highlights the need for a holistic view of the curriculum and building on the basics of literacy and numeracy to nurture a capacity for creativity, imagination and innovation. Yet this effort has been confounded in several countries, notably Australia, England and the United States, that continue to have faith in the transforming effects of narrowly focused high-stakes tests that have resulted in mis-alignment among a range of strategies that should be aligned and transforming.

The sidelining of the arts is one dysfunction in this mis-alignment despite the evidence that these are essential if the aim is to secure success for all students. Moreover, research has consistently shown that engagement in the arts is associated with improved outcomes in all areas of learning and with enhanced wellbeing. These findings, confirmed in the groundbreaking Australian research that forms the centre-piece of this book, have powerful policy implications as efforts are made to address problems of alienation of young people in many communities, especially those in disadvantaged settings.

While the focus has been on countries like Australia, England and the United States, there is universal concern about the place of the arts, as indicated in successive World Conferences on Arts Education sponsored by UNESCO. No fewer than 79 recommendations were made in a 'road map' for necessary change. Policymakers and practitioners cannot afford to ignore the case for urgent action.

At the same time that we draw attention to these dysfunctions and the need for change, we acknowledge the remarkable achievements of schools that have protected the arts in each of the three countries we have focused on and elsewhere around the world. It has required strong will and commitment to a compelling vision to achieve this. We acknowledge the work of the non-profit sector in supporting the cause, as exemplified in the efforts of TSR in Australia and the assistance of the philanthropic sector as well as government in many jurisdictions. An even greater effort will be required in the years ahead.

Toward a golden future

In Chapter 9 we canvassed a paradox. The idea of transformation in education that arises from 'disruptive innovation' is usually associated with the breathtaking developments in technology, but we suggested that the arts are so fragile that to establish or indeed re-establish their proper place in education will also constitute a 'disruptive innovation' that will have an impact in many domains within schools, across school systems and in other institutions. It has been pointed out that 'disruptive innovation' on the scale of technological change is largely driven from outside education, and it is hard to argue with that view. Schools and school systems seem to be in a state of non-stop 'catch-up' as every innovation makes its appearance. The same analysis might be made in respect to the arts, where the driving force for change is coming to a large extent from outside 'the system', albeit with the support of dedicated professionals in schools. Just as the 'disruptive innovation' arising from technology is associated with and, to some extent, depends on partnerships with and support of business and industry as well as the philanthropic sector, so too with 'disruptive innovation' that will arise from a resurgence in the arts.

We began Chapter 1 with the devastating critique of the narrowly focused high-stakes testing orientation to school reform in Australia offered by Richard Gill, former director of the Victorian Opera. It is appropriate that we conclude the book by returning to the Australian scene. In May 2011 *The Economist* published a lead article on the future of Australia under the heading 'The next Golden State' with a sub-title 'With a bit of self-belief, Australia could become a model nation' (*The Economist* 2011: 13–14). Much of the article contrasted the social and economic potential of the nation with the narrowly focused inward-looking discourse that it alleges is characteristic of politics in Australia. It looked at the characteristics of open, dynamic and creative societies as these have been created over the years in other nations and offered the following in respect to Australia:

> Such societies, the ones in which young and enterprising people want to live, cannot be conjured up overnight by a single agent, least of all by government. They are created by the alchemy of artists, entrepreneurs, philanthropists, civic institutions and governments coming together in the right combination at the right moment. And for Australia, economically strong as never before, this is surely such a moment.
>
> (*The Economist* 2011: 13)

The article makes the point that 'better themes for politicians would be their plans to develop first-class universities, nourish the arts, promote urban design and stimulate new industries' (*The Economist* 2011: 13). There could not be more powerful support for the themes in this book that apply to all nations that seek to create a 'golden future'.

Appendix

Effect sizes were calculated using the equation described by Hattie (2009):

$$\text{Effect size} = \frac{(\text{mean treatment}) - (\text{mean control})}{\text{pooled standard deviation}}$$

where pooled standard deviation (s_p) is equal to:

$$s_p = \sqrt{\frac{(n_1 - 1)s_1^2 + (n_2 - 1)s_2^2 + \ldots + (n_k - 1)s_k^2}{n_1 + n_2 + \ldots + n_k - k}}$$

- s_p is the pooled standard deviation
- n_1 is the sample size of the first sample
- n_2 is the sample size of the second sample
- s_1 is the standard deviation of the first sample
- k is the number of the samples combined

References

ACARA (2010a) *Draft Shape of the Australian Curriculum: The Arts*, Sydney: Australian Curriculum Assessment and Reporting Authority. Online. Available HTTP: <http://www.acara.edu.au/verve/_resources/Draft+Shape+Of+The+Australian+Curriculum+The+Arts-FINAL.pdf>, (accessed 13 May 2011).

—— (2010b) *National Assessment Program Literacy and Numeracy Summary Report: Achievement in Reading, Writing, Language Conventions and Numeracy*, Sydney: Australian Curriculum Assessment and Reporting Authority. Online. Available HTTP: <http://www.nap.edu.au/_Documents/National%20Report/NAPLAN_2010_Summary_Report.pdf>, (accessed 5 May 2011).

—— (2011a) 'Fact Sheet: About My School'. Online. Available HTTP: <http://www.acara.edu.au/verve/_resources/about_my_school.pdf>, (accessed 3 May 2011).

—— (2011b) 'My School: Glossary'. Online. Available HTTP: <http://www.acara.edu.au/myschool/myschool_glossary.html>, (accessed 5 April 2011).

—— (2011c) 'My School: Guide to Understanding ICSEA'. Online. Available HTTP: <http://www.acara.edu.au/verve/_resources/Guide_to_understanding_ICSEA.pdf>, (accessed 13 May 2011).

ACMF (The Australian Children's Music Foundation) (2009) 'The Australian Children's Music Foundation'. Online. Available HTTP: <http://www.acmf.com.au/>, (accessed 12 May 2011).

—— (2011a) 'About the Foundation . . .'. Online. Available HTTP: <http://www.acmf.com.au/>, (accessed 27 April 2011).

—— (2011b) 'Information on ACMF'. E-mail (27 April 2011).

Alexander, R. (ed.) (2010a) *Children, Their World, Their Education: Final Report and Recommendations of the Cambridge Primary Review*, London: Routledge.

—— (2010b) 'The Perils of Policy: Success, Amnesia and Collateral Damage in Systematic Educational Reform', paper presented at Miegunyah Distinguished Lecture in the Dean's Lecture Series in Melbourne Graduate School of Education, 10 March 2010.

Alleyne, R. (2011) 'Viewing art gives same pleasure as being in love', *The Telegraph*, 8 May 2011.

Anderson, M. (2011) 'Maximising the impact of philanthropy in education', *Teacher*, May: 56–59.

Australian Council for Educational Research (2010), *Social-Emotional Wellbeing Survey. Report: Educational Transformations' Schools September 2010*, Melbourne Australian Council for Educational Research.

Baker, J. (1998) *Juveniles in Crime – Part 1: Participation Rates and Risk Factors*, Sydney: NSW Bureau of Crime Statistics and Research. Online. Available HTTP: <http://www.lawlink.

nsw.gov.au/lawlink/bocsar/ll_bocsar.nsf/vwFiles/r45.pdf/$file/r45.pdf>, (accessed 13 May 2011).

Baltodano, H.M., Harris, P.J. and Rutherford, R.B. (2005) 'Academic Achievement in Juvenile Corrections: Examining the Impact of Age, Ethnicity and Disability', *Education and Treatment of Children*, 28: 361–79.

Bamford, A. (2006) *The Wow Factor: Global Research Compendium on the Impact of the Arts in Education*, Münster, Germany: Waxman.

—— (2009) *Arts and Cultural Education in Iceland*, Reykjavik: Ministry of Education, Science and Culture. Online. Available HTTP: <http://bella.mrn.stjr.is/utgafur/arts_and_culture_anne_bamford.pdf>, (accessed 7 April 2011).

Bandura, A., Barbaranelli, C., Caprara, G.V. and Pastorelli, C. (1996) 'Multifaceted Impact of Self-Efficacy Beliefs on Academic Functioning', *Child Development*, 67: 1206–22. Online. Available HTTP: <http://www.des.emory.edu/mfp/Bandura1996CD.pdf>, (accessed 19 April 2011).

Barber, M. and Mourshed, M. (2007) *How the World's Best-Performing School Systems Come Out on Top*, London: McKinsey & Company. Online. Available HTTP: <http://www.mckinsey.com/App_Media/Reports/SSO/Worlds_School_Systems_Final.pdf>, (accessed 29 May 2011).

Barnes, G. (2010) 'Report on the Generation of the 2010 Index of Community Socio-Educational Advantage (ICSEA)'. Online. Available HTTP: <http://www.acara.edu.au/verve/_resources/2010+ICSEA+generation+report.pdf>, (accessed 3 May 2011).

Bell Shakespeare (2011) 'Learning'. Online. Available HTTP: <http://www.bellshakespeare.com.au/learning/intro>, (accessed 15 September 2011).

Bernard, M.E., Stephanou, A. and Urbach, D. (2007) *Australian Scholarships Group (ASG) Student Social and Emotional Health Report: A Research Project Conducted by the Australian Council for Educational Research*, Melbourne: Australian Council for Educational Research. Online. Available HTTP: <http://www.asg.com.au/Page.aspx?ID=436>, (accessed 13 May 2011).

Brice Heath, S. (2002) 'Living the Arts Through Language and Learning: A Report on Community-Based Youth Organisations', in R.J. Deasy (ed.) *Critical Links: Learning in the Arts and Student Academic and Social Development*, Washington, DC: Arts Education Partnership. Online. Available HTTP: <http://www.aep-arts.org/files/publications/CriticalLinks.pdf>, (accessed 13 May 2011).

—— (2008) 'Foreword', in A. O'Brien and K. Donelan (eds) *The Arts and Youth at Risk: Global and Local Challenges*, Newcastle: Cambridge Scholars Publishing. Online. Available HTTP: <http://www.c-s-p.org/flyers/9781847186324-sample.pdf>, (accessed 27 April 2011).

Brice Heath, S. and Roach, A. (1999) 'Imaginative Actuality', in E.B. Fiske (ed.) *Champions of Change: The Impact of the Arts on Learning*. Washington, DC: The Arts Education Partnership, The President's Committee on the Arts and the Humanities, pp. 19–34.

Brown, C.J. (2010) *Great Foundations*, Melbourne: ACER Press.

Brown, G. (2007) 'Vision for Education: Speech at the University of Greenwich'. Online. Available HTTP: <http://www.ukpol.co.uk/mediawiki/index.php?title=Brown4>, (accessed 17 May 2011).

Bryce, J., Mendelovits, J., Beavis, A., McQueen, J. and Adams, I. (2004) *Evaluation of School-based Arts Education Programmes in Australian Schools*, Melbourne: Australian Council for Educational Research. Online. Available HTTP: <http://www.dest.gov.au/NR/rdonlyres/2E2FB54C-1DA2-43DE-BF40-9122DCD854DA/1631/evaluation_arts_education.pdf>, (accessed 13 May 2011).

Burnaford, G. (2003) 'Language Matters: Clarifying Partnerships between Teachers and Artists',

Teaching Artist Journal, 1: 168–71. Online. Available HTTP: <http://dx.doi.org/10.1207/ S1541180XTAJ0103_07>, (accessed 15 April 2011).

Burton, J.M., Horowitz, R. and Abeles, H. (2002) 'Learning in and through the Arts: The Question of Transfer', in R. Deasy (ed.) *Critical Links: Learning in the Arts and Student Academic and Social Development*, Washington, DC: Arts Education Partnership Online. Available HTTP: <http://www.aep-arts.org/files/publications/CriticalLinks.pdf>, (accessed 20 March 2011).

Business-School Connections Roundtable (2011) *Realising Potential: Businesses Helping Schools to Develop Australia's Future*, Canberra. Online. Available HTTP: <http://www.deewr.gov.au/ Schooling/Documents/RoundtableReport.pdf>, (accessed 23 May 2011).

Butzlaff, R. (2002) 'Can Music Be Used to Teach Reading?', in R.J. Deasy (ed.) *Critical Links: Learning in the Arts and Student Academic and Social Development*, Washington, DC: Arts Education Partnership. Online. Available HTTP: <http://aep-arts.org/files/research/CriticalLinks. pdf>.

Caldwell, B.J. (2010) 'How Can We Get Off This Bus?', paper presented at 2010 International Education Research Conference of the Australian Association of Research in Education (AARE) in University of Melbourne, 30 November 2010.

—— (2011a) 'My say', *The Age*, 4 May 2011.

—— (2011b) 'Reward teachers, by all means, but not in this ham-fisted way', *Sydney Morning Herald*, 4 May 2011.

Caldwell, B.J. and Harris, J. (2008) *Why Not the Best Schools? What We Have Learned from Outstanding Schools around the World*, Melbourne: ACER Press.

Caldwell, B.J. and Loader, D.N. (2010) *Our School Our Future*, Melbourne: Education Services Australia in association with the Australian Institute for Teaching and School Leadership.

Caldwell, B.J. and Spinks, J.M. (1992) *Leading the Self-Managing School*, London: Falmer.

—— (1998) *Beyond the Self-Managing School*, London: Falmer.

—— (2008) *Raising the Stakes: From Improvement to Transformation in the Reform of Schools*, London: Routledge.

Caldwell, B.J. and Vaughan, T. (2011a) 'Accountability and Assessment Measures', in J.C.K. Lee and B.J. Caldwell (eds) *Changing Schools in an Era of Globalization*, London: Routledge.

—— (2011b) 'Responses to the Educational Reform and Policy Agenda', in J.C.K. Lee and B.J. Caldwell (eds) *Changing Schools in an Era of Globalization*, London: Routledge.

Carroll, A., Hemingway, F., Bower, J., Ashman, A., Houghton, S. and Durkin, K. (2006) 'Impulsivity in Juvenile Delinquency: Differences Among Early-Onset, Late-Onset, and Non-Offenders', *Journal of Youth and Adolescence*, 35: 519–29.

Catterall, J.S. (2005) 'Conversation and Silence: Transfer of Learning through the Arts', *Journal for Learning through the Arts*, 1: 1–13.

Catterall, J.S., Chapleau, R. and Iwanaga, J. (1999) 'Involvement in the Arts and Human Development: General Involvement and Intensive Involvement in Music and Theater Arts', in E.B. Fiske (ed.) *Champions of Change: The Impact of the Arts on Learning*, The Arts Education Partnership, The President's Committee on the Arts and Humanities. Online. Available HTTP: <http://artsedge.kennedy-center.org/champions/pdfs/ChampsReport. pdf>, (accessed 27 April 2011).

Catterall, J.S. and Peppler, K.A. (2007) 'Learning in the Visual Arts and the Worldviews of Young People', *Cambridge Journal of Education*, 37: 543–60. Online. Available HTTP: <http:// gseis.ucla.edu/faculty/files/catterall/JC_CJEpublished.pdf>, (accessed 28 May 2011).

Chen, M. (2010) *Education Nation: Six Leading Edges of Innovation in our Schools*, San Francisco, CA: Jossey-Bass.

Chen, S., Martuglio, T., Weatherburn, D. and Hua, J. (2005) 'The Transition from Juvenile to

Adult Criminal Careers', *Crime and Justice Bulletin: Contemporary Issues in Crime and Justice*, 86: 1–12. Online. Available HTTP: <http://www.lawlink.nsw.gov.au/lawlink/bocsar/ll_bocsar.nsf/vwFiles/cjb86.pdf/$file/cjb86.pdf>, (accessed 28 April 2011).

Christensen, C., Johnson, C.W. and Horn, M.B. (2008) *Disrupting Class*, New York: McGraw-Hill.

Cisco (2008) *Equipping Every Learner for the 21st Century: A Cisco Futures Report*, San Jose, CA: Cisco Systems.

Commonwealth of Australia (2010) *Whole School Matters: Draft*, Canberra: Commonwealth of Australia. Online. Available HTTP: <http://www.mindmatters.edu.au/default.asp>, (accessed 30 May 2011).

Crafti, S. (2011) 'School inspired by Maori concept', *The Age*, 18 May 2011.

Craven, P. (2011) 'Scientists reinvent the wheel – art gives people pleasure', *The Age*, 19 May 2011.

Creedon, D.W. (2011) 'Fight the Stress of Urban Education with the Arts: The Arts not Only Build Our Brains, They Insulate Them from Our Stressful Urban Environments', *Phi Delta Kappan*, 92: 34–36.

Doidge, N. (2010) *The Brain That Changes Itself: Stories of Personal Triumph from the Frontiers of Brain Science*, Melbourne: Scribe Publications.

Dreeszen, C., Aprill, A. and Deasy, R. (1999) *A Guide to Arts and Education Collaboration, Learning Partnerships: Improving Learning in Schools with Arts Partners in the Community*, Washington, DC: Arts Education Partnerships.

El Sistema (2011) 'El Sistema: Venezuela'. Online. Available HTTP: <http://elsistemausa.org/el-sistema/venezuela/>, (accessed 13 May 2011).

El Sistema USA (2010) 'El Sistema: USA'. Online. Available HTTP: <http://elsistemausa.org/el-sistema/u-s-a/>, (accessed 12 May 2011).

EuroArts (2011a) 'El Sistema: The Story'. Online. Available HTTP: <http://www.el-sistema-film.com/el_Sistema_The_Story.html>, (accessed 12 May 2011).

—— (2011b) 'El Sistema: The Project'. Online. Available HTTP: <http://www.el-sistema-film.com/el_Sistema_The_Project.html>, (accessed 12 May 2011).

Ewing, R. (2010) *The Arts and Australian Education: Realising the Potential*, Camberwell: Australian Council for Educational Research. Online. Available HTTP: <www.acer.edu.au/documents/AER-58.pdf>, (accessed 21 April 2011).

Farrington, D.P. (2003) 'Key Results from the First Forty Years of the Cambridge Study in Delinquent Development', in P. Terence, T.P. Thornberry and M. Krohn (eds) *Taking Stock of Delinquency: An Overview of Findings from Contemporary Longitudinal Studies*, New York: Kluwer.

Finney, J. (2003) 'From Resentment to Enchantment: What a Class of Thirteen Year Olds and Their Music Teacher Tell Us About a Musical Education', *International Journal of Education and the Arts*, 4(6). Online. Available HTTP: <http://www.ijea.org/v4n6/>, (accessed 8 April 2011).

Finnish National Board of Education (2011) 'Basic Education in the Arts'. Online. Available HTTP: <http://www.oph.fi/english/education/basic_education_in_the_arts>, (accessed 22 May 2011).

Florida, R. (2005) *The Flight of the Creative Class*, New York: HarperBusiness.

Fritz, T., Jentscheke, S., Gosselin, N., Sammler, D., Peretz, I., Turner, R., Friederici, A.D. and Koelsch, S. (2009) 'Universal Recognition of Three Basic Emotions in Music', *Current Biology*, 19: 1–4.

Fullan, M. (2010) *All Systems Go: The Change Imperative for Whole System Reform*, Melbourne: Hawker Brownlow, in association with Corwin and Ontario Principals' Council.

Gardner, H. (2006) *Five Minds for the Future*, New York: Harvard Business School Press.

Garner, R. (2009) 'The big question: is the success of specialist schools an illusion resulting from extra funding?', *The Independent*, 23 January 2009.

Garvis, S. and Pendergast, D. (2010) 'Supporting Novice Teachers of the Arts', *International Journal of Education and the Arts*, 11: 1–22. Online. Available HTTP: <http://www.ijea.org/v11n8/v11n8.pdf>, (accessed 12 April 2011).

Gill, R. (2011) 'Focus on national tests robs children of true learning', *The Age*, 9 February 2011, p. 15.

Grossman, M. and Sonn, C. (2010) *New Moves: Understanding the Impacts of the Song Room Programs for Young People from Refugee Backgrounds: Executive Summary*, Melbourne: The Song Room. Online. Available HTTP: <http://www.songroom.org.au/images/stories/research/new%20moves%20executive%20summary%20report.pdf>, (accessed 30 May 2011).

Hallam, S., Rogers, L. and Creech, A. (2005) *Evaluation of a Voices Foundation Primer in Primary Schools*, London: Department for Education and Skills. Online. Available HTTP: <https://consumption.echannels.eduserv.org.uk/publications/eOrderingDownload/RR707.pdf>, (accessed 19 April 2011).

Hattie, J. (2009) *Visible Learning: A Synthesis of Over 800 Meta-analyses Relating to Achievement*, London: Routledge.

Hetland, L. and Winner, E. (2001) 'The Arts and Academic Achievement: What the Evidence Shows', *Arts Education Policy Review*, 102: 3–6.

Homel, R. (2005) 'Developmental Crime Prevention', in N. Tilley (ed.) *Handbook of Crime Prevention and Community Safety*, Uffculme, Devon: Willan Publishing, pp. 77–106.

Hopkins, D. (2007) *Every School a Great School*, Maidenhead, Berkshire: Open University Press.

Hopkins, D. and Craig, W. (2011) 'Powerful Learning: Taking Education Reform to Scale in the Northern Metropolitan Region', in D. Hopkins, W. Craig and J. Munro (eds) *Powerful Learning: A Strategy for Systemic Educational Improvement*, Melbourne: ACER Press.

Hopkins, D., Craig, W. and Munro, J. (eds) (2011) *Powerful Learning: A Strategy for Systemic Educational Improvement*, Melbourne: ACER Press.

Hughes, J. (2005) *Doing the Arts Justice: A Review of Research Literature, Practice and Theory*, in A. Miles and A. McLewin (eds), The Unit for the Arts and Offenders, London.

Hunter, M.A. (2005) *Education and the Arts Research Overview*, Strawberry Hills: Australia Council for the Arts. Online. Available HTTP: <http://www.australiacouncil.gov.au/__data/assets/pdf_file/0018/34083/EdArts_Research_Overview.pdf>, (accessed 13 May 2011).

James, S. (ed.) (2011) *Re-modelling Special Education: The Story of an Extraordinary School*. Melbourne: ACER Press.

Johnson, P. (2006) *Creators*, New York: Harper Perennial.

Jorgensen, E. (2003) 'What Philosophy Can Bring to Music Education: Musicianship as a Case in Point', *British Journal of Music Education*, 20: 197–214.

Kendall, L., Morrison, J., Sharp, C. and Yashanew, T. (2008) *The Longer-Term Impact of Creative Partnerships on the Attainment of Young People*, London: National Foundation for Educational Research. Online. Available HTTP: <http://www.creativitycultureeducation.org/data/files/nfer-2008-impact-of-creative-partnerships-on-yp-attainment-final-11-11-1-11.pdf>, (accessed 29 May 2011).

Koelsch, S., Fritz, T., Schulze, K., Alsop, D. and Schlaug, G. (2005) 'Adults and Children Processing Music: An fMRI Study', *NeuroImage*, 25: 1068–76. Online. Available HTTP: <http://www.musicianbrain.com/papers/Koelsch_adults+children_pr.pdf>, (accessed 29 May 2011).

Leadbeater, C. and Wong, A. (2010) *Learning from the Extremes*, San Jose, CA: Cisco Systems.

Levitin, D.J. and Triovolas, A.K. (2009) 'Current Advances in the Cognitive Neuroscience of

Music', *Annals of the New York Academy of Sciences*, 1156: 211–31. Online. Available HTTP: <http://levitin.mcgill.ca/articles/2009-Levitin-Tirovolas-Current_advances_in_the_cognitive.pdf>, (accessed 28 May 2011).

Little Kids Rock (2011a) 'About Us: Our History'. Online. Available HTTP: <http://littlekidsrock.org/our-history.html>, (accessed 19 April 2011).

—— (2011b) 'Every Child Deserves Music Education'. Online. Available HTTP: <http://littlekidsrock.org/>, (accessed 19 April 2011).

—— (2011c) 'Frequently Asked Questions by Teachers'. Online. Available HTTP: <http://littlekidsrock.org/teacher-faq.html>, (accessed 19 April 2011).

—— (2011d) 'News and Events: Press Releases'. Online. Available HTTP: <http://littlekidsrock.org/pr-122110.html>, (accessed 19 April 2011).

—— (2011e) 'The Program: How it Works'. Online. Available HTTP: <http://littlekidsrock.org/how-it-works.html>, (accessed 19 April 2011).

—— (2011f) 'Program: Methodology'. Online. Available HTTP: <http://littlekidsrock.org/methodology.html>, (accessed 19 April 2011).

—— (2011g) 'What We Do'. Online. Available HTTP: <http://littlekidsrock.org/what-we-do.html>, (accessed 19 April 2011).

Loveless, T. (2011) *How Well are American Students Learning? The 2010 Brown Centre Report on American Education*, Washington, DC: The Brookings Institution. Online. Available HTTP: <http://www.brookings.edu/~/media/Files/rc/reports/2011/0207_education_loveless/0207_education_loveless.pdf>, (accessed 27 April 2011).

Maguin, E. and Loeber, R. (1996) 'Academic Performance and Delinquency', *Crime and Justice*, 20: 145–264.

Manuel, J., Brock, P., Sawyer, W. and Carter, D. (2009) 'What is Within Becomes What is Around: Imagination, Innovation, Creativity', in J. Manuel *et al.* (eds) *Imagination Innovation Creativity: Re-visioning English in Education*, Putney, NSW: Phoenix Education.

Marks, G.N. (2009) 'Accounting for School-Sector Differences in University Entrance Performance', *Australian Journal of Education*, 48: 19–38.

McCarthy, K.F., Ondaatje, E.H., Zakaras, L. and Brooks, A. (2004) *Gifts of the Muse: Reframing the Debate about the Benefits of the Arts*, Santa Monica: The RAND Corporation. Online. Available HTTP: <http://www.rand.org/pubs/monographs/2005/RAND_MG218.pdf>, (accessed 3 May 2011).

MCEECDYA (2008) *Melbourne Declaration on Educational Goals for Young Australians*, Melbourne: MCEECDYA.

Ministry of Education (2010) *Ministry of Education Position Paper: Assessment*, Wellington: Ministry of Education. Online. Available HTTP: <http://www.minedu.govt.nz/~/media/MinEdu/Files/TheMinistry/AssessmentPositionPaperSep2010.pdf>, (accessed 18 February 2011).

Ministry of Education Singapore (2008) *Art Syllabus: Primary and Lower Secondary*, Singapore: Curriculum Planning and Development Division. Online. Available HTTP: <http://www.moe.gov.sg/education/syllabuses/aesthetics-health-and-moral-education/files/art-primary-and-lower-secondary-2009.pdf>, (accessed 19 May 2011).

Minnis Journals (2009) 'Expressing Emotion Through Performance: A Young Songwriter Embarks on Her Rise', *Education Today*. Online. Available HTTP: <http://www.minniscomms.com.au/educationtoday/articles.php?articleid=241>, (accessed 27 April 2011).

Mourshed, M., Chijioke, C. and Barber, M. (2010) *How the World's Most Improved School Systems Keep Getting Better*, London: McKinsey & Company.

Naisbitt, J. (1982) *Megatrends*, New York: Future Press.

Nathan, L. (2008) 'Why the Arts Make Sense in Education', *Phi Delta Kappan*, 90: 177–78.

National Commission on Excellence in Education (1983) *A Nation at Risk: The Imperative for Educational Reform*, Washington, DC: US Department of Education.

National Crime Prevention (1999) *Pathways to Prevention: Developmental and Early Intervention Approaches to Crime in Australia*, Canberra: Attorney-General's Department. Online. Available HTTP: <http://www98.griffith.edu.au/dspace/bitstream/10072/27168/1/11672_1.pdf>, (accessed 28 April 2011).

National Endowment for the Humanities (2002) 'Coming Up Taller Awards Program Marks Fifth Anniversary Celebration'. Online. Available HTTP: <http://www.neh.gov/news/archive/20021202.html>, (accessed 21 April 2011).

O'Toole, J. (2010) 'Foreword', in R. Ewing (ed.) *The Arts and Australian Education: Realising the Potential*, Melbourne: ACER Press. Online. Available HTTP: <www.acer.edu.au/documents/AER-58.pdf>, (accessed 21 April 2011).

Orchestras Canada (2009) 'El Sistema Comes to Canada'. Online. Available HTTP: <http://orchestrascanada.org/?p=2368>, (accessed 6 May 2011).

Oreck, B. (2004) 'The Artistic and Professional Development of Teachers: A Study of Teachers' Attitudes Toward and Use of the Arts in Teaching', *Journal of Teacher Education*, 55: 55–69. Online. Available HTTP: <http://www.sagepub.com/eis/Oreck.pdf>, (accessed 12 April 2011).

Oreck, B., Baum, S. and McCartney, H. (1999) 'Artistic Talent Development for Urban Youth', in E.B. Fiske (ed.) *Champions of Change: The Impact of the Arts on Learning*, The Arts Education Partnership, The President's Committee on the Arts and the Humanities. Online. Available HTTP: <http://artsedge.kennedy-center.org/champions/pdfs/ChampsReport.pdf>, (accessed 20 March 2011).

Papert, S. (1993) *The Children's Machine: Rethinking School in the Age of the Computer*, New York: Basic Books.

Parsons, L.M. (2001) 'Exploring the Functional Neuroanatomy of Music Performance, Perception, and Comprehension', *Annals of the New York Academy of Sciences*, 930: 211–31.

Pasko, L.J. (2006) *The Female Juvenile Offender in Hawaii: Understanding Gender Differences in Arrests Adjudications, and Social Characteristics of Juvenile Offenders*, Hawaii Research and Statistics Branch, Crime Prevention and Justice Assistance Division, Department of the Attorney General.

Pricewaterhouse Coopers (2010) *Creativity, Culture and Education: The Costs and Benefits of Creative Partnerships*, London: Pricewaterhouse Coopers. Online. Available HTTP: <http://www.creativitycultureeducation.org/data/files/pwc-report-236.pdf>, (accessed 5 May 2011).

Program for International Student Assessment (2007) *Program for International Student Assessment: Executive Summary*: OECD. Online. Available HTTP: <http://www.oecd.org/dataoecd/15/13/39725224.pdf>, (accessed 31 May 2011).

Quality of Education Review Committee (1985) *Quality of Education in Australia*, Canberra: Australian Government Publishing Service.

Ravitch, D. (2010) *The Death and Life of the Great American School System*, New York: Basic Books.

Renz, L. and Atienza, J. (2005) *Foundation Funding for Arts Education*, New York: The Foundation Center in cooperation with Grantmakers in the Arts. Online. Available HTTP: <http://www.fdncentre.org/gainknowledge/research/pdf/arted05.pdf>, (accessed 21 April 2011).

Richardson, J. (2011) 'Disrupting How and Where we Learn. An Interview with Clayton Christensen and Michael Horn', *Phi Delta Kappan*, 92: 32–38.

Robinson, K. (2009) *The Element*, New York: Viking.

Rogers, L., Hallam, S., Creech, A. and Preti, C. (2008) 'Learning about what Constitutes Effective Training from a Pilot Program to Improve Music Education in Primary Schools', *Music Education Research*, 10: 485–97.

Root-Bernstein, R. and Root-Bernstein, M. (1999) *Sparks of Genius, the 13 Thinking Tools of the World's Most Creative People*, Boston, MA: Houghton Mifflin.

—— (2010) 'Keynote Speech: Arts at the Center', paper presented at UNESCO Second World Conference on Arts Education in Seoul, 25–28 May 2010.

Rosen, J. (2008) 'Common Cause in Challenging Times', *Teaching Music*, 16: 20.

Russell-Bowie, D. (2009) 'What Me? Teach Music to My Primary Class? Challenges to Teaching Music in Primary Schools in Five Countries', *Music Education Research*, 11: 23–36. Online. Available HTTP: <http://pdfserve.informaworld.com/35327__925320436.pdf>, (accessed 21 April 2011).

—— (2010) 'Cross-National Comparisons of Background and Confidence in Visual Arts and Music Education of Pre-Service Primary Teachers', *Australian Journal of Teacher Education*, 34: 65–78.

Sacks, O. (2007) *Musicophilia: Tales of Music and the Brain*, New York: Random House.

Sarasota Ballet (2011a) 'Dance – The Next Generation'. Online. Available HTTP: <http://www.sarasotaballet.org/index.php/dng-information.html>, (accessed 21 April 2011).

—— (2011b) 'Dance – The Next Generation Success Stories'. Online. Available HTTP: <http://www.sarasotaballet.org/index.php/dng-success-stories.html>, (accessed 21 April 2011).

Saubern, R. (2010) 'Closing the Gap: Arts Education in the Top End', *Teacher*, 208: 10–15.

Schellenberg, E.G. (2006) 'Long-Term Positive Associations Between Music Lessons and IQ', *Journal of Educational Psychology*, 98: 457–68.

Schlaug, G., Jancke, L., Huang, Y. and Steinmetz, H. (1995a) 'In Vivo Evidence of Structural Brain Asymmetry in Musicians', *Science*, 267: 699–700. Online. Available HTTP: <http://www.musicianbrain.com/papers/Schlaug_HemDominance_1995a.pdf>, (accessed 28 May 2011).

Schlaug, G., Jancke, L., Huang, Y., Staiger, J.F. and Steinmetz, H. (1995b) 'Increased Corpus Callosum Size in Musicians', *Neuropsychologia*, 33: 1047–55. Online. Available HTTP: <http://www.musicianbrain.com/papers/Schlaug_CCallosum_1995b.pdf>, (accessed 18 May 2011).

Schlaug, G., Norton, A., Overy, K. and Winner, E. (2005) 'Effects of Music Training on the Child's Brain and Cognitive Development', *Annals of the New York Academy of Sciences*, 1060: 219–30. Online. Available HTTP: <http://www.musicianbrain.com/papers/Schlaug_Music_Child_Brain_NYAS2005.pdf>, (accessed 30 May 2011).

School of the Arts Singapore (2011) 'About School of the Arts Singapore'. Online. Available HTTP: <http://www.sota.edu.sg/TheSchool/AboutSOTA/tabid/70/Default.aspx>, (accessed 23 May 2011).

Schwartz, H.L., Hamilton, L.S., Stecher, B.M. and Steele, J.L. (2011) *Expanded Measures of School Performance*, Washington, DC: RAND Corporation. Online. Available HTTP: <http://www.rand.org/content/dam/rand/pubs/technical_reports/2011/RAND_TR968.pdf>, (accessed 27 April 2011).

Sluming, V., Brooks, B., Howard, M., Downes, J.J. and Roberts, N. (2007) 'Broca's Area Supports Enhanced Visuospatial Cognition in Orchestral Musicians', *The Journal of Neuroscience*, 27: 3799–806.

Southcott, J. and Crawford, R. (2011) 'The Intersections of Curriculum Development: Music, ICT and Australian Music Education', *Australasian Journal of Educational Technology*, 27: 122–36.

Specialist Schools and Academies Trust (n.d.) 'A Vision Paper for Arts Education', unpublished paper, London: Specialist Schools and Academies Trust.

Spillane, D. (2009) 'Boys in a Small Rural School: Developing a Culture of Confidence and

Success', in S.D. Harrison (ed.) *Male Voices, Stories of Boys Learning through Making Music,* Melbourne: ACER Press.

Stone, A., Bikson, T., Moini, J. and McArthur, D. (1998) 'The Arts and Prosocial Impact Study: Program Characteristics and Prosocial Effects'. Online. Available HTTP: <http://www. rand.org/pubs/drafts/2005/DRU1887.pdf>, (accessed 12 April 2011).

Tarica, E. (2011) 'Music failings spark chorus of complaint', *The Age,* 9 May 2011, p. 17.

Taylor, C. and Ryan, C. (2005) *Excellence in Education: The Making of Great Schools,* London: David Fulton.

The Economist (2009) *A New Ranking of the World's Most Innovative Countries,* London: Economist Intelligence Unit. Online. Available HTTP: <http://graphics.eiu.com/PDF/Cisco_ Innovation_Complete.pdf>, (accessed 30 May 2011).

—— (2011) 'The next Golden State', *The Economist,* 28 May: 13–14.

The National System of Youth and Children's Orchestras of Venezuela (2009) 'El Sistema methodology'. Online. Available HTTP: <http://www.fesnojiv.gob.ve/en/el-sistema-methodology.html>, (accessed 12 May 2011).

The Song Room (2011a) 'Introduction'. Online. Available HTTP: <http://www.songroom. org.au/home/introduction>, (accessed 24 May 2011).

—— (2011b) 'Music/Arts Workshops'. Online. Available HTTP: <http://www.songroom. org.au/programs/music-arts-workshops>, (accessed 12 April 2011).

The University of Sydney (2011) 'Bell Shakespeare Education'. Online. Available HTTP: <http://sydney.edu.au/education_social_work/professional_learning/teachers/bell-shakespeare/index.shtml>, (accessed 15 September 2011).

The Voices Foundation (2011a) 'History'. Online. Available HTTP: <http://www.voices.org. uk/aboutus/ourhistory/>, (accessed 27 April 2011).

—— (2011b) 'Our supporters and funders'. Online. Available HTTP: <http://www.voices. org.uk/funders/>, (accessed 27 April 2011).

Thorpe, V. (2011) 'Cultural figures and teachers denounce the abolition of the arts in schools project', *The Guardian,* 9 January 2011.

Toch, T. (2011) 'Education Entrepreneurs on the Potomac', *Phi Delta Kappan,* 97: 68–69.

UNESCO (2006) 'Road Map for Arts Education', report from The World Conference on Arts Education: Building Creative Capacities for the 21st Century in Lisbon, 6–9 March 2006. Online. Available HTTP: <http://portal.unesco.org/culture/en/ev.php-URL_ ID=30335&URL_DO=DO_TOPIC&URL_SECTION=201.html>, (accessed 6–9 March 2006).

Upitis, R. and Smithrim, K. (2003) *Learning Through the Arts: National Assessment: 1999–2002.* Final Report to The Royal Conservatory of Music, Toronto: Royal Conservatory of Music.

Vaughn, K. (2002) 'Music and Mathematics: Modest Support of the Oft-Claimed Relationship', in R. Deasy (ed.) *Critical Links: Learning in the Arts and Student Academic and Social Development,* Washington, DC: Arts Education Partnership. Online. Available HTTP: <http://www.aep-arts.org/files/publications/CriticalLinks.pdf>.

Vaughan, T., Harris, J. and Caldwell, B.J. (2011) *Bridging the Gap in School Achievement through the Arts: Summary Report,* Melbourne: The Song Room. Online. Available HTTP: <http://www. songroom.org.au/images/stories/Bridging%20the%20Gap%20in%20School%20Achieve ment%20through%20the%20Arts.pdf>, (accessed 30 May 2011).

Weatherburn, D., Cush, R. and Saunders, P. (2007) 'Screening Juvenile Offenders for Further Assessment and Intervention', *Crime and Justice Bulletin: Contemporary Issues in Crime and Justice,* 19: 1–11. Online. Available HTTP: <http://www.lawlink.nsw.gov.au/lawlink/bocsar/ll_ bocsar.nsf/vwFiles/cjb109.pdf/$file/cjb109.pdf>, (accessed 28 April 2011).

Weatherburn, D. and Lind, B. (1997) *Social and Economic Stress, Child Neglect and Juvenile Delinquency,*

Sydney: NSW Bureau of Crime Statistics and Research, Attorney General's Department. Online. Available HTTP: <http://www.criminologyresearchcouncil.gov.au/reports/17-95-6.pdf>, (accessed 28 April 2011).

Wetter, O.E., Koerner, F. and Schwaninger, A. (2009) 'Does Musical Training Improve School Performance?', *Journal of Instructional Science*, 37: 365–74. Online. Available HTTP: <http://www.casra.ch/publications/doc/WetKoeSch2009.pdf>, (accessed 28 May 2011).

Winner, E. and Cooper, M. (2000) 'Mute Those Claims: No Evidence (Yet) for a Causal Link between Arts Study and Academic Achievement', *Journal of Aesthetic Education*, 34: 3–10.

Winner, E. and Hetland, L. (2000) 'The Arts in Education: Evaluating the Evidence for a Causal Link', *Journal of Aesthetic Education*, 34: 3–10.

Zabel, R.H. and Nigro, F.A. (2001) 'The Influence of Special Education Experience and Gender of Juvenile Offenders on Academic Achievement Scores in Reading, Language, and Mathematics', *Behavioral Disorders*, 26: 164–72.

Zeki, S. (1993) *A Vision of the Brain*, Oxford: Oxford University Press.

—— (1999) *Inner Vision*, Oxford: Oxford University Press.

Zhao, Y. (2009) *Catching Up or Leading the Way: American Education in the Age of Globalization*, Alexandria, VA: ASCD.

—— (2011) 'Entrepreneurship and Creativity: Where Do They Come From and How Not to Destroy Them'. Online. Available HTTP: <http://zhaolearning.com/2011/02/26/entrepreneurship-and-creativity-where-do-they-come-from-and-how-not-to-destroy-them/>, (accessed 19 May 2011).

Index